BRENTWOOD

D0438537

Elizabeth I *and* Mary Stuart

Elizabeth I
and
Mary Stuart

The Perils of Marriage

ANKA MUHLSTEIN

Translated by John Brownjohn

WITHDRAWN

CONTRA COSTA COUNTY LIBRARY

3 1901 04231 9642

Copyright © 2007 Anka Muhlstein
Translation copyright © 2007 John Brownjohn

First published in Great Britain in 2007 by Haus Publishing,
26 Cadogan Court, Draycott Avenue, London SW3 3BX
www.hauspublishing.co.uk

The moral rights of the author have been asserted

A CIP catalogue record for this book is available from the British Library

ISBN 978-1-904950-85-1

Typeset in Garamond 3 by MacGuru Ltd
info@macguru.org.uk
Printed and bound by Graphicom in Vicenza, Italy
Jacket illustrations courtesy National Portrait Gallery, London

CONDITIONS OF SALE
All rights reserved. No part of this publication may be reproduced,
stored in a retrieval system, or transmitted in any form or by any means,
electronic, mechanical, photocopying, recording or otherwise, without the
prior permission of the publisher.

This book is sold subject to the condition that it shall not, by way of trade
or otherwise, be lent, re-sold, hired out or otherwise circulated without the
publisher's prior consent in any form of binding or cover other than that
in which it is published and without a similar condition including this
condition being imposed on the subsequent purchaser

Contents

For Louis

Introduction

I was prompted to write this book by my interest in the question of marriage as it affected queens regnant in the age of absolute monarchies. Marriage was a necessity for any monarch. No marriage, no offspring. No heir, no dynasty. Europe has never known a bachelor king. On the other hand, there have been queens – Elizabeth I of England and Christina of Sweden, to name but two – who remained unmarried, not for lack of suitors but by choice. This was because marriage posed special problems for a queen invested with genuine power and did not bring advantages alone. In the first place, even for the woman who occupied the throne, it detracted from her independence. Submission to her lord and master was the universal rule. The notion of a prince consort is a modern one. In the sixteenth century the queen's husband was king; he became, by force of circumstance, the couple's dominant partner. Thus a woman reigning in her own right might very well balk at the prospect of sharing her authority. Besides, whom should she marry?

Choosing a foreign husband was advisable only if his kingdom was contiguous and the marriage entailed a permanent union between the two countries, as in the case of Isabella of Castile and Ferdinand of Aragon. Marriage to a distant monarch was of little value, either politically

– the couple's interests might be divergent – or personally, because both spouses had to remain in their own countries and married life was restricted to rare, short-lived encounters. A prince of junior status, then? Given that such a match carried scant political weight, the man in question would have to be endowed with brilliant personal qualities. A subject, perhaps? That solution was dangerous because it inevitably gave rise to internal rivalries that threatened to degenerate, at worst, into civil war. It could not be ruled out, however, because queens were surrounded by men eager to please them; thus, love could take a hand and influence their choice.

In order to illustrate the complexity of the subject, I have chosen to compare two contemporaries: Elizabeth I and Mary Queen of Scots. Those two cousins, who shared the British Isles between them, adopted contrasting attitudes. Elizabeth, thinking like a queen, resisted her amorous inclinations and chose to remain unmarried; Mary, acting like a woman, and a woman in thrall to passion, married no less than three times. Those decisions affected their destinies, linked them inextricably, and culminated in Mary's execution at Elizabeth's behest.

1

The Bastard Princess

1533–53

That she had taken the trouble to be born was not enough to guarantee Elizabeth, daughter of King Henry VIII, the resplendent existence of an English princess. True, her birth on Sunday, 7 September 1533, was greeted with bonfires, interminable peals of bells and a solemn *Te Deum* in St Paul's Cathedral. Less than three years later, however, her mother, Anne Boleyn, was beheaded on grounds of adultery and the little princess forfeited her rank. The annulment of her parents' marriage had made a bastard of her.

Drama was the hallmark of life with Henry VIII, the king who had six queens of whom two were beheaded, two divorced, one died in childbirth, and only the last prevailed. His three children had three different mothers. The eldest, 'Bloody' Mary, was the fruit of his first marriage to Catherine of Aragon; Elizabeth was the daughter of his second wife; and his third wife, Jane Seymour, gave birth to his youngest child and only son, Edward VI. Elizabeth was seventeen years

Ancestry of Henry VII

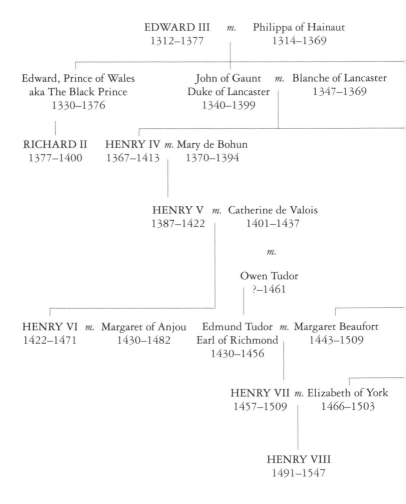

EDWARD III   *m.*   Philippa of Hainaut
1312–1377   1314–1369

Edward, Prince of Wales   John of Gaunt   *m.* Blanche of Lancaster
aka The Black Prince   Duke of Lancaster   1347–1369
1330–1376   1340–1399

RICHARD II   HENRY IV *m.* Mary de Bohun
1377–1400   1367–1413   1370–1394

HENRY V *m.* Catherine de Valois
1387–1422   1401–1437

m.

Owen Tudor
?–1461

HENRY VI *m.* Margaret of Anjou   Edmund Tudor *m.* Margaret Beaufort
1422–1471   1430–1482   Earl of Richmond   1443–1509
                       1430–1456

HENRY VII *m.* Elizabeth of York
1457–1509   1466–1503

HENRY VIII
1491–1547

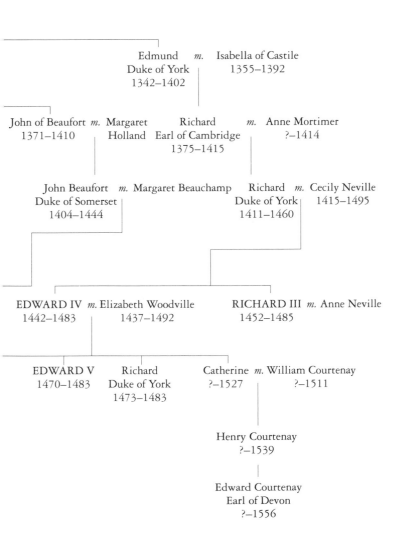

Edmund *m.* Isabella of Castile
Duke of York 1355–1392
1342–1402

John of Beaufort *m.* Margaret   Richard   *m.* Anne Mortimer
1371–1410   Holland Earl of Cambridge   ?–1414
                        1375–1415

John Beaufort *m.* Margaret Beauchamp   Richard *m.* Cecily Neville
Duke of Somerset   Duke of York 1415–1495
1404–1444   1411–1460

EDWARD IV *m.* Elizabeth Woodville   RICHARD III *m.* Anne Neville
1442–1483   1437–1492   1452–1485

EDWARD V   Richard   Catherine *m.* William Courtenay
1470–1483   Duke of York   ?–1527   ?–1511
             1473–1483

Henry Courtenay
?–1539

Edward Courtenay
Earl of Devon
?–1556

younger than Mary and four years older than her brother. If we are to gain an understanding of her childhood, adolescence and reign, we must go back in time and recall the volcanic family from which she sprang.

Elizabeth was a Tudor, a member of a family that had come to power thanks to the drive and initiative of her grandfather Henry VII and to the fact that the laws of succession prevailing in fifteenth-century England were not too well-defined or restrictive. Primogeniture, so firmly embedded in the royal traditions of France, was not recognized as a sufficient and necessary entitlement to the throne of England, hence the long power struggle waged by the descendants of Edward III. Royal authority was weakened by this civil war, known as the Wars of the Roses (the Lancastrians, the line that produced Henry IV, Henry V and Henry VI, took a red rose as their emblem, whereas a white rose symbolized the Yorkist branch, that of Edward IV and Richard III). Whoever wore the crown had to resist the unremitting pressure exerted on him in turn by the great rival houses of Lancaster, York and Warwick, which maintained veritable private armies.

On 22 August 1485, when Richard III was killed by Henry Tudor during the last battle of the Wars of the Roses, Henry, the last of the Lancastrian line, seized his opportunity without hesitation. Lord Stanley, who had facilitated his victory by deserting the king's party, retrieved the crown from the dust of the battlefield and placed it on his head to resounding cries of 'Long live King Henry!'

The new king set off for London, determined to assert his rights – somewhat dubious rights, as he himself was only too aware. He based his claim to the throne on the lineage of his mother, Margaret Beaufort. Margaret was the sole descendant of the Beauforts and a great-granddaughter of John of Gaunt, Duke of Lancaster, the fourth son of Edward III. During the oppressive reign of Richard III, fearing for the life of her son, the posthumous son of Edmund Tudor, Margaret sent him to Brittany, where he persistently plotted to reinstate the house of Lancaster. Having succeeded at the second attempt, he asserted his authority in the simplest manner: he proclaimed himself King Henry VII, summoned Parliament in November 1485 and, without entering into the details of his succession, argued that his victory had manifested the will of God. Henry's decisiveness, coupled with general lassitude and the fact that Richard III, the last sovereign of the Yorkist line, had not only left no descendants but contrived the murder of his nephews, the sons of Edward IV, clinched matters in his favour. It was only then that he married Elizabeth of York, thereby ending the rivalry between the two clans once and for all.

The young dynasty's position was consolidated by the birth of two sons and two daughters. Arthur, the eldest, married Catherine of Aragon in 1501 but died five months later, having already been languid and sickly at the time of the ceremony, and it appears that the adolescent couple's marriage was never consummated. However, the Spanish connection, accompanied by a favourable dowry, was too valuable to be lightly abandoned. Ever practical, Henry VII solved the problem by marrying his second son, Henry, who was now Prince of Wales, to the youthful widow. His two daughters also made brilliant marriages. Margaret wed James IV of Scotland – their granddaughter was Mary Stuart – and the younger, Mary, became the wife of Louis XII of France. The latter died not long afterwards, and his queen, who had not borne him any children, returned to England, where she married the Duke of Suffolk. Their descendants were exclusively female, and we shall later have occasion to speak of their granddaughters, Jane and Catherine Grey. In 1509, however, when Henry VII died and Henry VIII came to the throne, questions of succession were secondary.

The young king was eighteen years old. Robust, handsome and adept at all forms of physical exercise, he was also fond of music, dancing and poetry. Heir to a country eager to put an end to internal strife and married to a loving wife who lavished affection on him, he seemed destined for a glorious reign. The young couple and their entourage were not unduly worried by the ensuing series of miscarriages and stillbirths, especially as Catherine was delivered of a healthy daughter, Mary, in 1516. Although a trifle disappointed at not having had a son, the king felt sure that a boy would not be long in coming and displayed little ill humour. Daughters made good marriages, after all, and the little princess soon amused him with her quick wit. And so, since he continued to enjoy his conjugal duties, he persevered. The years went by, however, and still no male heir appeared. The slender, graceful young woman whom Henry had married was no more. The short, stout matron she had become was worn out by numerous pregnancies, and he wearied of her efforts to keep up with him, her caresses and attentions. The six-year gap between them abruptly widened. In 1525 the queen turned forty and reached the threshold of old age, whereas the king, at thirty-four, had never been more flamboyant – or more pragmatic. It was obvious that Catherine would bear him no more children, so the necessary conclusions had to be drawn.

Whispers began to circulate at court. The word 'annulment' went the rounds. There were plenty of dynastic justifications for a divorce. Memories of the Wars of the Roses were still vivid enough for everyone to want a clear-cut line of succession to the throne, and this problem was doubly acute because the Tudor family lacked male heirs. Although it was thoroughly accepted in England – as witness the Tudors' example – that regal power could be transmitted by the female line, people were chary of being ruled by a woman. Would a queen regnant be able to exert the requisite authority in an age when the sovereign still commanded his troops in battle? The role to be assigned to a potential husband was another question that aroused justifiable anxiety. A royal consort could easily seize power; worse still, a foreign prince, if he outlived his wife, might create dangerous dynastic complications. For the public good, it seemed essential that the king remarry. It is not beyond the bounds of possibility that Queen Catherine might have accepted this, had not the presence of a rival robbed the debate of all calm and objectivity, and had the lawyers devised a solution that would have safeguarded her daughter Mary's rights and status. A ferocious struggle ensued, for gentle, devout Catherine contested every inch of ground and proved dauntless and unyielding in the face of a powerful foe.

Henry VIII had had a number of mistresses during his marriage – one of them had even given him a son whom he acknowledged and created Duke of Richmond – but he had never been passionately in love with any of them. No woman ever resisted his advances, so his conquests soon bored him. Anne Boleyn, a young woman at court, was self-assured enough to play a different game. Once the king had succumbed to her charms, she kept him at arm's length. She had no intention of following in the footsteps of her elder sister, who had yielded to the king but, unable to retain his affections, had been compelled to contract a mediocre marriage a few months later. Anne's teasing tactics paid off, and Henry fell madly in love with her. His dynastic concerns were reinforced by the promptings of desire, and in 1527 he set about divorcing his wife. The conflict between them lasted for six years and culminated in a political and religious revolution affecting the entire kingdom.

Henry's pretext for requesting an annulment was that he had married his brother's widow, a union proscribed by the

Church. True, Pope Julius II had agreed to grant a dispensation, but it could be asserted that he was not entitled to set aside a prohibition contained in Holy Writ. Thus, Henry possessed an argument that carried some weight. Catherine countered it by claiming that her first marriage had never been consummated. Henry knew perfectly well that he had married a virgin and, consequently, that neither she nor her husband had lived in sin. However, he was so convinced that Pope Clement VII would quickly grant him satisfaction that this counter-attack did not seriously worry him. Plenty of sovereigns, notably his brother-in-law Louis XII,* had succeeded in getting their marriages dissolved. But Henry was wrong to underestimate the influence wielded over the Pope by Charles V, Catherine's nephew, and he failed to foresee the innumerable techniques of evasion that enabled the pontiff to play for time. The English king continued to exert pressure on Clement VII for four long years, but not even the threat of a schism was enough to make the Holy Father give way. Only Catherine's death could liberate Henry VIII, and, in view of the brutality he displayed when dealing with his subsequent wives, we are entitled to feel surprised that he did not have her poisoned. It was one of his advisers, Thomas Cromwell, who finally showed him that he

---

*Louis, Duke of Orleans, had married Jeanne, the daughter of Louis XI, who was incapable of having children. On becoming king he divorced her and married Anne of Brittany, the widow of his cousin and predecessor Charles VIII. When she died he married Mary Tudor, sister of Henry VIII.

Descendants of Henry VII

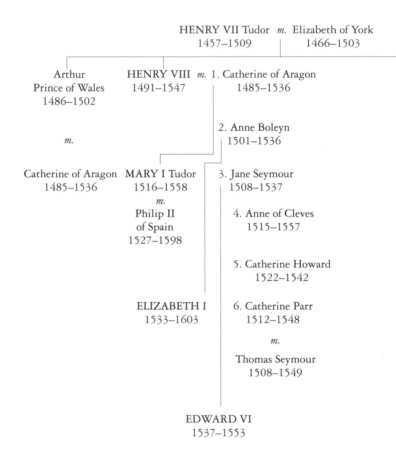

HENRY VII Tudor   *m.*   Elizabeth of York
1457–1509 | 1466–1503

Arthur   HENRY VIII *m.* 1. Catherine of Aragon
Prince of Wales   1491–1547   1485–1536
1486–1502

     2. Anne Boleyn
m.   1501–1536

Catherine of Aragon   MARY I Tudor   3. Jane Seymour
1485–1536   1516–1558   1508–1537
     m.
     Philip II   4. Anne of Cleves
     of Spain   1515–1557
     1527–1598

     5. Catherine Howard
     1522–1542

     ELIZABETH I   6. Catherine Parr
     1533–1603   1512–1548

     m.

     Thomas Seymour
     1508–1549

EDWARD VI
1537–1553

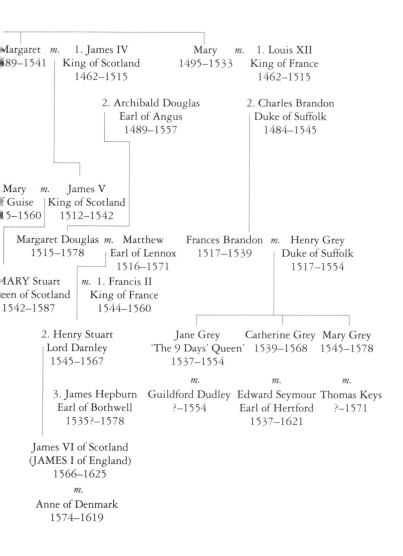

Margaret *m.* 1. James IV
189–1541 | King of Scotland
1462–1515

2. Archibald Douglas
Earl of Angus
1489–1557

Mary *m.* 1. Louis XII
1495–1533 | King of France
1462–1515

2. Charles Brandon
Duke of Suffolk
1484–1545

Mary *m.* James V
f Guise | King of Scotland
15–1560 | 1512–1542

Margaret Douglas *m.* Matthew
1515–1578 | Earl of Lennox
1516–1571

Frances Brandon *m.* Henry Grey
1517–1539 | Duke of Suffolk
1517–1554

MARY Stuart *m.* 1. Francis II
een of Scotland | King of France
1542–1587 | 1544–1560

2. Henry Stuart
Lord Darnley
1545–1567

Jane Grey
'The 9 Days' Queen'
1537–1554

Catherine Grey
1539–1568

Mary Grey
1545–1578

m.

3. James Hepburn
Earl of Bothwell
1535?–1578

m.

Guildford Dudley
?–1554

m.

Edward Seymour
Earl of Hertford
1537–1621

m.

Thomas Keys
?–1571

James VI of Scotland
(JAMES I of England)
1566–1625

m.

Anne of Denmark
1574–1619

was barking up the wrong tree, and that the solution to his problems lay in England, not Rome.

Going beyond the king's special case, Cromwell harped on the growing unpopularity of the Church, its taxes, abuses and influence. By so doing, he helped to found the English constitutional monarchy and organize the sovereign state. He did not seek the support of the House of Lords, half of whose members were ecclesiastics incapable of attacking a religious institution so profitable to them. Instead, he turned to the House of Commons, which was populated by merchants, lawyers and gentlemen who needed no encouragement to expose and deplore the misdeeds of bishops and priests. In 1532 the legislative independence of the Catholic Church in England was abolished. Appeals to the Pontifical Court relating to marriage or succession were prohibited. Having thus been released from papal jurisdiction, Henry VIII could at last divorce his wife. Another decision vital to the future of the kingdom freed the Church of England from the financial tutelage of Rome. Until the Reformation, every bishop who took possession of a diocese had to pay the Pope a tax, the annates, equivalent to a year's income from his domain. From now on, that sum was payable to the Crown. This revolution, for it genuinely was one, was cemented by state expropriation of the Church's vast estates, which comprised a quarter of the kingdom. Monasteries were dissolved and their lands sold off. The result, on the national plane, was the submission of the Church to civil authority. The king had arrogated all its temporal powers, that is to say, its rights of administration and taxation, of appointing its own dignitaries and controlling its own courts of justice. In 1535 Henry VIII assumed the title of supreme head of the Church of England.

Archbishop Cranmer, who was to direct the transformation of the Anglican Church, declared the marriage between Catherine and Henry null and void early in 1533, and on 25 January of that year the king married Anne Boleyn – an urgent and necessary denouement because the young woman had yielded to him at last and was pregnant. She was crowned Queen of England on 1 June and gave birth to a daughter, Elizabeth, in September. Regarded henceforward as her father's only legitimate daughter, Elizabeth assumed the title Princess Royal, which had previously been held by her older half-sister Mary, and took precedence over her. It should be noted that Anne was far from magnanimous in victory. She treated her stepdaughter harshly, displaying a severity towards her that was both cruel and offensive. Unfortunately for Anne, she was not content merely to bully the girl. Incapable of self-control, she made scenes, blamed her royal spouse for her own unpopularity, and ignored his mounting irritation. The trouble was, the hoped-for male heir still failed to appear.

A more equable, sensible and realistic young woman would have striven to allay her lord and master's disappointment and impatience. But Anne was not in the habit of putting herself out for anyone. Paradoxically, Catherine's existence was her sole protection. Henry VIII felt unable to dissolve his second marriage without opening the door to a revalidation of the first. But Catherine, debilitated by her virtual imprisonment, died on 7 January 1536. On the 29th, the very day of her predecessor's funeral, Anne gave birth to a stillborn child, a boy. Her bad luck persisted. Henry was not prepared to wait another seventeen years to rid himself of an exasperating wife. He accused Anne of adultery and instituted proceedings against her, being at pains to observe the formalities, but took no notice of his wife's denials: he had the marriage annulled and ordered Anne Boleyn's execution on 19 May 1536. He was considerate enough to spare her the axe, which was thought to be less efficient and more ignominious than the sword, and sent for a particularly skilful executioner from Calais to behead her. He married Jane Seymour eleven days later.

Elizabeth was now demoted in her turn. Although she and her half-sister Mary remained daughters of the king and were recognized and brought up as such, their dubious legitimacy deprived them of all claim to the title Princess Royal. The birth of a son to Jane Seymour, who gladdened the heart of Henry VIII by finally presenting him with a male heir, reduced their importance accordingly but had a pacifying effect on the royal family. Mary no longer had to give way to her younger sister and both girls deferred to their brother quite naturally and with good grace. Their presence at court created no problems. King Henry had no other son, so it was not in his interest to cast doubt on their competence to occupy the throne. This was because, by force of circumstance, they were being held in reserve. Granting them a respectable status was essential in order to maintain their value on the marriage market. There had been some question, when Elizabeth was born, of betrothing her to the Duke of Angoulême, son of Francis I. When Henry proposed to marry her off to a nephew of Charles V, the latter refused on the grounds of 'her mother's life and death'. The king did not wish his younger daughter's matrimonial stock to fall still further on the European market.

However, Henry's conjugal life was becoming more and more notoriously chaotic. Having done her duty by giving birth to a son, Jane Seymour died, carried off by puerperal fever like so many other women of her day. Next, the king sought to contract a political marriage. None of his attempts to forge an alliance with Francis I succeeded. His reputation did him no favours. Mary of Guise, who was approached because of her tall stature and good health, declined. 'I am tall,' she said, 'but I have a little neck.' And she set sail for Scotland, where she married James V. Henry then turned his attention to Germany and opted for Anne of Cleves on the strength of his ambassador's recommendation and a portrait by Holbein. He would have done better to listen to the French ambassador, who, weighing his words carefully, described her as 'tall and dignified, but of average comeliness.' The young woman landed at Dover and pressed on to London in spite of the atrocious weather, not wanting to delay her meeting with the king, who was awaiting her at Greenwich.

Dismayed by the sight of her, Henry exclaimed that he had – in modern parlance – been sold a pup. What should he do? He could not back out without causing serious diplomatic ructions, so the marriage went ahead at Greenwich in January 1540. After several effortful nights at Anne's side, however, Henry confided to his minister Cromwell that he found her 'abhorrent'. He did not blame his impotence on any mysterious factors such as spells or curses, but simply on the distaste inspired in him by his young bride's flabby breasts. Meantime, innocent as a nun and chirpy as a bird in springtime, Anne saw nothing abnormal about her undisturbed nights. Convinced that a kiss was enough to engender a child, she failed to comprehend the advice offered by her ladies-in-waiting, who were alarmed by her bridegroom's ill humour. The king persevered for another six months. Then, in July 1540, he decided to send 'the Flanders mare' home. Although naive and unsophisticated, Anne did not lack common sense. She willingly agreed to a divorce on condition that Henry did not send her back to Germany. Relieved to have avoided an unpleasant scandal, the king assigned her a royal residence and a comfortable pension. Thus provided for, she lived out her life in peace, on amicable terms with all the royal family.

Having burnt his fingers on a foreign bride and his ambassadors' over-indulgent reports, Henry VIII proceeded to choose himself a beautiful young bride in the person of

Catherine Howard. But she was too flighty, flirtatious and reckless to retain the favour of a man embittered by illness. Grossly overweight and suffering from horribly ulcerated legs, the king was incapable of satisfying his carnal desires even when they were aroused by a pair of shapely breasts. Catherine Howard was charged with adultery, like her cousin Anne, and beheaded in 1542. Henry VIII's sixth and last wife, Catherine Parr, married him in 1543. She did so with little enthusiasm, as one can imagine. Nevertheless, being a wise and sensible woman with the experience of two previous marriages to draw on, she held her own in an undramatic manner and proved an excellent and affectionate stepmother to Mary, Elizabeth and young Edward, the crown prince. It was then that Elizabeth began to spend more time at court and was able to observe her father at close quarters.

But to return to 1536, the year of Anne Boleyn's execution. How can we reflect on the person of Elizabeth without wondering how she reacted to her mother's death? This is a difficult question. We do not know when she heard the news or who informed her of it and in what terms. At two years and eight months old she would certainly have been affected by the drama had she been living with her parents, even allowing for the lack of family intimacy prevailing at the period and in her royal environment. But, in accordance with custom, she had been installed at Hatfield House, which was situated in the country some twenty miles from London. There she was provided with attendants and entrusted to a governess, Lady Bryan, who had fulfilled the same function for Mary, the king's elder daughter. The latter was thus compelled to share the home of the child who had usurped her title, her position and her father's affection. Whenever the king visited young Elizabeth, Mary was confined to her room because of her loyalty to her mother and her flat refusal to recognize Anne and her child. Anne's execution wrought another change in the half-sisters' relationship. Elizabeth was reduced to the simple status of the king's daughter and Mary regained precedence over her by virtue of their difference in age. Although the two girls continued to live together, Mary now had her own servants. No longer subjected to the humiliation of having to wait upon her sister, she gave free rein to the tender feelings aroused in her by an amusing and intelligent little girl who quickly grasped that she owed her elder sister some respect.

Although Henry VIII had little compunction in beheading those who displeased him, he did not vent his spleen on his victims' children. (In any case, a nobleman condemned to death traditionally entrusted his offspring to the sovereign's care.) In his younger daughter's case he continued to visit her, often invited her to court and was at pains to give her the best possible education. Thus, where Mary had suffered from the ill treatment inflicted on her mother, Elizabeth was spared the torment aroused by her own mother's tragic end. She never evinced any feelings of inferiority vis-à-vis her sister or brother that might have been fostered by her mother's disgrace, any more than she manifested resentment towards her father. On the contrary, she admired him, showed no fear in his presence and, once she became queen, often cited him as an example to be emulated. Besides, the scaffold that chills the modern imagination was then an instrument of government.

So many illustrious figures had been beheaded, whether for treason or for refusing to support the king in his quest for a divorce, that their descendants regarded such a death as honorable. As we shall see, Elizabeth's intimates included plenty of people who had been orphaned for reasons of state. Robert Dudley, her closest friend, the Duke of Norfolk, premier peer of the realm, her cousin Catherine Grey – all had lost a parent to the headsman's axe. Once on the throne, Elizabeth favoured her maternal kinsfolk and gladly accepted, from the Earl of Hertford, a locket ring containing two portraits of herself in profile and her mother full-face. But, although she never disowned Anne Boleyn, she made no attempt to rehabilitate her memory. Very sensibly, she was averse to rekindling the debate about her own legitimacy. What did remain with her was an extreme reluctance to order executions and – a rarity in the sixteenth century – a genuine respect for human life.

The long-awaited birth of the crown prince, Edward, in

October 1537, finally set Henry VIII's mind at rest about the future of his dynasty. As a result, he drew closer to his daughters and summoned them to London with greater frequency. His son's christening became the occasion of a regular family celebration. He named Mary Edward's godmother, a token of true reconciliation, and expressed a wish that Elizabeth should also attend the ceremony. Charged with presenting the chrismal bonnet to be placed on the infant's head after baptism, she herself was so small that she had to be carried to the altar by two noblemen. Until her father's last marriage, however, she never lingered at court. In any case, the little prince was sent to live in the country with his sisters. The royal children spent their life in one or another of the royal residences near London. Lady Bryan relinquished her duties with Elizabeth in order to take charge of Edward, and the little girl was entrusted to Catherine Champernon, known as Kate, to their mutual satisfaction. She remained in Elizabeth's service after her marriage to a cousin of Anne Boleyn, John Ashley, who was also a member of the princess's household.

Kate was instantly captivated by her young pupil, who displayed so much enthusiasm for her studies that it proved necessary to curb her somewhat. The royal children were taught Latin and the rudiments of rhetoric from the age of six, it being essential for a prince to be able to express himself. Elizabeth showed a remarkable aptitude for this art. The king's secretary, Thomas Wriothesley, who had come to settle some matter with Princess Mary, asked to see her younger sister, then aged six. Elizabeth addressed him, he was amused to report, with the self-assurance of a woman of forty. The princess was also instructed in French and Italian, music and astronomy. She proved to be a voracious reader. Her sister, although very painstakingly educated, was ignorant of the pleasures of intellectual speculation, whereas Elizabeth revelled in intellectual sparring matches throughout her life and seldom went anywhere without a large bag containing a book or two. She had been taught to judge a work by its stylistic elegance as well as its content, hence the love of rhythm and nuances of expression that made her such an exceptional public speaker.

Elizabeth was eleven years old when Catherine Parr, her last stepmother, came into her life just as her governess Kate had exhausted her store of knowledge, rendering the appointment of some tutors essential. The queen closely followed the progress of Elizabeth and Edward, who was quite as precocious and studious as his sister. The two children lived in separate residences, but their teachers, all Cambridge men, frequently conferred, employed the same methods, and often taught their pupils together. The only educational difference between them was that Elizabeth was not initiated into the practical aspect of politics. John Cheke, the most eminent of the tutors, took charge of the future king. For Elizabeth he recommended a young man named William

Grindal, an excellent Hellenist and Latinist, but no sooner was he appointed than he unfortunately died. Elizabeth then requested the services of Roger Ascham, Grindal's teacher and Cheke's favourite pupil. She got her way, and Ascham exerted a decisive influence on her. He complained of never being able to go to Cambridge because she refused to let him absent himself, even for a few days. He taught her a great deal more than Latin and Greek, in fact he was so successful that, at the age of sixteen, Elizabeth could express herself as fluently in the classical tongues as in French and Italian, the language that was replacing Latin in diplomatic circles. Fond of the open air, of physical exercise, games and sports, Ascham transmitted those likings to his young pupil, who always found it easy to alternate between intellectual pleasures and the more worldly delights of riding, dancing and the chase.

In 1544, by which time he was well aware that he would have no more children, Henry VIII resolved to settle the order of succession by officially rehabilitating his two daughters and designating them his successors in the event that his son died without issue. If they themselves had no children the crown would pass to the descendants of his younger sister Mary, who had married the Duke of Suffolk after the death of Louis XII. He debarred the offspring of his elder sister Margaret, Queen of Scotland, on the grounds that they were not pure English. A sovereign had to be born in England to rule the country, he considered, and the majority of his subjects endorsed that theory.

For Elizabeth, the death of Henry VIII on 29 January 1547 ushered in a period of dangerous uncertainty that did not end until eleven years later, when she finally inherited the throne. It was during this decade, which spanned the reigns of her brother and her sister and was marked by violent political and religious upheavals, that she underwent her political education. Constantly spied on and suspected, ostracized and courted in turn, she learned the virtues of prudence and dissimulation, grasped the absolute necessity of keeping her opinions a secret, and acquired the art of defending herself with perfect composure. The six-year reign of her brother, with whom she got on well, was a time of personal trial; under her sister's rule she experienced political danger of a potentially lethal nature.

Catherine Parr invited Elizabeth to share her London residence when she vacated the royal palace on the king's death. The queen dowager was gentle, affectionate and very devout. We might be tempted to picture her as a straight-laced widow, but this would be to ignore the fact that, at thirty-five, she was still a woman with blood in her veins. She had married Henry VIII reluctantly, being in love with Thomas Seymour, Jane's younger brother and, thus, the uncle of young King Edward VI. Seymour combined the audacity of a successful ladies' man with the insouciance of a reckless youth. He had not, of course, been unwise enough to dance attendance on the queen during the king's lifetime, but as soon as Henry died he reappeared, all the surer of himself because his brother, the Duke of Somerset, whom the Privy Council had appointed Lord Protector, fulfilled the functions of regent on the boy king's behalf. He would gladly have aimed still higher, in fact, and had briefly considered marrying Mary or Elizabeth, but was dissuaded from pursuing that objective. Catherine, still an attractive, good-looking woman, had retained her feelings for him. They were married in secret in May 1547, only five months after Henry's death, and Seymour did not wait long before moving in with his wife and her stepdaughter.

The handsome newcomer's temerity was remarkable. Although he had been unable to fulfil his ambition of marrying the king's younger daughter, she continued to interest him. Now fourteen, Elizabeth was a very comely and elegant girl, if we are to believe the portrait painted for her father just before his death. Illumined by a pair of dark eyes whose vivacity recalled her mother's, her regular, extremely pallid features were framed by a abundant head of hair with reddish glints. The picture shows her holding a book in her hands and posing in front of an open Bible as if to underline her decorous and studious disposition. But there was nothing of the bluestocking about Elizabeth, and she was not insusceptible to the attentions paid her by the handsome man who lived under the same roof and whose panache and gaiety had transformed the household's bookish atmosphere. Catherine, pregnant for the first time at thirty-six and blinded by affection for her fourth husband and first love, abandoned her authority and common sense. She allowed Seymour to play some dangerous games.

The master of the house took to visiting Elizabeth's bedchamber early in the morning. If she was still in bed he would draw aside the curtains and try to tickle her – although, according to her governess, she took refuge under the bedclothes. If he found her already up he would wish her good morning, accompanying this salutation by slapping her on the back or buttocks. He sometimes appeared bare-legged, clad only in a short nightgown. The outraged governess complained so vigorously that Catherine made an effort to accompany her husband on these early-morning visits, not that he behaved any better on that account. So afraid of vexing him that she played an equivocal role, Catherine once participated in an unlikely scene in the garden: she pinned Elizabeth's arms to her sides while Seymour cut her gown to shreds. However, she began to worry that she was being deceived, and that the flirtation was going too far. Elizabeth, for her part, pulled herself together and adopted a more circumspect attitude. Although she liked to sleep late, she was careful to rise and get dressed early enough to discourage Seymour's morning romps. Catherine was coming to term and her health gave rise to concern, so she seized the opportunity to remove the princess. The two women mutually decided to part without acrimony. Elizabeth and her suite installed themselves in the home of a gentleman and his wife who were friends of the queen dowager. The young princess conceded that it would be better to avoid intimacy with a man who may have attracted her more than she knew. But she had not seen the last of Seymour. Catherine failed to survive the birth of a daughter born in September 1548, and Seymour, liberated by her disappearance from the scene, fancied that marriage to the princess was within his reach at last.

Seymour's ambition was not matched by his intelligence, and his dreams of marrying Elizabeth prompted him to devise a grandiose scheme. For a start, he won over the governess to his way of thinking. Casting prudence and common sense to the winds in her turn, Kate broached the matter to Elizabeth, who smiled and blushed but did not appear to take the proposition amiss. Shocked by the financial machinations associated with it, however, she declined to commit herself. Seymour also endeavoured to gain the affections of the young king – they corresponded by means of notes concealed beneath a carpet – and strove to convince him that he would be able to request Parliament to end his minority. There took shape in Seymour's rather overheated imagination the prospect of removing his elder brother, the Lord Protector, in favour of himself. The truth was, he was conspiring against the established order, and the Privy Council reacted accordingly. On 17 January 1549 Seymour was arrested and consigned to the Tower of London, the prelude to a state trial.

Elizabeth was now in a very awkward position. Her governess, Kate Ashley, and her financial adviser, Thomas Parry, were also arrested on suspicion of having abetted

Seymour's plan to marry her without the Council's knowledge. That was where their error lay, and that was what warranted their detention and interrogation. Elizabeth could not escape the same suspicion, and she too was questioned by a special, Council-appointed commissioner, Sir Robert Tyrwhit. A lone girl of fifteen, she defended herself with remarkable skill and vigour.

Tyrwhit's object was to reinforce the charge against Seymour, but he misjudged the princess by advising her to lay responsibility for his schemes on her servants and gain the Council's indulgence by citing her youth and inexperience. She refused to give way, proclaimed her innocence, and took the offensive by accusing the Council, in her turn, of failing to defend the reputation of the king's sister by spreading rumours that she was with child by Seymour. The commissioner had to concede that he was dealing with someone more astute than himself. He reported to the Council that Elizabeth was a resolute young woman, and that nothing would be got out of her 'but by great polity' – in other words, except with great skill.

So Elizabeth won the day, but it had been a harsh lesson. She took back Kate Ashley, of whom she was very fond, but Parry never entirely regained her trust. Justifiably indignant that he had dabbled in the financial arrangements proposed by Seymour, she appointed another adviser to handle her affairs: William Cecil, who thereupon embarked on a great political career. Elizabeth displayed no outward sign of great emotion when Seymour was sentenced to death and beheaded. He was a man of spirit but lacking in judgement, she remarked coldly.

Some historians have chosen to regard this distasteful affair as the root of her distrust of men and marriage. In reality, however, although Elizabeth had no wish to marry, it did not detract from her liking for the company of men, and men of Seymour's stamp. Like him, all her favourites were handsome, amusing and intelligent but incapable of dominating her intellectually. This episode was important because it brought home to her, for the first time, that her proximity to the throne rendered her both exalted and vulnerable. It was only too easy for some conspirator to implicate her merely by association. From now on, her conduct was governed by extreme circumspection. The princess reimmersed herself in her books, dressed modestly and cultivated a low profile. She confined herself to exchanging letters, erudite and religious in tone, with her royal brother, who welcomed her with great ceremony whenever she came to court and kept her constantly at his side.

Edward VI, the boy king, was a frail and sickly youth but receptive to things of the mind and passionately interested in religious matters. Under the regency of his uncle the Duke of Somerset, the Lord Protector, Protestantism was consolidated first by the Act of Uniformity, which prohibited the celebration of the Catholic Mass, and then by the publication of the Book of Common Prayer, a prayerbook that facilitated the churches' transition from Latin to the vernacular.

The Lord Protector's authority, already weakened by

his brother's execution, was further eroded by a number of popular insurrections arising from the intensive development of sheep-farming, which was enriching the great landowners but ruining the peasants. Somerset was now challenged by his rival on the Council, John Dudley, an ambitious, determined and reckless man. Taking advantage of his influence over the young king, who was sufficiently under his sway to grant him honours, riches and the title Duke of Northumberland, the royal favourite rallied the malcontents around him. At his instigation, Somerset was arrested for treason and executed in February 1552.

At fifteen Edward was no longer a minor, properly speaking. He presided over the Council but left Northumberland to govern. Although the movement in favour of the Protestant Church was going from strength to strength, everything was thrown back into the melting pot by a deterioration in the young king's state of health. His sister Mary would succeed him, and it was common knowledge that she had never abandoned her Catholic beliefs. She had adopted the new religion under pressure from her father and had been unable to renounce it during her brother's reign, but no one doubted that her first step as queen would be to celebrate a Catholic Mass and remove the Protestants from power. This did not suit Northumberland.

He persuaded Edward VI to break his father's testament, set aside his two sisters on grounds of bastardy, and name as his successor Jane Grey, the granddaughter of Mary Tudor, queen dowager of France. Another advantage from

Northumberland's point of view was that Jane happened to be his daughter-in-law. When informed of this, Elizabeth was intelligent enough to avoid involvement by remaining at home instead of going to her dying brother's bedside. Mary's reaction was equally prompt. Alerted, strangely enough, by Robert Dudley, Northumberland's youngest son, she took refuge in Norfolk, where the Catholic party had remained powerful.

Edward VI died on 5 July 1553. Jane Grey was thereupon proclaimed queen in London, whereas Mary was recognized as such in Norfolk. The inevitable confrontation was over within a few days. The army raised by Northumberland with a view to seizing Mary disintegrated. Catholic or not, she was the daughter of Henry VIII. The crown passed to her by right, and she was acclaimed as queen on her arrival in London. As for Northumberland, he was escorted to the Tower amid jeering crowds, together with his young and luckless daughter-in-law Jane, the nine-days' queen, and his four sons.

Elizabeth had wisely remained aloof from all this turmoil, pleading ill health. As soon as Mary's triumph was beyond doubt, she made a miraculous recovery and joined her sister on the road to London. The queen welcomed her with numerous tokens of affection and accorded her second place in her train, and they entered the capital together. The coronation procession was as magnificent as custom prescribed. Elizabeth shared her carriage with the corpulent Anne of Cleves, the only one of Henry VIII's six wives to have survived, who made no secret of her pleasure at being included. Everyone was struck by the marked contrast between the two sisters. At thirty-seven, the queen had a face that bore the marks of an arduous life. She was not downright ugly, according to the Venetian ambassador, but his description of her lacked enthusiasm: 'Short rather than tall in height, of a pale complexion mingled with red, and very thin, she has big grey eyes, red hair and a round face, her nose being perhaps a trifle long and broad: all in all, if she were not beginning to approach her declining years by reason of age, one could call her handsome rather than ugly.'[1] But she was totally devoid of charm, and her short-sightedness lent her a distant air. Her young sister, on the other hand, radiated youth, elegance and majesty. Moreover, Elizabeth had mastered the art of waving to crowds, attracting their attention and acknowledging their plaudits with a happy smile. Although she undoubtedly represented the future, the present rather perturbed her. If her brother, who had always shown her great affection, had nonetheless tried on his deathbed to remove her right of succession, what did the coming-to-power of a sister with whom she had no affinity portend for her?

Thus began the reign of England's first queen, a difficult reign that justified all the fears Henry VIII had expressed at the prospect of leaving his throne to a daughter. One wonders what he would have said had he been able to foresee that not only England, but Scotland as well, would be ruled by women until the closing years of the century.

2

Mary Tudor: An Object Lesson

1553–8

Mary Tudor's reign was brief and unfortunate, not only for the country but for the sovereign herself. Her five years in power were marked by aberration and sterility. The queen's chequered existence had left its imprint on her mind as well as her features. She had felt her fall from grace far more than Elizabeth, if only because of her age, which enabled her to gauge the full extent of what she had lost. Furthermore, unlike her sister, who never questioned her duty of obedience to her father and was consequently not at odds with him, Mary had refused to bow to his will. Henry's response had been to keep her in a state of humiliating isolation. Entirely deprived of affection during her adolescence and inured to injustice, she never ceased to turn towards Spain, her mother's native land, for emotional solace and political support.

Yet as a little girl, while she was still Princess of Wales and first in line to the throne of England, Mary Tudor had been pampered by her father and made much of by his courtiers. Her childhood remained a happy one until 1527, when the question of her parents' divorce was raised for the first time. She was then eleven years old. The king was not at liberty to act quickly, as we have seen. He continued to pay the queen the minimum of consideration he owed her, like it or not, and the first few years of the dispute brought no change in the affection he had always shown their daughter. In 1531 his attitude hardened: the queen was packed off to Hertfordshire and Mary went to live in Richmond, a royal residence in Yorkshire far from the capital. Mother and daughter never saw each other again. Henry VIII forbade all contact and correspondence between them, and he himself did not receive his daughter for three years. Elizabeth's birth robbed Mary of her title and her independence. She was obliged to share her younger sister's abode, where she occupied a very inferior position, and Henry demanded the return of her silver plate and jewellery – an act of meanness that shocked his courtiers. Plenty of people supported the old queen in her struggle with Anne Boleyn, for everyone felt that the king had been goaded into such behaviour by his new wife. It seemed thoroughly excessive to harass the princess in this way and deprive her of her family circle. Mary, who steadfastly refused to recognize Anne as queen, was confined to her room and had her meals served there whenever the king was visiting little Princess Elizabeth. This severity only reinforced Mary's intransigence. The clandestine messages she received from her mother recommended a contradictory line of conduct: she must obey her father but never yield to him in religious matters. To Mary, fidelity to her religion demanded that she refuse to recognize her parents' divorce. Anne Boleyn's execution changed everything. Liberated by her own mother's death, which occurred the same year, Mary took the Spanish ambassador's advice and yielded to her royal father at last, renouncing the Catholic Church and regaining a respectable status at court.

Despite the snubs she had received, she remained dignified and charitable. She did not extend her contempt for Anne Boleyn to the latter's daughter, with whom she maintained relations which, if not cordial, were at least correct. On becoming queen she treated her political enemies leniently, her immediate impulse being to pardon them. Thus, she refused to order the execution of her cousin Jane Grey, whom she liked and knew too well not to be convinced that she had merely been a victim of her family's ambition. She proved uncompromising only in matters of religion. Her fanaticism earned her the sobriquet 'Bloody', for in re-establishing the Catholic Church on her accession she did not shrink from saving people's souls by burning them at the stake. It was her religious zeal and total lack of political instinct that spelled her downfall. She failed to grasp the absolute necessity of perpetuating the Tudors' unshakeable identification with England. On the contrary, what dominated her was pride in her Spanish blood and adherence to her religion. Before long she seemed a foreigner in her own land, and nothing could be more dangerous to a sovereign. By failing to gauge the extent of that danger, she incurred her subjects' hatred.

It was not solely a question of doctrine. Protestantism had not had time to become very deeply entrenched in England, and it is conceivable that many of its inhabitants would have accepted a return to the Latin Mass despite their loathing of priests and ecclesiastical authority, especially in London and the south of the kingdom. However, this would be to neglect the economic aspect of the matter. The sale of the monastic estates had enriched a substantial section of the population. Like the purchasers of national assets in France after the Revolution, the new owners had no intention of relinquishing their new acquisitions. Their attachment to the new Church was indissolubly bound up with their freshly acquired wealth. It was the financial interest of these purchasers – whether nobles, commoners or big peasant farmers – that safeguarded the Reformation in England.[1] The queen's religious policy was greeted with predictable discontent. A vigorous opposition made it clear that she would never be able to reconstitute the patrimony of the Catholic Church, and the first Masses to be celebrated in London were interrupted by riots. But the queen had no political antennae, and her matrimonial projects aggravated the prevailing religious unrest.

Being already thirty-seven when she came to the throne,

Mary had no time to lose if she wanted to produce an heir. In the view of her privy councillors and Parliament, there was one pre-eminently suitable candidate: Edward Courtenay, a great-grandson of Edward IV and last scion of the Yorks. Marriage to him would have consolidated the dynasty much as Henry VII's marriage to Elizabeth of York had done, and could have been speedily arranged. But Mary did not see it like that. Instead of thinking like a queen of England, she remained faithful to the principles that had guided her during her long years of waiting and disgrace, when the backing of Spain had been her only consolation. Charles V was still reigning when she ascended the throne. His son Philip, the widower of a Portuguese princess, was available. Irresistibly drawn to the idea of detaching England from an alliance with France and expanding Spain's sphere of influence still further, he proposed to Mary, and she, ignoring her subjects' widespread consternation, accepted him.

All attempts to marry her off had been doomed to failure once her parents' conjugal drama began. Francis I, who had considered her as a bride for the Dauphin, promptly dropped the idea. Who would have wanted to marry a princess virtually in disgrace, tainted with illegitimacy, bereft of all influence and covertly Catholic despite being the daughter of a heretic monarch? The question did not arise again during her brother's lifetime. Once free and on the throne, however, Mary willingly offered her hand to the heir to the kingdom of Spain. With the enthusiasm of an ageing spinster, she took to daydreaming in front of Titian's magnificent portrait of him, which Charles V had sent her, and soon fancied that she would be marrying for love. Her royal suitor was eleven years her junior. Although she confided to Simon Renard, the Spanish ambassador, that she was somewhat worried by her prospective husband's youth, Renard maintained that the young widower, who had fathered a child, Don Carlos, was exceptionally mature for his age. If Mary was troubled by her subjects' cold reaction and her advisers' disapproval, she did not show it, and obstinacy definitely remained her most typical characteristic. Elizabeth did not offer an unsolicited opinion on the matter, needless to say, but her silence did not preclude her from giving it some thought.

There was no reason why Elizabeth should have cherished any illusions about the felicities of marriage. Her father's conjugal balance sheet had been disastrous and the shenanigans of Thomas Seymour, her stepmother's husband, had left her scarred. But it was her observation of Mary's marriage – which was, as we shall see, disastrous on the personal as well as the political plane – that reinforced her innate distrust of the married state. The Spanish marriage succeeded in uniting two forms of opposition. The purely Protestant opposition was alarmed by the re-establishment of pontifical authority and the resurgence of Catholic strength; the so-called political opposition feared a Spanish takeover. Elizabeth was all the more concerned because, being unadulteratedly English and Protestant, she was by definition the contrary of her sister and, consequently, whether she liked it or not, situated at the interface between the two factions. Charles V's ambassador, Simon Renard, was well aware of this and viewed the princess's potential power with trepidation.

Elizabeth had learned in her father's time not to ask idle questions, not to pass judgement to no purpose, and to practise discretion and obedience. During her sister's reign her position was far more difficult and dangerous, if only because she could not afford to remain passive. She had, for example, to take up a position on religious matters. She began by shunning all Catholic ceremonies, but, in view of the queen's manifest displeasure, judged it expedient to ask to be instructed in the kingdom's former religion. Doubtful of the sincerity of Elizabeth's conversion and warned against her daily by Renard, who would have liked to see the princess incarcerated in the Tower or worse, Mary treated her young sister with such coldness – she even sought, against her ministers' advice, to challenge her place in the line of succession – that Elizabeth requested permission to retire to the country. She did so, ostentatiously taking with her the copes and chasubles essential to the celebration of the Catholic Mass. It was a timely departure.

She was not in London on 2 January 1553, when Charles V's envoys arrived in London charged with negotiating the terms of the marriage. They were greeted in the streets of the capital by scowling faces and even by a few snowballs, but there was worse to come. A veritable insurrection against the 'Spanish' queen took shape. It was led by Sir Thomas Wyatt, a Kentish gentleman who entered London at the head of three thousand men. The numerical superiority of the government troops compelled him to surrender, but the queen and her ministers had been badly frightened. Their reaction was illogical in its violence. That Wyatt and his principal lieutenants were executed was understandable enough, but it was incongruous that the same fate should be meted out to Jane Grey and her husband, who had been imprisoned in the Tower for months, completely ignorant of the conspiracy and cut off from the outside world. The queen and her ministers were, in fact, trying to intimidate Elizabeth, and they continued to pursue that policy at the prompting of Charles V's ambassador.

From Elizabeth's point of view, the great danger was that her mere existence represented a political threat to her sister. What could have been more useful to the opposition than a readily available replacement for the reigning queen? Elizabeth understood this so well that she remained obsessed throughout her life with the fear of naming her successor. She knew from experience – brutal experience, as it turned out – that the heir to a throne attracts dissidents like a magnet.

Once Wyatt's rebellion had been crushed, Mary faced up to the problem posed by her sister. Elizabeth had been at Ashridge since December, suffering from an attack of nephritis. She pronounced herself too ill to travel the thirty-odd miles between there and London, whither the queen had summoned her, but Mary would not accept this. When the physicians she dispatched to Elizabeth's bedside assured her that the journey would not prove fatal, she commanded her sister to present herself at court. Elizabeth wasted as much time as possible, travelling by litter and in very small stages, but she eventually entered the capital. Her pallor was so extreme that all who saw her were struck by it. She was conveyed to the palace of Whitehall, where she remained confined for a month while the Council debated her fate. Stephen Gardiner, the Bishop of Winchester, dug his heels in with Ambassador Renard's backing: Mary would never be able to reign in peace for as long as Elizabeth lived. As Mendoza, the future Spanish ambassador to England, wrote bluntly to the Bishop of Arras: 'It is considered that she will have to be executed, as while she lives it will be very difficult to make the Prince's [Philip's] entry here safe.'[2] But other councillors, notably Lord William Paget, the Secretary of State, firmly opposed this conclusion: to execute the princess, or even to arrest her, harboured a strong risk of fomenting a second rebellion underpinned by genuine popular enthusiasm. Mary vacillated until March. Then, unable to resist Spanish entreaties, she decided to confine Elizabeth in the Tower.

Elizabeth had always shown herself calm and dignified in times of trial. Under the circumstances, however, the mere mention of the Tower was enough to alarm her. At once a fortress, a royal palace, a prison and a place of execution for the great, it was in fact a group of buildings. Until now, Elizabeth had known only those reserved for the sovereign.

She had often entered the precincts to visit her father or her brother, who usually resided there. She had also played in the gardens as a child and spent a long time in front of the cages that held the lions in the Tower's menagerie, which were named after various kings. Quite recently she had accompanied her sister there on her triumphal entry into London. The Tower had been the point of departure for the great procession that had escorted Mary Tudor to Westminster for her coronation. This time, however, Elizabeth seemed likely to become acquainted with the fortress proper, its barred windows and dungeons hewn out of the living rock. Her imagination must have run riot because the Tower had a particularly sinister connotation for her: her mother had been executed and her mutilated body buried there, together with other victims of Henry VIII, in the Chapel of St Peter ad Vincula. Her transfer from Whitehall to the Tower could not but be a very bad omen. Her cousin Jane Grey had just been beheaded when everyone knew she had taken no part in Wyatt's rebellion. Why should her own fate be any more fortunate? She asked the two lords who had come to arrest her for an audience with her royal sister. Her request was denied. Would they at least give her time to write to her? The two men agreed, and Elizabeth composed her letter slowly – very slowly. She had learned that she would be taken to the Tower by boat because it was feared that conveying her there through the streets of London might provoke a surge of sympathy for her. She also knew that boats could not pass beneath London Bridge except at low tide, so the few hours she gained would gain her another whole day of relative freedom.

The letter is a heart-rending sight. Usually so neat, her handwriting is very irregular, and the numerous grammatical errors so uncharacteristic of her bear witness to her agitation and anxiety. In proof of her distrust she boldly scored the foot of the last page, which had remained blank, for fear that someone might forge her handwriting and add a confession of some kind. But the queen did not reply, and next day, a rainy Palm Sunday, Elizabeth's boat came to rest at the foot of the Tower. It had been decided that she should enter the precincts, not by the Queen's Stairs, but by Traitors' Gate, through which Anne Boleyn had passed as a prisoner escorted by her guards. Elizabeth drew herself up and declared: 'Here landeth as true a subject, being a prisoner, as ever landed at these steps, and before thee, O God, I speak it, having none other friends but thee.' As it happened, the state of the tide was such that she could not land there after all, so she came ashore at Tower Wharf and entered the fortress by way of the drawbridge.

On the queen's orders she was lodged in an apartment, not in a prisoner's cell, but deprived of all freedom of movement. For the first time in her life, perhaps, the princess who had always prided herself on being her father's daughter must have been haunted by the memory of her mother. Anne Boleyn had occupied these same rooms on two occasions: the eve of her marriage and the eve of her execution. Elizabeth was allowed to keep her attendants and have meals brought in from outside for fear of poison. After a few days she was even allowed to stroll along the battlements, but nothing could allay her agony of mind. Three executions took place during her imprisonment, and she several times asked if Jane Grey's scaffold had been dismantled. She lived in complete isolation, and no one was permitted to look in her direction on the occasions when she briefly left her quarters. One day a five-year-old boy, the son of one of her guards, presented her with a little bunch of flowers. They were promptly taken away from her in case a message was concealed in them. She was treated with respect, however. Elizabeth was a king's daughter, after all, and the future was uncertain. The Earl of Sussex warned his jailers to behave correctly, remarking that they might one day have to answer for their conduct.

The likelihood of that eventuality seemed to increase the more often Elizabeth's successive interrogations failed to elicit anything that might justify laying charges against her. Not only did she put up a spirited defence, but there was insufficient evidence – and, more important, perhaps, insufficient political determination – to convict her. The Spaniards urged the Council to act without delay, but to no avail; aware of the princess's popularity in London, the government fought shy of doing so, fearing that an utterly unwarranted execution – or even prolonged imprisonment – would set off an explosion of public resentment.

And so, two months after her arrest, Elizabeth was released, although the freedom granted her by her sister was heavily supervised. She was placed in the custody of Sir

Henry Bedingfield, the head of a prominent Norfolk family. Accompanied by a hundred men, he presented himself at the Tower to take possession of the prisoner. On 19 May the whole contingent set off for Woodstock, a somewhat dilapidated royal hunting lodge near Oxford. Elizabeth still feared for her safety, even though it became clear to her that imprisonment had not impaired her popularity. Far from it: on the short journey from London to Woodstock the scholars of Eton followed her litter, eager for a sight of her, and countryfolk pelted her with flowers and offered her cakes as she passed through their villages despite Bedingfield's efforts to keep them at a distance. When the cortège finally reached her modest new abode, Elizabeth pronounced it unworthy of her rank. Bedingfield ignored her protests and carefully examined all the locks. Having pessimistically reported that only three of the doors could be locked, he decided to install the princess in the caretaker's lodge.

Bedingfield proved finicky, pedantic and most concerned that his orders should be obeyed to the letter. He gave the princess a detailed account of these. All communication with the outside world was forbidden her, but she could rely on him in all matters affecting her safety. In other words, he had to ensure that the Protestants could not abduct her and the Catholics not assassinate her. Elizabeth recovered her composure and took great pleasure in being intractable: she complained incessantly, demanded justice, and preserved a stubborn silence when the priest prayed for the queen during Mass. Relations between the young girl and the old gentleman were excellent notwithstanding. Elizabeth teased him cruelly and called him her jailer; he considered himself her custodian and addressed her on bended knee.

Mary, relieved that there had been no need to cut off her sister's head and satisfied with the outcome of this tiresome episode, rather lost interest in Elizabeth's fate and directed all her attention to welcoming her future husband. The irruption of a man into an existence as sad, dreary and forlorn as hers was destined to bring her emotions to the boil. On the Spanish side, politics took pride of place. To Charles V, King of Spain, Emperor of Germany, Prince of the Netherlands and King of Sicily, a matrimonial alliance with England, whose four million inhabitants were outnumbered five to one by the population of France, counted for little on the European chessboard and was more of a prophylactic measure. It would enable him to counter the challenge posed by Henry II, King of France, who had secured the friendship of Scotland by marrying his son to Mary Stuart and advanced his pawns to the North Sea. Unrestricted trade between the English coast and Flanders was essential to Spain, which profited immensely from it: the entire Flemish textile industry depended on imports of cloth and raw wool from England. Thus, Charles V was reserving the possibility of taking concerted action to sever communication between France and Scotland. But his decision had been influenced by another factor. His son, who was hated in the Nether-lands, had little hope of succeeding him as elective emperor, so a supplementary crown, even if the title King of England conferred no power on him, was not to be sneezed at.

Kept informed by his ambassador, Charles V was well enough aware of the lack of enthusiasm shown by his son's future subjects to try to persuade him to be less Spanish in his ways and a trifle more broad-minded. Philip expressed his willingness to make a few concessions, especially as he did not propose to spend the rest of his life in England. He landed at Southampton on 19 July 1554. Five days later he made his entrance into Winchester, the diocese of Bishop Gardiner, one of the queen's most steadfast supporters. This was where the future spouses met on the eve of their marriage. Mary was not disappointed by her bridegroom's appearance. A slim, erect young man with very fair hair, pale skin and a heavy lower lip, he was entirely dressed in black in the Spanish manner and moved slowly and with dignity. He expressed himself in careful Latin, not knowing a word of English, and had to ask Mary, who spoke perfect Spanish, how to wish the company a good evening. We do not know how he reacted to the little woman who stood facing him in all her finery, flushed with excitement, but eye-witnesses reported that he was tactful enough to greet her with delight and affection. The wedding ceremony was suitably splendid, and after spending several days at Windsor the newly-weds entered London. Philip made a genuine effort to surround himself with Englishmen and conform to their ways. He even drank some English ale without pulling a face.

Nevertheless, foreign ambassadors stressed that political tension was mounting, engendered less by the Spanish marriage than by Mary's efforts to bring about a full re-establishment the Catholic religion and restore the Pope's spiritual authority over her realm. Paradoxically, Charles V's political realism dissuaded him from prodding Mary in that direction. Reluctant to see his son to become the focus of religious strife, he urged the Pope to delay sending a legate to England to put an end to the schism. It was not until the Pope had accepted the irrevocable loss of the Church's properties that his representative, Reginald Pole, the only English cardinal, could land at Dover. His arrival coincided with the election of a new Parliament, which displayed greater flexibility in religious matters. All antipontifical legislation was repealed and new laws directed against traitors and heretics were enacted. Henry VIII's work had been obliterated. It is conceivable that the country would have accepted these measures, had not Mary been so brutally overzealous.

Supported by Cardinal Pole – and by him alone, for it should again be emphasized that Philip took no part in this initiative – she instituted proceedings designed to combat heresy in January 1555. Those who refused to recant were burned alive. There were nearly three hundred such martyrs, most of them humble folk of whom many were women and very young people. The local inhabitants were compelled to witness these public executions by fire, which were all the more frightful because the weather was so exceptionally wet that it prolonged the unfortunate victims' sufferings while simultaneously enabling them to display immense courage. The queen's reputation, to which she owed her terrible nickname, 'Bloody Mary', never recovered. She was not only bloodthirsty but foolish into the bargain, for the effect of all this cruel, futile persecution was to infect her kingdom with a positive detestation of the Pope and the Catholic Church. Even if she realized this, she was too fanatical to draw back. Besides, she considered herself justified by a mark of divine favour: she had been expecting a child since November of the previous year. Her bishops ordained the singing of *Te Deum*s and she prostrated herself before every altar in sight. Her husband Philip, with an eye to the future, did not pin too many hopes on his prospective heir. He himself was a prey to darker and more realistic thoughts: his second wife seemed no more robust than his first, and the latter had died in childbirth.

In the event that neither Mary nor her child survived, would it not be wiser to make a friend of Princess Elizabeth, her heir apparent? Accordingly, Philip pressed for the complete rehabilitation of his young sister-in-law, summoned her to court, and reportedly took pleasure in her company and conversation. Then he waited and waited while a sinister farce unfolded in the queen's apartment. As 1555 wore on, Mary inevitably realized that her pregnancy was illusory, but she said nothing. Did she hope that this would keep her husband at her side? Did she believe that a miracle would occur? She had announcements prepared, withdrew from public life a month before the putative date of the child's birth, as custom prescribed, and organized processions and public prayers, but the baby failed to appear for the very good reason that there *was* no baby. The whole affair was becoming absurd and distressing. Philip left as soon as he decently could, and by August 1555 Mary found herself humiliated, ill, childless, and without a husband. She had few illusions: the future, she realized, belonged to Elizabeth. She tried hard to unload her by suggesting that she marry the Duke of Savoy, but Elizabeth refused so bluntly that the plan was abandoned. 'The afflictions suffered by her were such,' she informed the queen, 'that they had ... ridded her of any wish for a husband.'[3] Without much hope, Philip offered her his son Don Carlos, who was eleven at the time. Elizabeth would not be tempted, any more than she was by the King of Sweden, who offered her the hand of his son, Prince Eric. Once again, she informed her sister that she was too attached to her unmarried state to wish to exchange it.

She was granted permission to reconstitute her personal household and take up residence at Hatfield. Although delighted to have regained her independence and escaped the vigilance of her 'protectors', alias guards, she was so afraid of some reckless initiative on the part of her supporters that she took innumerable precautions. Because a single word might incriminate her, she could not afford to trust a soul. The danger confronting her was twofold: primarily political but also, and more threateningly still, religious. Mary would have hesitated to execute her sister for reasons of state, but she would have had no compunction in sacrificing her to the demands of her conscience. The laws against heretics were rigorously enforced until Mary's death, so it was not inconceivable that an ecclesiastical court composed of bishops determined to keep the kingdom under Catholic jurisdiction would have condemned Elizabeth to death on suspicion of Protestantism. Accordingly, the young princess compelled herself to maintain the strictest observance in matters of religion.

If she was not uneasier still, this was probably thanks to her brother-in-law, who kept an eye on her from far-off Spain. Convinced by now that Mary was terminally ill, Philip concentrated his diplomacy on Elizabeth. He was anxious to maintain the Habsburg-Tudor alliance and very much afraid that France would impose Mary Stuart, maternal great-granddaughter of Henry VII, as Queen of England if Elizabeth were removed by force. Did he contemplate marrying her after Mary's death? Some have said so, although he was well aware that, under the circumstances, a solid rapprochement would be worth more than a matrimonial alliance. Furthermore, he knew that Elizabeth would be hard to sway. His ambassador had reported that, when urged once more to marry, the princess had told him that she could not forget that her sister had forfeited the affection of her people by marrying a foreigner.[4] Besides, Mary was still alive.

Philip paid a second visit to England in 1557. By this time

his father Charles V had retired to the monastery of San Geronimo de Yuste and entrusted him with responsibility for his various kingdoms. Philip nonetheless considered it necessary to absent himself from Spain because he wanted England to participate in the war he was waging against France, and only his presence there would bring the requisite pressure to bear on Mary. He also thought it essential that Elizabeth should be present during his visit, not only so that he could cajole her – which he did by treating her with the greatest consideration – but also to associate his foreign policy with an extremely popular English princess. She was the only member of the royal party to be cheered at it made its way through the streets of London.

Philip departed for the Low Countries less than three months later, even though Mary had again announced that she was expecting a child. No one believed her this time, and she did not maintain the charade for long. The Spanish king had left his sick, lonely, pathetic wife to cope with a difficult situation. Totally subservient to her husband, she had agreed to take part in his continental war, a step that resulted in the loss of Calais, which the English had held for more than two centuries. Although this remnant of their French possessions may not have retained much strategic importance, its loss underlined the futility of the Spanish alliance. Ambassador Renard had no illusions about the success of this policy. A long report he wrote in March 1558 stated that it was 'impossible to stand between her [Elizabeth] and the throne', she being 'held in the highest honour and regard'. She was widely respected and supported by a powerful and well-organized political faction, and it was clear that, on her accession, England would become Protestant once more and leave the orbit of Spain.[5]

Mary was driven to despair by Philip's refusal to return from Brussels, where he still was, and console her. Demoralized and convinced that her enemies harboured designs on her life, she doubled her bodyguard and wore a coat of mail day and night. Only five persons were permitted access to her. She spent the last few months of her existence like a woman buried alive, as Elizabeth put it when recalling this period in later years. Elizabeth herself, who shunned the court from now on, devoted herself to curbing the enthusiasm of her supporters – who would gladly have hastened her accession – and to reflecting on the causes of the queen's failure. The Venetian ambassador observed that Mary's misfortunes stemmed from two sources: her unbridled and excessive love for an indifferent husband, and the hatred she had felt, ever since her accession, for her sister.

Hatred was a strong and surprising word to use in view of Mary's extremely cordial attitude towards her younger sister during the upheavals that ensued on the death of Edward VI and delayed her coronation. But everything changed after her humiliating phantom pregnancy. It was no use shutting her eyes: she knew that the nation's hopes were centred on Elizabeth, her successor and diametrical opposite. What exasperated the queen more than anything else was her certainty that Elizabeth was deceiving her, and that, all her denials notwithstanding, she would revoke the re-establishment of the Roman Catholic Church. She said she was a Catholic, but how could she not be suspected of duplicity? She proclaimed her ignorance of all Protestant conspiracies, but how could she be believed? She was keeping her cards close to her chest as circumstances prescribed, a game with which Mary herself was only too familiar, having played the Anglican at her father's insistence and maintained that pose until her accession. Thus the queen stubbornly declined to name Elizabeth her successor – an absurd refusal, given that Elizabeth was past removing.

Philip, who knew this better than anyone, dispatched a special envoy, Count de Feria, who arrived in England a week before Mary's death. On the instructions of his royal master, who was nominally King of England, he presided over a meeting of the Council at which Elizabeth's right of succession was confirmed and arrangements were made for the transfer of power in consultation with William Cecil, the princess's private secretary. Mary died early on the morning of 17 November 1558. At midday Elizabeth was proclaimed queen and the change of government took place without a hitch. The young queen formed her government within two days, even before leaving Hatfield House for London. Her first step was to appoint Cecil to the vital post of Chief Secretary of State. He owed his important status entirely to her, an essential guarantee of any royal adviser's loyalty. She had complete confidence in his judgement and made it clear to him 'that you will be faithful to the state, and that without respect of my private will, you will give me that counsel you think best, and if you shall know anything necessary to be declared to me of secrecy, you shall show it to myself only. And assure yourself I will not fail to keep taciturnity therein, and therefore herewith I charge you.'[6] Cecil often gave her advice she would sooner not have heard and did not invariably follow, but this independence formed part of their agreement. The new sovereign's second step was to effect a considerable reduction in the size of the Council: 'I do consider that a multitude doth make rather discord and confusion than good counsel.'[7]

If Philip thought his benevolence had earned him his sister-in-law's gratitude, he was mistaken. The new queen lost no time in distancing herself from Spain. When Feria came to congratulate her, expecting some sign of appreciation, she briskly informed him that she owed her accession, not to his master's protection, but solely to the will of her people. Compelled to swallow his pride, Feria rather sheepishly reported to Philip that he had been received rather like a man who came bearing 'bulls from a dead Pope'. The kingdom he said, was now in the hands of young people, traitors and heretics all. The old and the Catholics were dissatisfied but dared not open their mouths. Elizabeth seemed to Feria 'incomparably more feared than her sister, and gives her orders and has her way as absolutely as her father did.' Spain had lost a kingdom 'body and soul'.[8] The Spanish marriage had been a total failure.

One wonders sometimes whether bad examples may not be more salutary than good ones. Elizabeth became a great queen by turning all of Mary Tudor's initiatives on their head. A refusal to embark on a continental war was one of her political constants; she flaunted her pride in being purely English and her conduct was guided by the danger of marrying a foreigner. Religious fanaticism, whether Catholic or Protestant, always horrified her. Convinced of the absolute necessity to govern in accord with Parliament, she accepted the idea of compromise. More surprising still was the conclusion of a speech to Parliament delivered by her Lord Keeper of the Great Seal. The queen had charged him to inform the House that she would never be governed by her will or whim to such an extent that, in order to satisfy them, she imposed chains upon her subjects or gave them cause to manifest their grievances by engaging in riot or disorder.[9] This was a statement of paramount importance. For the first time, a monarch had acknowledged that subjects could rebel in consequence of their sovereign's folly and conceded that the divine right of kings must be tempered by reason. Finally, personal experience had also acquainted Elizabeth with the attraction inevitably exerted by a successor. Opposition became consolidated and crystallized around a pretender to the throne. Like her sister, she did not name her successor until the very last moment; but, unlike her sister, she had to deal with a pretender as dangerous in captivity as at liberty. That pretender's name was Mary Stuart.

3

The 'Reinette'

1542–63

If Elizabeth's birth had been a sore disappointment, that of Mary Stuart nine years later, on 8 December 1542, was greeted no more warmly. Her ailing, bedridden father, James V of Scotland, had already been stricken by the death of his two sons the previous year, and by his defeat by English forces at Solway Moss on 24 November, which left his country open to invasion. On hearing the news, he turned his face to the wall, predicted the end of his kingdom, and died within a few days. Thus his daughter became Queen of Scotland to the sound of universal lamentations. She was less than a week old.

The Scottish debacle was so complete that the English did not follow up their advance. Henry VIII's victorious general justified the granting of a truce by emphasizing that it would be dishonourable of him to trample on a corpse or attack a widow and an infant at the very moment when the king, their husband and father, was being buried. War gave way to diplomacy. Henry recalled his general and sent Sir Ralph

Sadler, a trusted envoy who knew Scotland well, to examine the situation in general and the infant queen in particular.

The baby was disrobed in his presence, and the widowed queen, Mary of Guise, proudly remarked that she was a robust child who would one day be as tall as her mother. Sadler, who acknowledged this, addressed himself to the crucial question of who would govern the kingdom during Mary Stuart's minority. The Englishman, who distrusted Mary of Guise and her French connections, supported the candidacy of the Earl of Arran, a direct descendant of James III's sister and, thus, second in line of succession. Despite his lack of personal authority, Arran was duly appointed regent in preference to the queen mother. His feeble intellect, docile nature and lack of realism – which became steadily more pronounced – did not displease the English, who glimpsed the possibility of seizing Scotland without recourse to war: it would be sufficient to marry the Queen of Scotland to Edward, son and heir of Henry VIII. The future king was five, the queen only a few weeks old, but no matter.

The Earl of Arran consented to this idea, and the requisite agreements were signed. The two parties solemnly committed themselves to the marriage. In view of the youthful fiancée's age it was agreed that she would remain in Scotland until she turned eleven, at which time she would be married by proxy and come to England. Meanwhile, Henry VIII proposed to send an English tutor to Scotland to live with Mary. He and his wife would attend to the little girl's health and wellbeing and, later on, to her education. It went without saying that the English king promised to respect the Scottish kingdom's independence both before and after her marriage.

The Scots had little faith in their powerful neighbour's sincerity, and Henry VIII had failed to allow for violent fluctuations in Scottish political life. The treaties were denounced, whereupon Henry VIII, ever impatient and irascible, took up arms once more and embarked on a relentless military campaign. The Earl of Hertford, who commanded his forces, was instructed to burn Edinburgh and raze it to the ground, so that its ruins would be a reminder of its inhabitants' duplicity and disloyalty for generations to come. Hertford carried out his orders with great zeal. This brutal war went on for two years, during which the infant queen was transported from one castle to another to prevent her from being abducted by the English. The year 1544 saw the birth in France of a first child to Henry, son and heir of Francis I, and Catherine de Médicis. By opening up the possibility of an alternative matrimonial policy – one particularly acceptable to Mary of Guise – this led to a complete reversal of Scottish public opinion.

Factors that also favoured a French marriage included the brutality of the English armies, which were continuing their offensive; the personal authority and composure of Mary of Guise, queen dowager of Scotland, which secured her the regency a few years later; and the accession in 1547 of Henry II of France, who was very amenable to taking action in defence of a Scotland under merciless attack by its neighbour. Defeated at Pinkie Cleugh, compelled to submit to occupation by English troops and to seek assistance from France, the Scots briefly forgot their internal squabbles. In July 1548 their parliament agreed to give Mary in marriage to the eldest son of the King of France on condition that the latter defended Scotland as if it were his own kingdom but undertook not to annex it. The prompt departure of the *reinette,* the 'little queen', to use her French sobriquet, had become an urgent necessity because it would have been imprudent to keep her within her own dominions, which were partly under English occupation. And so, on 29 July 1549, Mary left the shores of Scotland bound for a new life in France. She was six-and-a-half years old.

Mary Stuart is the kind of historical figure that kindles controversy and fires the imagination. The various episodes in her short and dramatic life possess an aesthetic quality, not necessarily attributable to her beauty, that encourages one to fantasize. How can anyone fail to be stirred by the vision of a little girl taking leave of her tearful mother and going aboard a beflagged royal ship, its sails flapping in the wind, accompanied by four pretty little companions no taller than the sea boots of the bearded, smiling sailors who gently shepherded them up the gangplank? Mary had not been parted from those four scions of great Scottish families, all named Mary like herself and assigned to her as companions at her birth. Entranced by this novel experience and heedless of the boat's violent motion, the carefree little girls proceeded to laugh and frolic amid the ropes and cannon unsupervised by their charming governess, Lady Fleming, an illegitimate daughter of James IV, who had succumbed to seasickness.

It took them six days and nights of stormy weather on the high seas to reach Roscoff, where they were introduced to the delights of *la belle France*. Their onward journey from Brittany to the Île-de-France was punctuated by festivities and fireworks. To the sound of fifes and drums, the youthful queen was preceded through the streets of the towns on her route by a contingent of children attired in white and armed with miniature pikes and halberds. The royal family gave her an affectionate welcome at the Château de Saint-Germain, and Henry II told the *reinette* – her official designation at the French court – that she was 'the most perfect child' he had ever seen. In 1548, Henry II and Catherine de Médicis still had only three children: Francis, the Dauphin, who was one year younger than his little fiancée, and two daughters, Elizabeth, who later married Philip II of Spain, and Claude, the future Duchess of Lorraine. The four children were brought up together in a pampered, protected environment. Need one stress the difference between Mary's childhood, as it unfolded from then on, and Elizabeth's? The former was flattered by the finest poets – 'Be content, mine eyes,' wrote du Bellay, 'you will never see a lovelier sight' – and could bask in the prospect of a brilliant future; the latter was forever a prey to doubt, danger and loneliness. Their upbringing differed too. Elizabeth, as we have seen, underwent a very bookish, highly political education supplemented by observation of the events unfolding around her. Mary was brought up to be an ideal queen consort. Music, dancing, poetry, deportment, Latin and Italian (though not English, which she did not learn until much later, during her captivity) – all these were taught her with the greatest success.

Her status as queen regnant of Scotland was forgotten. True, she occasionally dressed in Scottish costume, a woollen plaid cloak in which she draped herself when dancing, and she continued to speak Scottish with her Maries, her nursemaid and her governess, the beautiful Lady Fleming. But it soon became apparent that the latter was more interested in King Henry II than in her young charge. Having consequently incurred the wrath of Diane de Poitiers, the king's official mistress, who was unaccustomed to competing for her royal lover's affections although she was twenty years his senior, the attractive interloper was sent home after giving birth to a son, the bastard d'Angoulême, who was brought up with Henry II's other children. Her place was taken by a Frenchwoman.

So Scotland featured very little in the young queen's existence. Although her mother, Mary of Guise, wrote her detailed reports on the state of her kingdom, it seems that, even when she nominally assumed power at the age of twelve, she confined herself to signing blank sheets and sending them to the regent without enquiring too deeply into what was going on. More serious were the secret treaties she endorsed some years later, in 1558. She was then sixteen and, unlike her future husband, very intelligent and sharp-witted, so it is hard to imagine that she failed to appreciate their significance. Under the terms of those agreements, she bequeathed Scotland to the King of France in the event of her dying without issue. She also undertook, on behalf of her subjects, to reimburse France for the sums expended on their defence and her own education. The treaties were secret but the taxes to be raised were real, and their effects on Scotland did not take long to make themselves felt.

Scotland was cold and misty, the amenities in its castles were rudimentary, and its inhabitants were unfamiliar with the choice refinements devised by the French of the Renaissance (when they were not busy slaughtering one another in the name of religion). However, the sophisticates of Fontainebleau or Chambord were wrong to underestimate the Scots' self-pride, their intellectual and religious passions, and their knack of shrewdly enlisting English or French support according to circumstances. The fact remains that, incensed by the growing burden of the taxes that were swelling France's coffers, a number of Scottish noblemen decided to go over to the Protestants – the English, in other words – in opposition to the steadfastly Catholic policy pursued by their regent, Mary of Guise. These noblemen, who assumed the name 'Lords of the Congregation', banded together in an association termed the Covenant. Based on religion, unlike the Scots' fluctuating family alliances, this association not only survived but was renewed several times and constituted an important factor in Scottish politics until the seventeenth century. Eighteen months later, in May 1559, Elizabeth substantially reinforced it by facilitating the return of John Knox.

Knox, the acknowledged leader of the Scottish Reformation, was a redoubtable preacher – redoubtable in the truest sense of the word, given his extremely violent nature. The French had sent him to the galleys for complicity in the murder of a cardinal. Released at the request of the English, he was enrolled in the band of preachers and religious propagandists whom Edward VI employed to tour his kingdom and reinforce the Reformation. Knox's eloquence and power of persuasion made numerous converts, but he became a victim of his own renown. Compelled to go into exile on the accession of Mary Tudor, he fled to Geneva, the capital of Calvinism. Although Elizabeth disliked him because he fulminated against female monarchs, she seized the opportunity to weaken the Scottish Catholics and permitted him to return to England, whence he slipped into Scotland. He stiffened the resolve of Protestant adherents wherever he went, and his political acumen and extraordinary personal authority proved vital to the Protestant cause, which was powerfully supported by English troops and money.

In France, however, this development caused little concern. Everyone at court was too preoccupied with social functions, excursions on horseback and enjoyable visits to the châteaux of the Loire Valley. Rather surprisingly, the wedding of Mary Stuart and the Dauphin, who had both attained the customary age for marriage, was postponed because it was still hoped to remedy the simple-mindedness and physical debility of the heir to the French throne. The royal youth had no time for anything but hunting – and his betrothed. All contemporary observers agree that he was passionately devoted to her, and that she always treated him with great affection. At long last, on 24 April 1558, the wedding took place. Francis of Valois and Mary Stuart were married with great pomp at Notre Dame. Mary thus became the Dauphine and Francis became King of Scotland. Henry II requested the Scots to dispatch the crown matrimonial* to Paris. The Scots procrastinated, rightly considering that a crown was worth a visit to their country. Discussions dragged on until the onset of a series of events so grave that they rendered the question of Francis's coronation secondary and the Scots retained their precious symbol.

The years 1558 and 1559 brought some major changes in Europe. Elizabeth ascended the throne in November 1558, six months after Mary Stuart's nuptials. Charles V had died several weeks earlier and Henry II was mortally wounded in a tournament in Paris seven months later, in June 1559.

---

*The crown matrimonial was reserved for the sovereign's consort.

The former left a mature successor, Philip II, Mary Tudor's widower, who married Elizabeth of Valois, daughter of Henry II and Catherine de Médicis.* By contrast, Francis II's successor as King of France was, as we have seen, an incompetent and somewhat retarded youth. Elizabeth of England would not have worried overmuch had not the young king married her cousin Mary Stuart, Queen of Scotland, who thus became Queen of France. Mary's first step thereafter was to proclaim herself Queen of England as well, by line of descent from Henry VII.

As the granddaughter of Margaret Tudor, Henry VIII's elder sister, Mary based her claim on Elizabeth's illegitimacy, which was commonly accepted by Catholics, who had never acknowledged the validity of Henry VIII's divorce from Catherine of Aragon and thus considered his marriage to Anne Boleyn null and void. Mary Stuart's stance was of little consequence in 1559 because Elizabeth's right of succession had not been contested by anyone, and because a queen reigning and residing in France had no chance of winning widespread support in England, even among Catholics. But the situation was transformed by the death of Francis II in 1560, after a reign of one year's duration: having now become queen dowager, Mary had regained a freedom of action Elizabeth found disquieting. It was traditional for queens of France whose husbands had just died to dress in white

---

*Philip II had not succeeded his father as Holy Roman Emperor. The elective crown had passed to his uncle, Ferdinand I. It thus remained in the family.

and closet themselves for forty days, weeping and praying, in a room draped in black with the curtains drawn and only a few close friends or relations for company. Mary wept copiously and observed this custom – for a fortnight. That done, she opened her door and received a bevy of ambassadors, ministers and prominent figures. The question of her remarriage was already acute.

Mary Tudor had demonstrated the drawbacks of marrying a foreign prince who was heir to a distant kingdom. A consort entirely devoted to the interests of his own country could not fail to arouse virulent unpopularity in that of his spouse. If, in addition, he spent very little time with her, he afforded her no moral or emotional support. By marrying the Dauphin, Mary Stuart had compounded this disadvantage. She had left her kingdom in early childhood to be reared as a French princess at the side of her betrothed. Thirteen years went by before she considered returning. By then, Mary knew nothing of her country or its inhabitants. Worse still, the interests of Scotland had been subordinated to those of France to such an extent that it had become a French colony in all but name. Last but not least, Scotland had become Protestant during Mary's absence, whereas she herself had remained a Catholic. To return there after her husband's death would inevitably present problems. The question, under existing circumstances, was whether she wanted to return there at all. As she saw it, other options were open to her.

A childless queen dowager at the age of eighteen, Mary Stuart had six months earlier lost her mother, the only person who could have guided her in her native land. She did not have a future all mapped out for her. The path of personal ambition should have led her straight back to Scotland, there to wield an authority that had devolved upon her by birth; the easiest and pleasantest course of action would have been to remain at the French court; and, finally, considerations of prestige should have prompted her seek a second marriage as glittering as the first. She very soon grasped the limits of her range of possibilities.

She may briefly have dreamed, not only of remaining in France, but of regaining the full splendour of her rank by marrying her brother-in-law Charles IX, but he was only ten years old. In any case, Catherine de Médicis had now become regent and, thus, all-powerful, and she was quite determined to get rid of a daughter-in-law who, confident of the support of her maternal uncles, the powerful, aggressive and troublesome Guises, had not always treated her, Catherine, with due respect. Accordingly, Mary turned her attention to Don Carlos, the son of Philip II of Spain. On paper he represented the most attractive match in Catholic Europe; in reality, he was an alarming candidate. Mary was undiscouraged by the fact that he was misshapen, mentally unbalanced and subject to murderous tantrums, which proved that she was then thinking in purely political terms and not of her personal happiness. But Philip II did not pursue negotiations, deterred by the hostility of France and England, which feared encirclement by the Habsburg domination of the Netherlands as well as Spain. Other royal suitors such as the Kings of Sweden and Denmark presented more modest prospects. Mary did not take them up and prepared to return to Scotland.

Although her mother's death had left her without support and advice, she still had a brother, or rather, a half-brother, in the person of James Stewart, the illegitimate son of James V, who was twelve years older. If the customs of ancient Egypt had been acceptable in Scotland they could have married like Cleopatra and Ptolemy, and Mary might possibly have had a bright and happy future. James Stewart was a Protestant but far from being a religious fanatic. Thoughtful and rather solemn by nature, he was well regarded in England, where he conferred with Elizabeth's ministers before going to France to arrange for his sister's return. The religious question was the main problem to be resolved.

Mary's Catholicism had become unacceptable to the vast majority of her subjects. In 1560 the Scottish Parliament had promulgated a law establishing the Reformation as the state religion, abolished papal jurisdiction over the country and prohibited the celebration of the Mass throughout its territory. James Stewart suggested that Mary abjure, but she flatly refused. To get round this impasse, however, she declared that she would not seek to impose Catholicism on her kingdom and would be content to hear Mass in her private chapel. Her brother, who thought this a reasonable compromise, undertook to secure its acceptance in Scotland. Sir Nicholas Throckmorton, Elizabeth's ambassador to France, was favourably impressed by the queen's moderation. She had shown 'great wisdom for her years, modesty, and also...great judgment in the wise handling of herself and her matters, which, increasing with her years, cannot but turn greatly to her commendation, reputation, honour and great benefit of her and her country. [...] I see her behaviour to be such, and her wisdom and kingly modesty so great, in that she thinketh herself not too wise, but is content to be ruled by good counsel and wise men (which is a great virtue in a Prince or Princess, and which argueth a great judgement and wisdom in her).'[1] Contemporary observers detected in the ambassador's encomium an undercurrent of regret that his own queen was more inclined to enjoy herself and act according to her own ideas than to take his advice.

There remained a political problem: the ratification of the Treaty of Edinburgh, which had been negotiated in May 1560, or before the death of Francis II. This treaty represented a victory for the Scottish Protestants in that it secured the withdrawal from their territory of both the French and the English. One article stipulated that the queen could no longer display the arms of England. Mary was reluctant to give way on this point, and this point alone, because it would have meant abandoning all claim to the English succession and unequivocally acknowledging Elizabeth's right to wear the crown. She prevaricated and played for time, claiming that she could not sign before returning to Scotland and securing the consent of her Council. This greatly annoyed her cousin the English queen.

However, Mary's departure was decided upon once James Stewart had persuaded the Scottish nobles, without overmuch difficulty, that substantial advantages could accrue from a young and malleable queen who occupied a favourable position on the European chessboard. The splendid farewell festivities organized at Saint-Germain by Catherine de Médicis lasted four whole days, and Pierre de Ronsard composed an elegy on the departure of her who was 'the flower, colour and light' of France. Mary set off for Calais accompanied by a large retinue. Elizabeth had refused her safe-conduct, which would have enabled her to land on English soil in the event of a storm, but Mary did not care. With a touch of bravado, she informed her royal cousin that she had made the crossing in even more perilous conditions at the age of six, so she would doubtless avoid any reefs or encounters with English vessels. She also – with a sarcastic smile, one presumes – declined an offer by Charles of Guise, Cardinal of Lorraine, to keep her jewels for safety's sake.

She embarked for Scotland on 14 August 1561, accompanied by her four Maries, three uncles, Brantôme the chronicler and Châtelard the court poet. The little, laughing girl who had made the crossing in the opposite direction in

1549 was now a very tall, slender young woman saddened and somewhat disheartened by the prospect of leaving a country familiar to her since childhood, bound for unknown trials and tribulations. The fog that enshrouded Calais and the shore seemed a foretaste of Scotland's rain and mist. Brantôme described the queen standing in the stern of her galleass, gazing at the French coast as it quickly receded into the murk and sobbing: 'Adieu, France, adieu, France! Adieu, my beloved France… Methinks I shall never see you again.'[2] But Mary was a resilient young woman, and her moods, as if wafted along by the sea breezes, were forever changing.

An encounter with Elizabeth's ships resulted in an exchange of courtesies, not cannon balls. The crossing, which took only five days, was not delayed by this. By the morning of 19 August, the two galleons and their convoy of more modest vessels were manoeuvring in the fog prior to sailing up the Firth of Forth and entering Leith, the port of Edinburgh. The captain fired a salvo and dropped anchor. It had been pouring with rain for two days, and John Knox, the implacable preacher, wryly remarked that the heavens were bearing witness to what the young queen was bringing in her train: 'sorrow, dolour, darkness and impiety.' She had not been expected so soon, and no one was there to welcome her, but the inhabitants, alerted by the gunfire, came running at the news of her arrival. All agog, they saw a tall figure dressed in black step ashore and surrounded by gentlemen in sumptuous attire. James Stewart was summoned from Edinburgh. In the meantime, a wealthy merchant named

Andrew Lamb offered the travellers his home as a place of refreshment. The official welcome began a few hours later.

Determined to charm her subjects, Mary refused to be demoralized either by the elements or by the sound of fifes, which grated on ears accustomed to more sophisticated music-making. She kindled the inhabitants' curiosity. Her graceful bearing, her elegance on horseback, her enthusiasm and the fluency with which she thanked them in Scottish – all these aroused popular rejoicing, and she entered Holyrood Palace wreathed in smiles. A handsome stone building situated in open country outside the walls of the city, Holyrood was a former monastery remodelled in the French style by her father. It seemed an almost cheerful place compared to Edinburgh Castle, which dwarfed and overwhelmed the buildings around it. Mary pronounced herself satisfied with the suite of rooms assigned her in Holyrood's most comfortable tower. Her subjects assembled to welcome her that same evening. To Brantôme's extreme distaste, they treated her to a rather discordant serenade while she was receiving the noble families who would make up her court and her entourage.

It must be borne in mind that the entire population of Scotland numbered no more than five or six hundred thousand. Of these the Scottish nobility formed a tiny group in which family ties, ramified and complicated by intermarriage, divorce and illegitimacy, promoted ferocious rivalries and unexpected volte-faces. The impossibility of relying on ever-changing alliances rendered political life exceptionally turbulent, the more so since the clan chieftains' acceptance of royal authority was only half-hearted and they refused to be bound by the law, hence their incessant recourse to the dagger when disputes arose.

Mary began by taking her half-brother's advice, from which she benefited considerably. James Stewart risked his own skin by stationing himself at the door of her chapel to prevent Protestant demonstrators from disrupting the celebration of Sunday Mass on his half-sister's arrival. This earned him her trust, and she left him to govern. She attended meetings of the Council with a piece of embroidery in her hand but took no part in its deliberations. Only one political problem exercised her: the English succession. This was a strange preoccupation in the autumn of 1561. Neither of the two queens was married, but it was quite conceivable that one or the other would easily remedy this situation by producing a natural heir. On the one hand, therefore, the problem did not present any particular urgency; on the other, if Elizabeth died first, other potential claimants had the advantage over the Queen of Scotland of having been born in England and of residing there. Despite this, Mary dispatched William Maitland to London in September to extract Elizabeth's endorsement of the validity of her claim.

Maitland, one of the queen's most faithful servants, was also one of the few Scottish diplomats of the time. He had served Mary of Guise in both London and Paris. An extremely well-educated and practical man, he differed from many of his compatriots in his absence of religious fanaticism. The Protestant in him was not offended by his queen's religion. His mission was impossible and he knew it, but he did succeed in eliciting the English queen's candid comments on the question, an awkward and delicate matter in view of her own avowed intention to marry and have children.

Mary was not the only pretender, and besides, the weight of her claim left something to be desired. If the provisions of Henry VIII's testament were to be observed, they automatically disqualified her by reason of her birth on foreign soil. Her French upbringing constituted another disadvantage because it underlined her cosmopolitanism, and her Catholicism rendered her undesirable in the eyes of a Puritan Parliament. For all that, Elizabeth probably preferred her at this stage to the other candidate, Catherine Grey, sister of Jane, the ill-starred nine days' queen, for, to her ministers' great regret, there was no man in the running.

Elizabeth had summoned her cousin Catherine to court, but she disliked her and made little attempt to disguise the fact. In 1560 Catherine had committed the irredeemable folly of marrying the Earl of Hertford in secret, thereby arousing the queen's fury. Elizabeth, as we shall see later, reacted in an unpredictable way to the matrimonial plans of her relations and ladies-in-waiting. Thus, when Maitland visited her in 1561, she displayed no animosity towards her Scottish cousin even though she refused to name her her heir for very precise and personal reasons.

She had already conceded to Maitland that Mary's request was sound by refraining from citing the testamentary dispositions of her father, who, as we have seen, wished to exclude from the succession any prince born beyond his frontiers. Given that, as Elizabeth saw it, no other valid candidate existed, and that the prospect of a union with Scotland was desirable, the solution did not displease her in principle. However, she justified her refusal to make a formal decision on the grounds that it would be impossible for her to maintain good relations with her successor. To nominate Mary, she explained to the Scottish envoy, would inevitably cause her to hate her. 'The desire is without example, to require me in mine own life, to set my winding sheet before my eyes. Think you that I could love my own winding sheet?'[3] She then went still further – further than any father or mother would have ventured to go: 'Princes cannot like their own children, those that should succeed unto them. How then shall I, think you, like my cousin, being declared my Heir Apparent?'[4] This provocative statement, so utterly devoid of hypocrisy and sentimentality, affords striking evidence of the queen's relentless introspection and illustrates her attitude to marriage and motherhood. Why bear a child, only to repudiate it? But she was not finished with Maitland. She had another argument to put forward: 'I know the inconstancy of the people of England, how they ever mislike the present government and have their eyes fixed upon that person that is next to succeed.' And she concluded with the following words in Latin: 'They are more prone to worship the rising than the setting sun.'[5] She knew what she was talking about, she assured Maitland, for she had represented the dawn of her sister Mary's night. Although there was nothing left to be negotiated under the circumstances, Elizabeth did not demand that Mary renounce her claim and even advised Maitland to pursue the matter with her minister, Cecil.

Thus, although Elizabeth had made no concessions, cordiality between her and her cousin was the order of the day. In May 1562, confident of her much-vaunted charm and reassured by the manner in which her own subjects had accepted her, Mary took the initiative of arranging a meeting in England at York. To permit a Catholic queen to visit her kingdom seemed a reasonable risk to Elizabeth, who obtained her Council's agreement even though it would present the Papist party with an opportunity to pluck up its courage and rally its forces. The two ministers, Maitland and Cecil, both of whom regularly lamented being subject to a woman's authority, offered no objection despite the expense of such a meeting. The two queens exchanged letters, portraits and gifts. Notwithstanding the frightful weather, which rendered the roads almost impassable, preparations were well advanced when some news from France stopped the project in its tracks. In January 1562 the Huguenots had secured the right to hold services in a number of protected places. This measure provoked a furious reaction by the most extreme wing of the Catholic party, which was led by the Guises. A Protestant congregation was massacred at Wassy, in Champagne, on the orders of the Duke of Guise. Within a month the country was ablaze with religious strife. The Huguenots appealed to England, the Catholics turned to Spain. Elizabeth could not, of course, leave London under these circumstances, least of all to consort with a niece of the Guises. The meeting was postponed and the queens resumed their respective occupations.

This was when Mary discovered how violent rivalry between the Scottish clans could be. She wished to reward her half-brother for his loyalty by granting him the prosperous earldom of Moray. The title had fallen into abeyance and the land was administered by the Earl of Huntly. Furious at being deprived of a major source of income, Huntly took up arms against his sovereign. Although his son already had a wife, he felt confident of getting that obstructive marriage annulled and boasted that he would abduct Mary and marry her to him. James Stewart took command of the royal army, and the ensuing battle proved decisive: the rebels were routed and the Earl of Huntly was captured. Fatally wounded at that precise moment, he fell from his horse and died. His embalmed body was then conveyed to Edinburgh, where Parliament met to sit in judgement on the traitor. The fact that the traitor was a corpse did not prevent him from being tried. The coffin was stood on end in front of the parliamentarians, who pronounced Huntly guilty. They found a more animate culprit in the person of his son, who was likewise tried and condemned to be beheaded.

Peace had been restored, but a few months later the court was thrown into turmoil by another incident. The poet Pierre Châtelard, who had accompanied Mary to Scotland, professed himself enamoured of the young queen in a courtly way. He did not leave it at that, however, and one night, whether for fun or in bravado, he hid beneath her bed. Discovered there by the servants who inspected the queen's chamber every night before she retired to bed, he was ejected. Mary demanded that he leave court. Châtelard refused to take her at her word, and the next day, thrusting aside the sentry guarding her door, he rushed at her while she was alone with two female attendants. In response to Mary's cries for help, her guards seized Châtelard and threw him into the dungeon. Tried and condemned to death, he was beheaded in the queen's presence after reciting Ronsard's *Hymne à la mort* by way of a prayer:

I salute thee, happy and beneficent Death,
medicine and solace for extreme distress.

Châtelard's lunatic behaviour led Mary's entourage to wonder if he had been an instrument employed to tarnish her reputation. Whatever the truth, a husband was becoming a royal necessity because the queen's unmarried state could not fail to provoke dangerous agitation and stimulate rivalry between the clans. The preacher John Knox remarked that the queen's marriage was a universal topic of conversation. Equal concern was felt on the other side of the border.

In 1562 Queen Elizabeth collapsed, struck down by a bad case of smallpox, and for several hours was given up for lost. Cecil, urgently summoned to the palace in the middle of the night, convened a meeting of the Council. All it did was to register differences of opinion on the problem of the succession. Some opted for Catherine Grey, a descendant of the Suffolk line favoured by Henry VIII; others considered bestowing the crown on a more distant cousin, the Earl of Huntingdon, who had the great advantage of being a man. No one declared for Mary. The queen recovered, but everyone – ministers, courtiers, churchmen and ordinary citizens alike – became preoccupied with the need for her to marry.

In 1563, therefore, the two queens were in a comparable position: both were experiencing political problems, but those problems – the lot of every sovereign – were not insurmountable. Although neither of these husbandless, childless queens was under immediate threat, their future was fraught with uncertainty. The question of marriage was destined to link them inextricably.

4

Handsome Dudley

1563–5

The two young women's parity was deceptive. Personal authority is a monarch's most indispensable attribute. Elizabeth, despite her difficult, lonely and often humiliating childhood, had displayed it from the outset; Mary, a queen from birth, forever flattered but never consulted, was wholly devoid of it. An enthusiastic horsewoman and intrepid huntress, she did not lack courage or shrink from fatigue. She was capable of riding for hours at the head of her retinue while engaged in punitive expeditions against overly independent nobles, and she took pleasure in doing so. What she did lack was intellectual self-assurance and the knack of playing one person off against another in order to dominate both – in short, political acumen. The price she had to pay for her charm and physical attraction was to seem utterly feminine and, thus, in a position of weakness vis-à-vis an uncouth society in which disputes were often settled by force. Mary's opponents were no more affected by the tears to which she often resorted than they were by her fits of hysterics or bouts of depression. All these manifestations were adjudged to be symptomatic of a young woman in need of a husband. This was meat and drink to James Stewart, whom we shall henceforth call by his title, the Earl of Moray, because he felt convinced that she would leave him to wield power indefinitely.

Elizabeth, for her part, remained an enigma after five years on the throne. The members of her immediate circle were disconcerted by her combination of intellectual vigour and thoroughly feminine coquetry. She liked men, but – incomprehensibly, as it seemed to her contemporaries – evinced no desire to get married. Although her favourite companions were young and handsome, she did not allow herself to be carried away by their ardour and enthusiasm. William Cecil remained her most valued adviser and closest associate. Many years older than his queen – she was only sixteen when he began to manage her affairs – and of relatively humble stock, his background being that of a Cambridge intellectual, he did not share her love of dancing, music and the chase. When entrusting him with the post of Chief Secretary of State on her accession, Elizabeth had told him that she was counting on him to advise her 'without respect of my private will'[1] and promised him 'taciturnity', thereby enabling him to address her with absolute candour. Cecil remained at her side for the next forty years. If we are to believe his son Robert, who succeeded him, the confabulations between the sovereign and her chief secretary resembled the endless private conversations between two lovers. No one knew the queen better than Cecil. He respected her political instinct and the gracious way she charmed the crowds during her appearances in public. He admired her use of feminine guile to attain her ends, was the first to take her tears, sulks and smiles seriously, and did not put them down to girlish emotionalism. He patiently endured her vacillations and changes of heart, but on one matter – the vital question of her marriage – he never tired of trying to sway her until their difference of opinion was rendered redundant by the queen's advancing years.

Why did Elizabeth persist in rejecting all her suitors, whose numbers had swelled since her accession? Her spirit of independence and the extreme pleasure she took in her pre-eminent status cannot be doubted. James Melville, Mary Stuart's ambassador to the English court, was quick to discern that her imperious nature would prove an impediment to marriage. When Elizabeth declared that she would marry only if the Queen of Scotland's conduct obliged her to do so, Melville shook his head and replied that he knew full well she would never take a husband whatever her cousin did. 'Madam,' he said, 'I know your stately stomach; ye think if ye were married, ye would be but Queen of England, and now ye are King and Queen both; ye may not suffer a commander.'[2] According to one theory, which was often advanced and did not depend on the psychological aspect of her decision, Elizabeth knew herself to be infertile. This is doubtful, given that she enjoyed excellent health and menstruated regularly, as witness the espionage conducted by her ladies-in-waiting, nor did her physicians, whom Cecil often questioned, ever mention any physical defect that might have inhibited conception. The fact remained that she had always said – ever since refusing to marry the Duke of Savoy at her sister Mary Tudor's suggestion in 1557 – that she was not bent on marriage, and that her unmarried state suited her perfectly well. This did not, however, mean that she was averse to contemplating some politically advantageous marriage in the abstract or to dreaming of a life of greater sexual fulfilment, nor did it prevent her from basking in male admiration.

By 1560 her reputation for playing hard to get was well established in the courts of Europe. Nothing amused her more than to tease a suitor. Once she had declined the Spanish proposals, rejected a second approach by the Swedish crown prince, and seen off the Dukes of Savoy, Nemours and Ferrara, the Earl of Arran and the Earl of Arundel, a scion of one of England's most ancient families, Emperor Ferdinand offered her his son, Archduke Charles. Elizabeth lent an attentive and inquisitive ear to Baron von Breumer, the archduke's chamberlain, who came to England to extol his royal master's merits. She requested a detailed account of his proficiency as a horseman, dancer and musician. A man content to spend his days beside the fire would not suit her, she declared. Aware that Breumer was not at liberty to be objective, she sent her own ambassador in Augsburg a regular questionnaire relating to the young man's physical appearance, likings and religion, and even demanded to know 'whether he hath been noted to have loved any woman, and in what sort.'[3]

After three months of enquiries, she rejected Archduke Charles with the utmost courtesy. While conceding that such a marriage would greatly enhance her prestige throughout Europe, she informed Breumer that, having 'consulted her heart', she had found there no wish to abandon her solitary state. The baron was nonetheless taken aback by the favour she suddenly showed him after this refusal. He was on the Thames some days later when the royal barge glided alongside. The queen invited him aboard and played the lute to him. The following day she requested his presence at breakfast – a rare privilege – and invited him for another boat trip that evening. In a very cheerful mood, Elizabeth chatted incessantly and plied him with questions about the archduke. She explained at great length, not for the first time, that she would never commit herself without having seen a prospective husband in person. Under instructions from Emperor Ferdinand, who was stung by the notion that his son should be compelled to make such a 'puerile and inconvenient' visit, Breumer remarked that few men would consent to be submitted to prior inspection. Strongly encouraged by her amiable manner, however, he assured her that he did not consider negotiations to be at an end.

Meanwhile, King Eric of Sweden, who had been marking time for months, undeterred by the queen's prevarication, announced his intention of coming to woo her in person. Although Elizabeth had intimated to him many times that their kingdoms were too far apart to favour a matrimonial alliance between them, he persevered with his suit and wrote her long, amorous letters in Latin. She always rejected him, but with such tact, gaiety and ambiguity that he persisted in his advances for a long time, though not without casting an occasional glance in the direction of Mary Stuart. In the end, Eric the indefatigable was conquered and deposed by his neighbour, John of Finland, which put paid to his career as a suitor. At a pinch, Elizabeth could always justify her lack of enthusiasm for marriage by citing the difficulty of finding an adequate partner.

If only Mary Stuart had been a man! Clearly, Elizabeth's ideal course of action would have been to marry the king of an adjacent country. Her reluctance to tie herself to the ruler of a distant land was perfectly rational. There remained the possibility of marrying some lesser prince for the purpose of procreation, even if he carried little political clout. In that case it was quite reasonable, albeit not customary, for the queen to wish to satisfy herself that he shared her tastes and was physically attractive. She also had to unearth a prince willing to submit to inspection. Finally, most of the European royal families were Catholic, which posed an additional problem. Elizabeth's persistent rebuffs were understandable, therefore, but her stubborn refusal to settle the succession was surprisingly perverse. By declining to marry *and* nominate her successor she risked provoking the gravest internal dissension if she died prematurely. The undue severity with which she behaved towards her Protestant cousin, Catherine Grey, who had been born in England and included in the line of succession by Henry VIII, is illustrative of this inconsistency.

In Tudor England a relative's disgrace did not entail that of his or her family. Thus, although Mary Tudor had ordered the execution of Jane Grey, Catherine's sister, she never ceased to treat the young woman kindly and appointed her a Lady of the Bedchamber. (Mary, the youngest of the Grey sisters, was then far too young to come to court.) Catherine remained at court on Elizabeth's accession, but in an uneasy, joyless frame of mind. The queen, who disliked her, did not conceal how little she admired her intellect and personal qualities. The poor creature possessed neither 'power or force',[4] she told Maitland one day. Moreover, she had promptly downgraded her from Lady of the Bedchamber to the less intimate post of Lady of the Privy Chamber. Catherine, for her part, was afraid of her cousin and resented this lack of respect for her rank. Her fear of the queen was such that she dared not inform her that the Earl of Hertford had asked her to marry him.* All this had happened in 1560, even before Mary Stuart's return to Scotland.

---

*The Earl of Hertford was the son of the Lord Protector and, thus, a nephew of the Thomas Seymour who had risked a dangerous dalliance with Elizabeth in her girlhood. His father and uncle had both been executed.

Displaying a combination of impatience and irresponsibility, young Catherine thereupon married her suitor in secret. The queen had left London for a few days' hunting on a nearby estate, and Catherine got out of accompanying her by pleading toothache. At eight the next morning, accompanied by her future sister-in-law, Lady Jane Seymour, she left the palace of Whitehall by an inconspicuous door that led through an orchard to the river and made her way to Hertford's residence. The earl was already waiting for them, but the clergyman was late. Energetic Lady Jane went off to look for the man and brought him back with her. He did not give his name and no one asked it. The couple later described him as an elderly, ruddy-cheeked man with a red beard. He conducted the service without delay and took his leave, but not before Lady Jane had given him ten sovereigns for his trouble. The newly-weds having partaken of a glass of wine and some sweetmeats, she then withdrew.

The couple wasted no time in going to bed and engaging in 'carnal copulation'.* They had to be quick because Lady Catherine could not afford to miss dinner with the comptroller of the queen's household in the middle of the day, so they got dressed in a hurry. That a lady of Catherine's rank could have donned her garments unaided aroused the gravest doubts in the minds of the investigators who examined

---

*This account of the whole episode is taken from the earl's subsequent testimony (see Alison Plowden, *Lady Jane Grey, Nine Days Queen* (Sutton, Stroud: 2003) p 150).

the matter later on, but the earl stated that his bride had managed to get dressed in a quarter of an hour. He had then accompanied her to the gateway overlooking the river, where his sister was waiting. Since the tide was now high, the two young women had returned to the palace by boat.

What followed smacks more of pulp fiction than a royal palace. Catherine, who still dared not breathe a word, saw her husband from time to time thanks to her obliging sister-in-law and a sympathetic chambermaid. But Jane Seymour died in March 1561 and the chambermaid took fright and left Lady Catherine's service. In April the queen requested Hertford to accompany Robert Cecil, her minister's son, to France. No one declined a royal request lightly and for no good reason. Although Hertford had an excellent reason for not going, he could not take advantage of it: Lady Catherine believed – without as yet being certain – that she was expecting a child. Her fears were soon confirmed. Some months later, unable to conceal her condition and lacking any moral support, her mother being dead and her sister far too young to be of any help, she confided her great distress to Elizabeth Saintlow, an old family friend.* Old friend or not, she refused to intercede on her behalf. Catherine then decided to seek help from her brother-in-law Robert Dudley,† the queen's Master

---

*The same Elizabeth Saintlow reappears some years later as the wife of the Earl of Shrewsbury, Mary Stuart's custodian.

†Robert Dudley's brother Guildford had married Jane Grey and shared her fate.

of the Horse. She entered his chamber at night and, seated on the edge of his bed, poured out all her woes, confessing her extreme reluctance to confide in the queen and beseeching him to intercede for her. That Dudley was dumbfounded by this nocturnal visit may well be imagined. He put Elizabeth in the picture the very next morning, but without pleading the unfortunate young woman's case.

The queen immediately vented her royal spleen on the poor little goose. Catherine was imprisoned in the Tower the same day, big belly and all, and the Earl of Hertford was urgently recalled. Elizabeth, who was not disposed to be lenient, reacted with undue severity. Hertford was escorted to the Tower on arrival and an inquiry opened into the validity of the marriage, which had been tainted with illegality by Jane Seymour's death and the impossibility of finding the priest who had conducted it. For a clandestine marriage to be recognized, the participants had to produce two witnesses and prove that the officiating priest had been ordained. Catherine gave birth to a boy, who was christened Edward in the very chapel where the headless cadavers of her grandfather and her aunt Jane lay buried.

Far from being mollified, Elizabeth showed no inclination to pardon the couple and referred the whole case to the ecclesiastical authorities. Alive to her wishes, the Archbishop of Canterbury ruled that no valid marriage between Lady Catherine and Lord Hertford had taken place, and that they were consequently guilty of the sin of fornication. He imposed a heavy fine and recommended that they be held in prison at Her Majesty's pleasure. The governor of the Tower treated them with some leniency, especially as Elizabeth fell gravely ill at this time and many members of the Council favoured Lady Catherine's accession if the queen should die. Reluctant to persecute a woman who might possibly become his queen and at pains to entertain her, he sent for her semi-tame monkeys and favourite dogs. More to the point, he neglected to lock the couple's doors, with the result that their regular reunions produced a second child, which was born in February 1563. Elizabeth's fury knew no bounds. The people of London felt sorry for such a luckless, romantic couple and would have preferred the queen to treat them less harshly, but Elizabeth, usually so alert to public opinion, did not relent. The governor of the Tower was imprisoned in his own stronghold and the erring couple were banished to the country. The earl was placed under his mother's supervision, together with the elder child. Lady Catherine was allowed to keep the baby but committed to the custody of her uncle.

However, the alarm caused by the queen's illness in 1562 necessitated that a solution be found. The House of Commons presented her with a petition that laid less stress on her need to marry than on the naming of a successor. If the queen were unfortunately to die, the House foresaw 'the great dangers, the unspeakable miseries of civil wars: the perilous intermeddlings of foreign princes' and 'the unsurety of all men's possessions, lives, and estates.'[5] Imperturbably, Elizabeth replied that she well understood her parliamentarians' anxiety, but that the question was so serious and so important that she could not give them an immediate answer. They could trust her, however: she considered herself the mother of her subjects and would never be neglectful of them. The House of Lords chimed in with a plea that she should marry 'where it shall please you, with whom it shall please you, and as soon as it shall please you'[6] and, in the interim, that she should determine who should succeed her. The queen briskly replied that, although her skin undoubtedly bore the marks of smallpox, she was not wrinkled. She might be old – she was then twenty-nine – but God could yet send her children as he had to St Elizabeth, and to designate a successor might unleash a sanguinary conflict in England. Besides, not only had negotiations been reopened with Charles of Habsburg, but Catherine de Médicis, apprehensive of their potential outcome, proposed her son Charles IX, who was still a minor, in February 1565. Elizabeth had laughed at this and remarked to Paul de Foix, the French ambassador, that she feared his master would find her 'old and thus unpleasing'.[7] But, faithful to her tactic of prevarication, she stated that she would submit the question to her nobility, and the two candidates were held in reserve for several months.

Although exasperating, Elizabeth's refusal to make a decision may not have been as irrational as it seems. She knew she could never choose a successor who would meet with unanimous approval. Despite her Catholicism, Mary

Stuart had displayed great religious moderation and scrupulously adhered to the agreements made prior to her return, and Elizabeth felt in her heart of hearts that Mary was better placed than her own scatter-brained cousin Catherine by reason of her experience, her connections and the patent advantage of a union between their two kingdoms. However, all depended on what husband the Scottish queen chose.

There were not many candidates available, even though Mary had the advantage over Elizabeth of being able to wed a Catholic. She had long hoped that her plan to marry Don Carlos would succeed, but Philip II, compelled to acknowledge that his son's incurable insanity ruled him out as a husband, had broken off negotiations for good. That left Archduke Charles, the Emperor's son, who was also in the running for the hand of the Queen of England and, consequently, unenthusiastic because he would have preferred London to Edinburgh. After two years of widowhood, Mary's grand aspirations were dashed by reality. The opposition of Catherine de Médicis debarred her from setting her sights on France, and Elizabeth had informed her that she would regard marriage to a Spanish, French or Austrian prince as a hostile act. To choose a Scottish husband might destabilize relations between the clans. Moreover, the only obvious candidate by reason of his family status – he was Mary's natural successor if she remained childless – was the Earl of Arran, the man who had considered marrying Elizabeth, a dreamer who was also going insane.

It was then that an idea took shape in Elizabeth's fertile

brain. Who better qualified than herself to choose a husband – an English husband, naturally – for her widowed cousin? A marriage that met with her approval would not be decisive – she did not go as far as that – but it would at least be a step in the direction of an arrangement, an implicit undertaking to recognize Mary as her successor. Accordingly, she sent for Maitland and submitted a startling proposal. On mature reflection, she announced, she had come to the conclusion that only one man would be capable of satisfying her cousin's requirements: someone so perfect and so well endowed with all the graces that she herself would willingly have wed him had she been tempted to marry. The man in question was none other than Robert Dudley, her closest friend. Maitland must have had legs of steel, or his knees would have buckled at this insane suggestion. Robert Dudley? He couldn't even imagine how he was going to inform Mary of the queen's proposal, and as soon as he had taken his leave he hastened to confide in the Spanish ambassador. Why did Robert Dudley's name inspire such dread?

Here we must go back in time, for Robert Dudley's friendship with Queen Elizabeth was of long standing. His family had experienced some spectacular ups and downs. Edmund, Robert's grandfather, had served Henry VII as a kind of tax inspector whose task it was to comb the records in search of estates that had failed to pay their taxes and demand retrospective payments from their owners. Edmund became a past master at resurrecting old ordinances that would enable the king to recover more money still. Needless to say, he was not only generously rewarded by Henry VII but accused, probably rightly, of accepting bribes from those whom he inspected. Not unnaturally, he was hated, and Henry VIII – less from conviction than for popularity's sake – had him arrested and executed when he came to the throne. This dishonour did not extend to his family, however. His widow married Arthur Plantagenet, an illegitimate son of Edward IV, who served as an equerry to Henry VIII and was granted the dead man's confiscated estates.

Edmund's son John became a ward of the Crown, the usual practice when someone died leaving an heir who was still under age. John Dudley was brought up by an old friend of his father's, Sir Edward Guildford, who had purchased wardship of the youth from the state (the point of such an arrangement being that, on attaining his majority, the ward would in his turn buy back his right of succession). John married Jane, his guardian's daughter, distinguished himself in the army and soon appeared at court. Despite the shadow of the scaffold, Henry VIII made him one of his favourite companions. Extremely ambitious and determined to rebuild his fortunes, he enjoyed a distinguished public career and a happy private life, as witness the birth of thirteen children, one of whom, Robert, was born in the same year as Elizabeth, 1533.

Ten years later, in 1543, Henry VIII married his last wife,

Catherine Parr, a great friend of Jane Dudley's. As children they had both been chosen by Catherine of Aragon to undergo tuition with her daughter, Mary Tudor. They remained friends, and Catherine Parr's marriage prompted Jane to introduce young Robert into the new queen's household. Very mindful of her stepchildren's education, Catherine perpetuated the tradition of finding fellow pupils for the royal offspring, and it delighted her to include Robert in the tutorials attended by Elizabeth and her brother Edward when they were together. Although Elizabeth was more precociously intelligent than Robert, she enjoyed his company. Like her, he was fond of hunting, riding and dancing, a pastime at which he excelled, so they spent a great deal of time together. Then life became more complicated.

As we have seen above, John Dudley, Duke of Northumberland, led the conspiracy against Mary Tudor on her accession and was thrown into prison with his four sons. John was summarily executed. One year later his son Guildford and his daughter-in-law, Jane Grey, the nine days' queen, were beheaded while the other three boys, Robert included, continued to languish in their cells. We are now in 1554, the year when Elizabeth herself was imprisoned in the Tower. The two friends could not, of course, communicate during their captivity, nor even after their release. Elizabeth seldom came to court, and Robert displayed a spirit of magnanimity by offering his sword to Philip of Spain, Mary Tudor's consort, who benefited considerably as a result. Robert Dudley fought on Spain's behalf in various battles on the Continent and was rewarded for his outstanding services by the restoration of some of his estates. By the time Elizabeth came to the throne, therefore, Robert Dudley cut a good figure. No only had he demonstrated his courage, but his personal assets were far from negligible. By marrying Amy Robsart – a love match, it should be emphasized – he had become a major landowner in Norfolk.

Robert was among the first to pay homage to Elizabeth. Happy to be reunited with this friend of her youth, she welcomed him with delight and promptly appointed him Master of the Horse. This judicious choice aroused no comment, his brother having held the same post under Edward VI. No sinecure, it entailed responsibility for all the royal stables and for organizing the court's travels.[8] An unrivalled horseman, an excellent judge of horseflesh and thoroughly conversant with court ceremonial, Robert Dudley possessed all the qualities he needed to perform his duties well. He was allotted official quarters in the palace – and left his wife in the country. This was quite customary, because wives ran their husbands' estates, brought up their children and seldom came to court. Although Elizabeth did have some women friends, she much preferred the company of men, and it soon became apparent that she preferred Robert Dudley's company to any other.

He encouraged her to go riding every day, which she gladly did. As if to compensate for the tribulations of their youth, he arranged the most elaborate entertainments for Elizabeth – tournaments and banquets, masques and theatrical performances – but gratified the frugal housewife in her by avoiding reckless expenditure. Unlike so many others, he did not amass a fortune in her service; on the contrary, he devoted much of his remuneration to presenting her with magnificent gifts. Elizabeth adored mixing business with pleasure, and Dudley was just as capable as his queen of lightning transitions from the serious to the trivial. Intellectually, however, Elizabeth always retained the upper hand. Robert Dudley did not threaten her, he amused her. More important still to a young woman surrounded by the ponderous machinery of a court populated by old gentlemen – councillors, heads of distinguished families, ambassadors, officials – he was a friend of her own age with whom she could exchange pleasantries in a remarkably nimble, allusive idiom incomprehensible to others, and on whom she could rely to the hilt. Tall, handsome and elegant, he bore himself with a pride she did not find displeasing.

Jealous courtiers nicknamed Dudley 'the Gypsy' because he was forever on the move, danced indefatigably and had a swarthy complexion reminiscent more of the southern sun than the mists of England. To Elizabeth he was simply 'Two Eyes', and he signed the letters he sent her 'Ô Ô'. Tongues began to wag, of course, and diplomatic dispatches devoted considerable space to tittle-tattle. 'Lord Robert,' reported Feria, Philip II's ambassador, 'has come so much into favour that he does whatever he pleases with her affairs, and it is even said that Her Majesty visits him in his chamber day and night.'[9] Even more significantly, Feria passed on a rumour that was circulating at court: Dudley's wife, Amy Robsart, was said to be suffering from 'a malady in one of her breasts' and the queen was only waiting for her to die to marry her lover. The Spanish ambassador concluded by suggesting that it might be opportune to open negotiations with Lord Robert with a view to securing his goodwill. The Venetians made similar insinuations: Robert Dudley was a very handsome young man to whom the queen showed so much favour and affection that many people believed that if his wife were to die – she had been ill for some time – the queen would be more than happy to marry him.[10] Mary Stuart, still in France at this time, expressed malicious surprise that the Queen of England should be on the point of marrying her equerry. Most serious of all was a conversation William Cecil had with the Spanish ambassador – a far from innocent conversation intended to be repeated. That a paragon of loyalty and integrity like Cecil could resort to this subterfuge was a measure of his uneasiness. It would be better for all concerned, he said, if Robert Dudley were in paradise rather than on earth. Worse still, he added that he strongly suspected him of wishing to get rid of his wife. This exchange took place on 7 September 1560. The very next day Lady Dudley was found dead at the foot of a staircase, her neck broken. Had she deliberately thrown herself down the stairs, or had she been pushed? The whole affair seemed suspicious.

Elizabeth, who grasped this at once, requested Dudley to leave court and await the outcome of an inquiry before reappearing in her presence. She could hardly fail to be disturbed by such a bizarre accident. Amy Robsart had for several months been staying with some friends, Anthony and Ursula Foster, in their big fourteenth-century manor house. The Fosters occupied one wing, Anthony's old mother, Mrs Owen, an apartment of her own, and Lady Dudley and her companion, Elizabeth Odingsells, a suite of rooms above the big entrance hall. September 8th was the first day of a fair in the nearby town of Abingdon. Amy gave all her servants leave to attend it and urged her friend Elizabeth to do likewise. The latter was far from eager to go because the town would be swarming with yokels on a Sunday, but she ended by yielding to Amy's entreaties. Having dined *à deux* with old Mrs Owen, Amy retired to her room.

On returning from the fair, the servants found her dead at the foot of the stairs leading to her apartment. Robert Dudley was summoned without delay and an inquest held. The unusual behaviour of the deceased, who seemed to have been at pains to send all her companions away, pointed in the direction of suicide. Despite the denials of her lady's maid, the theory that she had yielded to this temptation could not be discounted: Amy had indeed been suffering from cancer of a very advanced and painful nature, and she was also depressed by her husband's neglect. A more modern theory, based on the extreme decalcification caused by her disease, suggests that one false step could have resulted in a fatal fall. Although Robert Dudley was cleared, nothing could dispel the mystery – and to be cleared was insufficient to qualify a man for marriage to the Queen of England.

Elizabeth, who had seemed unusually edgy throughout

the week the inquest lasted, was immensely relieved. She pronounced the matter closed and speedily summoned her 'Ô Ô' back to court, which went into mourning for three weeks. Amy was buried at Oxford with great ceremony – buried but far from forgotten by her contemporaries. Rumours never ceased, not only in the vicinity of the tragedy but in London and Paris as well.* Infuriated by this, the queen defended Dudley by citing the conclusions of the inquest, showered him with favours and assigned him a residence near her own in Greenwich Palace. 'I cannot do without my Lord Robert, for he is like my little dog, and whenever he comes into a room, everyone at once assumes that I myself am near.'[11] Not content to make jokes about her favourite, she appointed him to the Council.

Seats at the Council table were not numerous, but Dudley had earned his place by giving Elizabeth some very sound advice on military matters in October 1562. He had also been of great service to her in setting up a European spy ring that kept her better informed than before. But there was no question of his marrying her, even though, being less politically astute than the queen, he persevered with his suit and did not abandon hope. All the ambassadors'

---

*Alexis de Tocqueville, who visited the ruined manor house in the nineteenth century, conjured up the memory of 'charming, delightful' Amy Robsart 'falling into the chasm laid for her' (letter to Mary Mottley dated 30 August 1833 in *Œuvres, papiers et correspondance,* vol. XIV, p. 392). He had probably seen *Amy Robsart,* the romantic melodrama staged by Victor Hugo ten years earlier.

reports bore witness to the deplorable effects of the scandal. As Throckmorton wrote from Paris: 'One laugheth at us, another threateneth, another revileth the Queen.' People, he declared, were saying things 'which every hair of my head stareth at and my ears glow to hear.'[12] Elizabeth, who was too mindful of her reputation to yield to her personal feelings, reassured Cecil by telling him that if she married 'it would be as a Queen and not as Elizabeth'.[13]

That autumn she had once more to endure her parliamentarians' remarks on the absolute necessity of her marrying. Her cryptic response was that, where the succession was concerned, other solutions had been devised as much for their welfare as for her own safety.[14] In March 1963 she offered her 'Eyes' to Mary by way of Maitland, who thought the proposal a joke in bad taste and sidestepped it. He expressed his pleasure that Elizabeth should be demonstrating her great affection for Mary Stuart by wishing to give her what she cherished most, but said that his queen would be reluctant to deprive her of the pleasure and solace Lord Robert afforded her. Despite this, Elizabeth refused to be disconcerted or discouraged.

Personal feelings are not always easy to decipher, and the task becomes more difficult the greater the distance in time, especially when one is dealing with a secretive and often contradictory person not given to revealing her emotions. But how can one resist trying to find some explanation for such a surprising move? We must, I think, bear in mind the genuine drawbacks Elizabeth's marriage to Dudley would have presented. First and foremost, there was the dust raised by his wife's death. The effect of slander on the queen cannot be underestimated, for it was impossible to reign without exercising absolute moral authority, particularly in the case of a woman. Then again, Elizabeth knew that Dudley had aroused a great deal of envy, and that his family history was not such as to allay it. Marrying him carried a genuine risk of inciting the seditious to rebel. Finally, a husband, even one as attractive as Dudley, would weigh upon her. She was unprepared to submit to a man's authority. For as long as his existing marriage precluded him from marrying her, Elizabeth dreamed of love; confronted by the possibility of committing herself, she recoiled, and the more Dudley pressed her the more she shied away. It saddened her to deny him a crown, but then, with a flash of inspiration, she thought of offering him another.

The scheme was not without its advantages. On the personal level, of course, she would be depriving herself of his company, but that loss would be offset by her pleasure in making a king of him. On the political level his presence would bring about a peaceful rapprochement between the two nations and weaken French and Spanish influence, and, if she were going to have a successor, she would have just as soon liked him to be Robert's son. Cecil, always a trifle jealous of handsome Dudley, was very favourably disposed towards the queen's proposal, which would have removed her favourite from the scene. He wrote as much to Maitland, enumerating all Dudley's qualities, stating that 'he was singularly esteemed of the Queen'* and emphasizing that he possessed gifts and qualities not to be found in many princes. However, the interested parties displayed little enthusiasm.

Robert Dudley had no desire to be transplanted to Scotland, even as husband of the queen, because he had still not given up hope of marrying his own queen. Besides, he felt convinced that this was a plot concocted by Cecil to get rid of him. In reality, he had little to fear, knowing full well that the Scottish queen would not accept him. In October 1563, however, when Lord Randolph, Elizabeth's emissary, came to convey her insulting proposal, Mary controlled her annoyance. In return for her potential consent, she demanded that Elizabeth name her her successor and that Parliament ratify the decision. Well aware that the English queen would never agree, Mary gained time by engaging in futile negotiations. She herself had another idea in mind. If she had to marry an English nobleman, it would be better to reinforce her own claim to the English throne by choosing one of royal blood. Such a young man existed. His name was Henry Stewart, Lord Darnley, and he was a descendant of Margaret Tudor, sister of Henry VIII, by her second marriage. Margaret's first husband had been James IV of Scotland. On his

---

*The manuscript displays an interesting amendment. Cecil had written that Dudley was 'singularly beloved of the Queen's majesty'. On reflection, he struck out 'beloved' and substituted 'esteemed' (see D Wilson, *Sweet Robin* (Allison & Busby, London: 1997) p 144).

death she had married a Scot of exalted birth, the Earl of Angus, by whom she had had a daughter, Margaret, Countess of Lennox, Darnley's mother. Thus Mary and Darnley shared the same grandmother and the same religion.

Elizabeth intimated to Melville that she knew of Mary's interest in Darnley. The Scottish envoy, who refused to be drawn, confined himself to remarking, jocularly, that the beardless young man carried no weight. He had to keep his cards close to his chest because neither Darnley nor his family could leave England without the queen's consent. Elizabeth made another effort to promote Robert Dudley: she gave him the earldom of Leicester, hoping to render him more acceptable to her cousin, but her own enthusiasm was beginning to wane. The affair dragged on for another few months. At last, weary of what she called the Scottish labyrinth, Elizabeth consented to Darnley's departure for Edinburgh. Had Dudley convinced her that their separation would be too painful? Had she realized that Darnley represented the lesser of two evils to the extent that she could not prevent Mary from taking a husband indefinitely, and that an English Catholic would be better than a Duke of Guise or an Austrian archduke? Whatever the truth, Darnley left his mother behind in England as a hostage and took himself off to Mary Stuart's court in February 1565. The pace of events was about to quicken.

5

Mary Marries

1565–6

Darnley arrived in Edinburgh on 13 February 1565 and was warmly welcomed by the queen and her entourage. No one apart from his mother had ever boasted of his intellectual qualities, but he was tall and slim – attributes of considerable importance to Mary. She herself, being five feet eleven inches in height,* topped everyone around her by a head. With her young cousin – he was three years her junior – she could at last enjoy looking a partner in the eye while dancing a galliard. Darnley had got off to a good start. Despite his slight build he rode well, hunted with enthusiasm, and made a generally favourable impression. He also made a point of attending a sermon preached by the redoubtable John Knox to emphasize that, like Mary's, his Catholicism was not that of a proselytizer. Without abandoning her dignity, Mary seemed more than satisfied.

---

*The recumbent figure on her tomb in Westminster Abbey is just short of 5 feet 11 inches.

When Darnley caught measles and was confined to his chamber, she hurried to his bedside. An experienced nurse, having tended her frail husband, Francis II, throughout her girlhood, she lavished remedies and caresses on the young man. Darnley recovered after several weeks; Mary emerged from his sickroom smitten with love and determined to cure herself by marrying him as soon as possible.

Formerly a cold, ambitious young woman indifferent to the homage paid her and of unblemished reputation – unlike Elizabeth, whose own reputation had been tarnished by the Dudley affair – Mary now seemed a different person. Randolph, the English ambassador, was shocked and at a loss to describe the pitiful change that had come over the 'poor Queen whom ever before I esteemed so worthy, so wise, so honourable in all her doings', but who was now so altered by love of Lord Darnley that he could scarcely recognize her. As for Darnley himself, he had 'grown so proud' that he was 'intolerable to all honest men' and almost forgetful of his duty to the queen, and Randolph could not imagine what their life together would be like.[1] Events were to justify his worst fears.

Mary's fundamental error was to brook no delay in fulfilling her wishes. Far from exploiting her freedom of choice and the rare advantage of being able to inspect a suitor in person, she did not take the time to sound Darnley out and discover his true character, which was execrable. His pretty manners, feminine traits and smooth skin concealed a spoilt and vindictive nature. Once assured of Mary's feelings for him, he displayed such brutality that he lashed out with his fists at underlings who dared not return his blows. He also indulged in unbridled drunken orgies. 'His manner of speech is so proud and disagreeable that one would think him the king of the world, him who was but the Lord Darnley so short a time before,' declared one courtier, speaking on behalf of all his friends. It should be added that Darnley's membership of the Lennox clan badly threatened the equilibrium established by Moray and risked provoking more tension among the Scottish nobility. Randolph, noting the contempt and hatred aroused by Darnley's behaviour, wrote to Cecil: 'I know not, but it is greatly to be feared that he can have no long life among these people.'[2] Darnley's metamorphosis was almost instantaneous, and it is surprising and tragic that Mary did not take fright at it before the wedding. Worse still, she herself had changed beyond recognition. Randolph wrote that she had lost all her majesty, and that even her looks had suffered. Her spirits and conduct had undergone such a transformation that he was at a loss to describe them.[3]

Elizabeth, kept informed of developments by Maitland during April, expressed displeasure at her subject's disobedience, for Darnley had not sought her permission to marry. She informed Mary that she considered such a marriage unseemly, disadvantageous and a threat to their friendship. With a metaphorical shrug, Mary replied that she was at liberty to exercise her own judgement in choosing a husband. She immediately lost the support of her brother Moray, who tried to warn her against the danger of a rebellion by the clans. Faced with the rejection of his advice and the animosity of the future king, which he rightly foresaw, he left court. Maitland, the faithful minister whose experience and patience had been so useful to the young queen, was alarmed by the threat to her country's internal stability and only too well aware of the problems posed by the accession of a Catholic prince. But his advice, too, fell on deaf ears. Consumed with passion, Mary cast caution to the winds. Without giving any more thought to the consequences of her decision, she prepared to marry Darnley, 'the properest and best proportioned long [tall] man that ever she had seen',[4] on 29 July 1565. Darnley's brief, violent and murderous reign was about to begin.

Although he enjoyed the queen's favour and was bound to become their king, the courtiers shunned him. His sole companion during his first few months in Scotland was David Riccio, an Italian musician who acted as Mary's secretary for her French correspondence. Riccio had arrived in Scotland in 1561, in the train of the ambassador of Savoy. Remarkably ugly, short of stature and even slightly humpbacked but endowed with a fine bass voice, he soon attracted Mary's attention. She had a passion for music, and her evenings in private were enlivened by various forms of musical entertainment, so she asked him to remain at her court. Riccio climbed another few rungs of the social ladder when the queen discovered that he wrote good French and entrusted him with all her correspondence in that language. Although Riccio's was not a political post, he ended by becoming very well acquainted with current affairs because of the importance of Mary's relations with her adoptive country. His ease of access to the queen lent him a certain standing of which he was imprudent enough to boast. He shamelessly ingratiated himself with Darnley by organizing wild debauches, and his influence became far greater than his intellect warranted.

Riccio got busy as soon as he saw that Mary was determined to marry, and it was he that drafted the letter requesting the papal dispensation essential to a marriage between cousins. The Vatican chancellery dragged its feet, and Mary, impatient and self-assured, made arrangements for the ceremony without waiting for a reply. She also, as we have seen, dispensed with Elizabeth's consent. Having created Darnley the Duke of Albany on 22 July 1565, she then, on her own authority and without consulting Parliament, proclaimed him king on the eve of her wedding.* Gone was the moderate Mary who had been careful to avoid provoking the Queen of England and her own nobles for no good reason; who had rightly believed that she could not dispense with her brother's advice and was too mindful of her own 'majesty' to conceive of making other than a great and glorious marriage. What remained was a woman infatuated with a debauched and brutal nincompoop devoid of common sense and political support. Randolph, who was distressed by this development, reported that he had never seen a woman

---

*The title brought him no political authority. Only the crown matrimonial, which Mary had bestowed on Francis II, conferred authority to govern.

more headstrong or more rooted in her own opinion, bereft of self-discipline, reason and discernment.

What could have accounted for this sudden transformation, if not a physical passion that was all the more violent because Mary Stuart seems until now to have been exempt from any titillation of the senses? Elizabeth, who was always interested in the opposite sex, had been strongly tempted to marry Dudley for the simple reason that she found him attractive, whereas Mary had never shown the slightest interest in such matters. Having been chastely married to a physically and mentally immature boy and then transported to Scotland under her brother's aegis, she had continued to live in semi-spinsterdom, and however much she had wanted to marry Don Carlos, it was certainly not for the sake of his physical charms. A contemporary observer invited to predict which of the two queens would marry out of erotic passion would have bet on Elizabeth – and lost.

The wedding took place on Sunday, 29 July 1565. The contrast between this occasion and the sumptuous ceremonial of Mary's first marriage to the Dauphin verged on the tragic. In Paris in April 1558 a jubilant, glittering throng had come flocking from all directions and crowded around the blue, lily-embroidered carpet that led from the Seine to a pavilion erected in front of Notre Dame – a pavilion roofed with Cyprus silk sprinkled with gold lilies – to see the royal procession 'all resplendent in gold and silver'. Musicians clad in yellow and red were the first to set foot on the carpet. Following them, preceded by a mounted escort, came the princes of the Church attired in their most ornate robes and carrying crucifixes encrusted with precious stones, who advanced towards the cathedral with slow and dignified tread. Next to make their entrance were the Dauphin, his brothers and cousins. Then, walking at the side of King Henry II, appeared the Queen of Scots, a radiant figure acclaimed by the crowd and followed by Catherine de Médicis, the princesses, the grand dignitaries of the French court, and the ambassadors. Contrary to custom, Mary had chosen to wear white, a colour traditionally worn by French queens in mourning, but no one could have mistaken her fabulous, heavily embroidered gown, which sparkled in the sunlight, for mourning attire. In Edinburgh seven years later it was a grave-faced young woman in black, the traditional colour of full mourning, who emerged from her apartment at six in the morning and made her way to Holyrood's chapel royal on the arm of the Earl of Lennox, Darnley's father. What accounted for the unaccustomed hour and the absence of onlookers was the fact that the marriage service had to be Catholic and, thus, absolutely private.

Mary had chosen her costume to emphasize that the King of Scotland – as Darnley had now been proclaimed – was marrying the Queen Dowager of France, not a virgin bride. Standing alone before the altar, she awaited the arrival of her betrothed. They exchanged vows in accordance with the Catholic rite. Then Darnley withdrew, leaving Mary alone once more to hear Mass, her face hidden beneath her black hood. On emerging from the chapel she symbolically changed her attire by permitting each of those around her to remove one pin. That done, she withdrew to her chamber and re-emerged wearing a dazzling white gown appropriate to one embarking on a second life of happiness. The newlyweds were then joined by their nobles at a banquet held to the strains of trumpets and viols. The crowd gaily jostled for an abundance of coins thrown from the palace windows. The banqueters dined and danced. Finally, as the English ambassador reported, the couple retired to bed. One would like to believe that Mary's enjoyment of her wedding night was worth the price she would have to pay for it.

The political consequences of this marriage took only a week to make themselves felt. The clan chieftains resented the barely veiled threats of Darnley, who was annoyed at the concessions Mary had granted them at the beginning of her reign, and rose in revolt. The rebellion was swiftly crushed. Mary, displaying her usual courage, did not hesitate. The intrepid horsewoman mustered her loyalists, leapt into the saddle, and led them against the insurgents accompanied by her husband, who sported a suit of gilt armour for the occasion. Surprised by the speed of her reaction and bereft of Queen Elizabeth's support, on which they had been counting, all the rebels surrendered except her brother, Moray, who crossed the border and installed himself in England.

Mary had won the day, but not for long. She tried to establish a different equilibrium between the clans by favouring those who had always been opposed to her brother. One of them was the Earl of Bothwell, who was to play a vital role in the months ahead. Previously banished by Moray, he now returned from exile. The heir of a great family in the south of Scotland, the Hepburns, Bothwell had led an exceptionally adventurous life. Although a Protestant, he had supported Mary of Guise. When she died he joined Mary Stuart in France and returned to Scotland with her. He was appointed a member of the Council, but in March 1562 the Earl of Arran accused him of planning to abduct the queen – probably wrongly, since Arran was known to be insane. Arrested and imprisoned in Edinburgh Castle, he managed to escape and reach England. There he was rearrested and confined in the Tower but allowed to cross over to France a few months later. Mary recalled him on the occasion of one of her nobles' first rebellions, and he hired a fishing boat so as to land unobtrusively. He married Jean Gordon, a member of the Huntly clan, but this robust, brutal 'ape in purple' was a lady's man for all his unlovely features, broken nose and protruding ears, and was no respecter of conjugal fidelity.

The queen did not trust her nobles despite this changing of the guard. She cherished few illusions about them and, like many monarchs, preferred not to employ their services when it came to handling her confidential reports. That was how David Riccio, who was always at her side, came to be entrusted with tasks of growing importance. Here again, Mary demonstrated her lack of political acumen. She needed an adviser capable of guiding her through the clans' political maze, not an amusing private secretary. In this respect a foreigner like Riccio was quite as naive as Mary, and he also aroused the jealousy of numerous Scottish grandees. An adviser from a humble background should have cultivated humility and, above all, avoided drawing attention to himself by indulging in undue ostentation, but Riccio blithely discarded his original black livery and strutted around in multicoloured satins and silks. He also incurred Darnley's wrath because of his intimacy with the queen. Mary Stuart's marriage disintegrated with a rapidity that was, perhaps, the most curious feature of her matrimonial venture, but not before she had conceived a child.

Darnley, on whom his wife had lavished gifts and marks of affection, had gone too far. Loud-mouthed and rude, insolent to the Council and obnoxious to everyone in general, shockingly ignorant and insufferably boorish in private, often drunk and invariably bad-tempered, he disgusted Mary as quickly as he had charmed her. Having once sought his company all the time, she now barred her door to him, especially as she no longer required his services as a stallion. Having originally meant to entrust him with genuine political responsibility, she omitted to notify him of Council meetings and refused him permission to bear the royal arms. Even the medallions and coins adorned with their effigies and names, 'Henricus' and 'Maria' (his was on the left in the place of honour), were withdrawn from circulation. Mary did not fear Darnley – he could do nothing, so notorious was his incompetence and so absolute his isolation – but she failed to appreciate the danger represented by her nobles, who were furious at being more or less sidelined. Hitherto held in check by the authority of Moray and Maitland but chafing at the favour shown to Riccio, they were at boiling point. Once the dissension in the royal household became public knowledge, they thought they could use Darnley to humiliate the queen. The result was an ignoble rapprochement between a prince consort and those who were conspiring against their sovereign, his wife.

The rebel lords' manoeuvre succeeded with ease. Darnley's vanity had convinced him that 'the marriage was done with the consent of the nobility, who thought him worthy of the place; that the whole kingdom had their eyes upon him; [and that] they would follow and serve him upon the fields [of battle], where it was a shame a woman should command.'[5] Mary, for her part, seemed strangely untroubled by her perilous situation. The opposition comprised the Protestant lords who had been banished from court like Moray; the Protestant Church, still headed by Knox, which was concerned that Mary, with the support of France and Spain and the financial backing of the Pope, had abandoned her policy of conciliation with England; and, lastly, the political lords who had formerly wielded influence within the Council. These were led by Maitland and Morton, who bitterly resented the contemptible Riccio's advancement. It was the widespread jealousy inspired by the royal favour shown him that united this disparate opposition. The Protestants were indignant at the status accorded to a Catholic suspected of being an agent of the Pope, the politicians held him responsible for their fall from grace. As for Darnley, incensed at being denied access to the queen's bedchamber, he had turned on his former friend and boon companion in the belief that Mary was rejecting him because she had become Riccio's mistress. Needless to say, the plotters encouraged him in that belief to ensure his complicity.

Assassination, a political instrument often employed at this period, was practised in Scotland with a certain formality. The conspirators agreed on what was to be done, but they knew each other too well to be satisfied with a mere promise or word of honour. Accordingly, they drew up a document or 'bond' that defined the role of each and bore his signature and seal. Displaying attitudes as transitory as they were cynical, the parties to the plot met to sign this agreement, which stipulated that the crown matrimonial would be offered to Darnley, the exiles recalled and the Protestant religion reaffirmed. Maitland withheld his signature, possibly prompted by an access of good sense, if not of integrity. Darnley, on the other hand, initialled the document. The signatories did not specify that Riccio would be assassinated, but the Italian's murder was the prime essential from Darnley's point of view. Although Randolph, Elizabeth's ambassador, kept her informed of his spies' reports, she made no move to warn Mary. In any case, the Scottish queen would not have listened to her any more than she listened to Melville, her former ambassador in London, who warned her of the sinister rumours circulating in Edinburgh. She shrugged her shoulders and assured him that her compatriots were all talk and no action. Riccio, who was also warned, responded in the same vein: 'Paroles, paroles, nothing but words. The Scots will boast but rarely perform their brags.'[6]

On Saturday, 9 March 1566, by which time she was six months pregnant, Mary was dining in her private apartment in the tower at Holyrood, which was cosier at that time of year than the big rooms on the ground floor. Her companions included David Riccio, Lady Argyll, an illegitimate daughter of James IV and thus her half-sister, and one or two other guests, among them her equerry Arthur Erskine. The small size of the premises must thus be borne in mind, because the table could accommodate eight persons at most. The little supper room was next door to Mary's bedchamber, which was connected by a privy staircase to Darnley's apartment on the floor below. Riccio, sumptuously attired in a damask doublet trimmed with fur, was chatting gaily when Darnley, drawing aside the curtain over the doorway to the bedchamber, made an unheralded appearance. The others moved up to make room for him and went on with their meal. Minutes later Lord Ruthven appeared wearing armour, sword in hand and deathly pale. Mary, dumbfounded because only her husband was entitled to use the privy staircase, curtly demanded to know the reason for his presence. Ruthven replied that he had come to settle accounts with 'this poltroon David', who was guilty of having offended against the sovereign's honour. Riccio, unarmed and understandably terrified, clung to the queen's skirts with both hands and implored her to save him, but the rest of the conspirators, two of them armed with pistols and three with daggers drawn, had already climbed the narrow staircase in single file and burst into the supper room. Some barred the exits while others hurled themselves on the unfortunate man. Deaf to his cries of *'Justizia, justizia, sauvez ma vie, Madame!'*, they prized his fingers away and dragged him out of the room. Then, wielding their fists and daggers indiscriminately, they lashed out at him with such fury that they cut each other's hands. Finally they threw his mutilated, bleeding carcass down the stairwell. Fifty-three wounds were found on his hideously disfigured corpse.

Darnley had not joined in. He remained at Mary's side in an endeavour to persuade her that he was not complicit, but his perfidy was so obvious that she was not deceived for a moment. Furthermore, she persisted in believing that her own life and that of her unborn child had been deliberately endangered, for why else had the conspirators chosen to assassinate Riccio within a few feet of her? She heaped reproaches on the nonentity whom she had raised to become a king, upbraiding and hurling the vilest abuse at him. Darnley, shaken by the carnage, responded with a string of complaints: she had ceased to love him since Riccio's elevation, she no longer trusted him and never joined him in his bedchamber. He whined like the spoilt child he had always been, and by so doing lost the initiative. He was a traitor and a coward, Mary told him, and she would draw her own conclusions.

At this moment of danger and extreme violence she displayed an admirable degree of intelligence – and dissimulation. She was unarmed, vulnerable and utterly alone, and she knew it. The conspirators' men were barring all the doors, so no one could come to her aid. Alerted by the unwonted commotion, a crowd had assembled outside. Darnley appeared at the window and spoke some reassuring words: an Italian spy had been killed but the queen was in no danger. She was resting. Everyone should do likewise and go to bed.

In reality, Mary was a prisoner. The nobles on whom she knew she could rely, Bothwell and Huntly, had managed to escape by boldly swinging across the lion pit on the end of a rope. She realized that the victors might spare her life until she gave birth to an heir, but that her days as queen were numbered. With remarkable coolness and composure, she decided to revenge herself by playing the only trump in her hand: Darnley, her squalid husband.

After addressing the crowd, Darnley repaired to the queen's chamber. Swallowing her disgust, anger and pride, she greeted her husband politely and set to work on him.

They shared the same interests, she said. How could he possibly imagine that the nobles would permit him to wield power? If only he would think for a moment, he would realize that he was a puppet in their hands. Had he forgotten the contempt with which they had treated him? She continued to cite arguments, stopping only when she saw him waver. This did not take long: having betrayed his wife in the evening, he had abandoned his accomplices by morning. Mary then acted with great speed, being well aware that there was nothing to prevent him from changing tack again. The following morning she rose at the usual hour and got dressed in time to receive Moray, who had hurried to her side in the hope of regaining his influential status, accompanied by Morton, Maitland, and even the terrifying Ruthven. Showing none of the fear she felt, she placed herself under Moray's protection and greeted him with well-feigned relief. 'If my brother had been here,' she cried, throwing herself into his arms, 'he would never have suffered me to have been thus cruelly handled!' Moray took charge and suggested a compromise: if Mary would undertake to pardon the conspirators, they would withdraw their guards. But the conspirators, being mistrustful, would have preferred a promise of pardon in writing. The day passed in negotiations. When evening came Mary finally pleaded exhaustion, saying she felt so ill that a midwife was sent for at her request. This put her mind at rest: no one would take the liberty of disturbing her repose, nor, as luck would have it, had anyone noticed that she had summoned her page and the captain of her guard to her apartment and conferred with them briefly.

There were no apparent losers in this curious situation. Moray, his peace of mind restored, was feeling indispensable again; the conspirators congratulated themselves on having got the better of their queen at small cost – the murder of a buffoon; and Darnley, full of himself once more, came and went between the wife he had betrayed two nights before and the friends he had betrayed the day before. The triumphant conspirators decided that it was time to relax, to eat and drink and leave the womenfolk to their stomach cramps and vapours. Within a few hours they were all dead drunk.

Mary, who had kept watch, was reassured by the silence. Opening her door, she stole carefully down the darkened tower staircase and emerged by way of a subterranean passage that came out in the castle's small graveyard, where the others were waiting for her. Darnley, in a hurry to escape, galloped on ahead. Mary got up behind Arthur Erskine, her equerry, followed by the captain of her guard, her page and several other faithful retainers. Six months pregnant, she rode hell for leather to the castle of Lord Seton, the father of one of her Maries. There she was given an omelette for breakfast, a fresh horse and a mounted escort of two hundred men. Late that morning she reached Dunbar Castle, a fortress guarding the coast some twenty-five miles south-east of Edinburgh. Once there, she took matters in hand again.

Speed, daring and a vigour remarkable for a woman in her condition had won the day. Instead of being paralysed by the horrifying incident of two nights before, she had found the strength to manipulate a contemptible husband who was in league with her enemies, undertake a mad dash on horseback, and galvanize her supporters. She followed up her successful initiative by assembling an army with Bothwell's assistance, for Mary was no Amazon: she needed a man, and Bothwell – sturdy, dashing and courageous – was the opposite of Darnley. They prepared to enter Edinburgh, where the conspirators discovered that they had been duped. The most compromised among them fled. John Knox disappeared, and Maitland, although he had prudently absented himself on the night of the murder, deemed it advisable to leave the city.

Mary made peace with her brother and invited him to re-form her privy council in company with Bothwell and several other leading nobles who had refrained from dabbling in the conspiracy. But what to do with Darnley, her treacherous, doubly dishonoured husband? Mary found his presence loathsome and made no secret of it in private. In public, however, she remained extremely circumspect. Darnley was the father of her unborn child, after all. If the spineless creature decided to question its paternity, it would be tainted with bastardy; but if she tried to get rid of her unwanted spouse by seeking an annulment, the same problem would arise. An annulled marriage vitiated the legitimacy of its offspring – a disability from which Mary Tudor and Elizabeth had long suffered – so she had to suffer in silence and make a triumphal but conjugal return to her capital city.

But Darnley, of course, was finished. No one wanted to be in his entourage, which was henceforth confined to a handful of servitors. By contrast, James Stewart, Earl of Moray, became reconciled with Bothwell and resumed a preponderant influence that expressed itself in improved relations between Scotland and England.

Elizabeth's response to her cousin's adventure was spontaneous and extremely vigorous: in the first place because professional loyalty caused her to be horrified on principle by any attack on a legitimate sovereign; and, secondly, out of womanly solidarity. Appalled by the truly horrifying details Mary gave her in a personal letter sent from Dunbar, she took to wearing a miniature of Mary at her waist, the Spanish ambassador reported, and she told him that in Mary's place she would have transfixed her husband's heart with her own dagger. She must also have privately reflected that all this butchery furnished additional proof of the perils of marriage.

The ensuing months were months of truce. Heavily pregnant and exhausted after all her ordeals, Mary seemed to be at the end of her tether. She refused to return to Holyrood and took up residence in Edinburgh Castle, which was more austere and uncomfortable but a great deal easier to defend. There, on 19 June 1566, in a big four-poster bed draped in taffeta and velvet, she was delivered of a male child, born with a caul, who gave immediate evidence of health and strength. He was given the name James. Although the birth had been a very arduous one, Mary did not rest. Having summoned all the leading courtiers to her bedchamber and sent for Darnley, who had not been present at the birth, she pointed to the child and said: 'God has given you and me a son, begotten by none but you.'[7] Darnley made no reply. Everyone knew that it was only his jealous tittle-tattle about David Riccio's* influence over the queen that had cast doubt on the little prince's paternity. Taking the baby in her arms, Mary continued in a loud voice: 'Here I protest to God, as I shall answer to him at the great day of Judgment, that this is your son and no other man's son. I am desirous that all here, with ladies and others, bear witness. For he is so much your own son, that I fear it will be the worse for him hereafter.'[8] The child's father bowed his head and left the room without a word.

---

*This slur resisted the passage of time. In private, Henry IV of France used refer to James as 'Solomon', a jocular allusion to David Riccio's alleged paternity.

6

Political Assassination or Crime of Passion?

1566–7

The birth of a healthy son deprived Darnley of his only asset. Mary had no further need of her parasitic spouse and did not mind letting him know it. What did a husband matter, now that she had a child? Mary had also regained the advantage over Elizabeth, who now had to confront a pretender provided with an heir, which greatly strengthened her position. The advent of James redoubled England's eagerness to see Elizabeth married at last. She needed a husband without delay if she wished to avoid the eventual accession of a Catholic queen. As she herself admitted to the Hapsburgs' envoy, 'she had formerly purposed by all means to remain single, but in consequence of the insistent pressure that was brought to bear upon her by the Estates of her realm, she was now resolved to marry.'[1]

So negotiations with Archduke Charles now became brisker and more specific. The ambassadors and councillors devoted less time to his appearance and physical charms than to the religious freedom he would be granted if he persisted in his Catholicism. The odds in London were in favour of marriage. Tension at Elizabeth's court had become palpable since the Scottish crown prince's birth, and the possibility of finally settling the succession was being openly mooted by many English noblemen, foremost among them Robert Dudley but including the Duke of Norfolk, the Earl of Pembroke and others. What rendered the matter more urgent still was that Mary's political position seemed strengthened. Her own nobles, shaken by the failure of the conspiracy and well aware that the existence of a child would augment their queen's self-confidence, rallied to her more unitedly than ever before. This apparent lull was rare for Scotland. In fact, the semblance of unity stemmed solely from a common hatred of Darnley.

Mary did not support her husband. People despised, shunned and scarcely troubled to greet him, the more so since Darnley, champing at the bit with fury, vituperated against the queen in the presence of his servants, who broadcast and embellished his complaints. To make matters worse, he sought support from abroad. Accusing her to Philip II of being 'dubious in the faith',[2] he represented himself as the only true defender of Catholicism at court and threatened to leave for the Continent a few days after his son's official baptism. This worried Mary, who feared that he would proclaim that he was not the boy's father. All these altercations made her physically ill. Maitland clearly discerned that the cause of the queen's dark mood was displeasure with her disastrous marriage. She had showered Darnley with honours, contrary to her subjects' wishes, and he had rewarded her with such ingratitude and behaved so badly towards her that it broke her heart to know that he was her husband, but that she could see no way out of her predicament.[3] The French ambassador, du Croc, also noted that a reconciliation seemed impossible under the circumstances. Not only was Darnley's conduct intolerable, but the queen distrusted him so greatly that she had only to see him in conversation with some nobleman to fancy that another plot was being hatched against her.[4] Du Croc described the atmosphere at court in a long letter to Catherine de Médicis. The queen and her lords were on the best of terms, he reported, whereas the king was universally disliked. 'He cannot be otherwise, given the manner in which he conducts himself, for he wishes to be everything and to be in command of everything, and is taking a path that will end in his being nothing. [...] He often complains to me...and I assure him that the queen, being offended in her person, [will never give him back] the authority he possessed heretofore, and that he [should be] content with the honour she does him and good cheer she grants him.'[5] Du Croc concluded by saying that the worst thing from the queen's point of view, perhaps, was the knowledge that she herself was responsible for her own misfortune. Her incessant altercations with Darnley were causing her to fear that he would abduct their son. In August she decided that the boy would be safer if removed from Edinburgh to Stirling Castle, the most secure fortress in Scotland, where he would live under the protection of Lord Mar.*

We now come to a shady episode in the history of Scotland. At the end of November 1566 the queen conferred with her principal advisers at Craigmillar Castle, near Edinburgh. On the agenda: What to do about Darnley? In the course of a conversation with the Scottish ambassador to France, Maitland confided his despair at the thought that their queen was tied to such a man, but said that she herself could see no way of getting rid of him. He was concerned by her extreme lassitude and exhaustion, which were such that one evening, in Moray's presence, she confessed that she had 'no pleasure to live, and if she could find no other remedy, she would slay herself.'[6]

As we have seen above, she could not contemplate an annulment, or even divorce, because that would have entailed young James's bastardy. All that remained were solutions more drastic than those sanctioned by law. We do not know the terms of the agreement that was reached, but Mary must have obtained sufficient assurances because she agreed to rehabilitate Riccio's assassins and permit the guilty lords to return from exile. Darnley was dismayed by this news, knowing that his erstwhile accomplices would never forgive his treachery. Thus a secret pact was signed

---

*To illustrate the complex relationships existing between the various Scottish clans, it may be mentioned that the Earl of Mar's sister was Margaret Erskine, the mother of James Stewart, James V's illegitimate son.

by the queen's councillors but not by the queen herself. The meeting broke up, and Mary concentrated on preparations for her son's baptism, which was to take place at Stirling on 12 December.

Celebrated in accordance with the Catholic rite and accompanied by festivities, balls and masques, the baptism was as splendid as befitted a child whose godmother and godfather were, respectively, the Queen of England and the King of France. Those monarchs did not attend in person, of course, but they sent suitably magnificent gifts. A more disconcerting absence was that of the father, who sulked in his room and did not show his face during the ceremony or the revels that followed, leaving Bothwell to do the honours. Although it did not detract from the splendour of the festivities, Darnley's gesture presaged disaster. Du Croc, who was sure the whole affair would end badly, confided as much to Archbishop Beaton, his opposite number in Paris, but 'preferred not to commit to paper' the reasons why he felt convinced that 'no improvement in the situation could be expected.'[7] Darnley must also have been convinced of it, because he decided to leave for Glasgow, the seat of his family, the Lennoxes. Did he plan to steal a march on his enemies and resort to force?

Rumours of a conspiracy became so persistent that Mary recalled the young prince for fear her husband would abduct him, Stirling being nearer Glasgow than Edinburgh. In fact, her husband had caught smallpox so badly that he was confined to his bed and did not leave it for two months.

Mary then took her most controversial step ever: she went to Glasgow in January 1567 and brought Darnley back to Edinburgh with her. Why?*

Those biographers of the queen who are in love with their subject have theorized that her soft heart melted at the thought that the poor, ailing young man was lonely without her. Those of a more political complexion reckon that she feared the influence of his father, the Earl of Lennox, and thought it safer to keep an eye on him, even though his pitiful condition rendered a major initiative on his part unlikely. Cynics, of whom the present author is one, think the worst: that Mary and her loyalists had concluded a pact. Even if we concede that she may not have undertaken to play a personal part, she did, at the very least, agree to give them a free hand. So Darnley's presence was essential. He would never have gone with Bothwell, Morton or Moray of his own free will. Only the queen could bring him back, nor did she doubt her ability to do so. 'She knew that his heart was "of wax", whereas hers was "of diamond".'[8]

Employing a shrewd combination of charm and authority, Mary persuaded Darnley to come with her and resume his place at the palace. The unfortunate man, racked with shivering fits and wearing a taffeta mask over his pustulated face that left only his oozing eyelids visible, made

---

*The vast bibliography on the subject compiled by A Weir for her *Mary, Queen of Scots and the Murder of Lord Darnley* (Ballantine, New York: 2003) lists over 500 titles.

the journey lying in a litter. It seemed easier, as he himself admitted, not to nurse him in Edinburgh Castle, which was so dark and dank at this time of year, or even at Holyrood, but in a smaller, healthier and more comfortable house that happened to belong to Moray. This residence, which stood in its own garden, was known as Kirk o'Field. It was adjacent to the church of St-Mary-in-the-Field and situated a short distance from Holyrood, where the queen resided. Mary gave orders for various items to be sent over from the palace: some tapestries to protect Darnley from the cold, some pieces of furniture and a tub for the patient to bathe in. A door served as a stretcher on which to transport him from room to room. The bedchamber he had been allotted was on the first floor, and another room was made ready for the queen on the ground floor. Having stated that she meant to keep her husband company as often as possible, she had her own handsome bed, which was draped in violet velvet, installed there in case she chose to spend the night on the premises. Darnley moved into Kirk o'Field on Saturday, 1 February 1567.

Mary kept her word and became once more the attentive nurse she had been in the first flush of their relationship. Once Darnley felt better, she organized card games and intimate dinners. As if to signify that their reconciliation was complete, she remained with him so late on the Wednesday and Friday nights that she did not return to Holyrood to sleep. On Sunday, 9 February, it was announced that Darnley had recovered and would resume his place at court on the morrow. This being the last Sunday before Lent, Mary had a busy day ahead. In the morning she attended the wedding of two members of her household, in the afternoon a farewell dinner for the Savoyard ambassador. Finally, accompanied by Bothwell, Huntly and Kennedy, she went to spend the evening with Darnley at Kirk o'Field. Moray, who had a singular knack of absenting himself at crucial moments, especially when a murder was in the offing, had gone to visit his sick wife, and Maitland and Morton were equally careful not to be there. It was a convivial evening. The gentlemen played dice while Mary sat at her husband's bedside and chatted with him. At eleven she rose to return to Holyrood. Darnley protested, wanting her to stay overnight, but she insisted and rode back to the palace with her escort.

At Holyrood the sound of viols and bagpipes denoted that the wedding ball was still in progress, so the queen went to the ballroom and mingled with the guests. On retiring to her chamber she asked Bothwell and John Stewart of Traquair, a loyalist who had helped her to escape on the night of Riccio's murder, to accompany her because she wanted a word with them. Traquair left first, and she remained alone with Bothwell for another few minutes. At last the candles were extinguished and silence descended on the palace.

At two in the morning the inhabitants of Edinburgh were roused by a violent explosion. The queen immediately sent for news. She was informed that Kirk o'Field had been blown to smithereens and that Darnley and his manservant had been found strangled at the bottom of the garden. It appeared that a suspicious noise had alerted them to the presence of a band of silent men surrounding the house. Terrified, Darnley had attempted to escape by sliding down a rope, but he failed to elude his assailants. Bothwell, who hurried to the scene, had his body carried to the house next door, where it was examined by surgeons, members of the Council and local inhabitants before being placed in a litter and taken to the palace. Meanwhile, he returned to confer with Mary. They had plenty to talk about.

If Bothwell had been cool-headed, chivalrous and politically astute, he would have persuaded Mary to shut herself up in her apartment, put on deepest mourning and ordain a serious investigation. But Bothwell did not think like a statesman and lacked courtesy in his dealings with women.

The murderers had chosen to strike in the dark. A dagger or harquebus did not guarantee anonymity – an eyewitness might prevent the culprit from denying his guilt – but an explosive charge was the ideal weapon for a collective crime, and its use had the advantage of a certain imprecision. Everything indicated that Bothwell was responsible and he knew it, but the queen's role was less apparent. She could easily have chosen to linger at Kirk o'Field, in which case she would have been killed with the other occupants. Had the man who lit the fuse deliberately waited for her to leave before doing so? How could this be proved? In order to banish all suspicion, it was essential for her to distance herself from Bothwell and avoid the smallest appearance of complicity and, thus, of guilt.

Catherine de Médicis and Elizabeth immediately sent off long personal letters urging Mary to act with the utmost vigour. If she failed to punish those responsible, she herself would remain suspect. Elizabeth had not been personally tainted by the scandal surrounding the death of Robert Dudley's wife because she had promptly severed contact with him while awaiting the results of the inquest. Darnley's murder could have far more serious repercussions. The Queen of England took a very grave view of the risks incurred by sovereigns who suffered themselves to be attacked or slandered by their subjects. Writing to Mary in French on 24 February 1567, she advised her as follows: 'My ears have been so deafened, my understanding so vexed and my heart so affrighted to hear the horrid sound of the abominable murder of your late husband and my slain cousin that I have no wish, even now, to write of it. [Although his death affects me extremely, since he is so close a kinsman of mine,] I would boldly tell you what I think of it. I cannot conceal that I mourn more for you than for him. Oh, Madame, I would not be fulfilling the office of a faithful cousin or affectionate friend, were I to attempt to gratify your ears rather than devoting myself to the preservation of your honour. I will not disguise from you that most people believe you will wink at avenging this deed, and that you will be careful not to touch those who have done you such a favour. It could be thought that the murderers had been assured they would go unpunished.... I exhort you, I counsel and entreat you, to take the matter so seriously that you will not shrink from touching him who is closest to you, should the matter concern him, and that nothing will prevent you from ordaining an exemplary punishment.'[9]

Mary Stuart took no notice of this anxious letter, whose urgent tone should have impressed her. It is not surprising that her life has spawned so many novels, plays, operas, legends and impassioned accounts, because we do not know the gist of the remarks she exchanged with those close to her at many of the turning points in her existence. Her most crucial conversations often took place without witnesses, and the authenticity of many of her letters cannot be guaranteed beyond doubt. We reconstruct; we reflect on psychological data that are merely hypotheses because the incessant upheavals that occurred in the relations between the various actors give rise to a troublesome discontinuity that thwarts all our efforts to discern some method in their doings. The intellect always seeks a logical connection between various events. Nothing is more disconcerting than to find oneself faced with a series of actions and to be unable to detect the thread that links them together. Nothing is harder to admit than incomprehension. It is, in fact, impossible to find a logical and satisfactory explanation of Mary Stuart's behaviour during the tragedy that was about to unfold. This is because she was not a rational being but a kaleidoscope in which the most incoherent images kept colliding, disintegrating and reconstructing themselves.

What is beyond dispute is that the Scottish queen's conduct at the time of this crisis was downright demented. By 9 February 1567 Mary was already in love with Bothwell – infatuated in the true sense – and no member of her entourage wielded sufficient influence over her to restrain her amorous impulses. Her doubly adulterous passion was reprehensible, she knew, and it must have tormented her to be unable to confide in anyone. Du Croc, the elderly ambassador who cherished a genuine affection for the woman who had been his youthful queen and had experienced so many tragedies in so short a time, was the only person to detect that she was suffering from a secret wound. In whom could she have confided her shame and desire? Unlike Elizabeth, who possessed a man of incontestable loyalty and devotion in William Cecil, Mary Stuart did not have an adviser who was solely dependent on and absolutely devoted to her. All the members of her entourage cherished ambitions of their own. Differences of opinion among her closest associates were coloured by personal emotion. Yet she badly needed guidance. She did not possess the authority or knowledge required to govern, but she never managed to relegate her favourites to a secondary role, distinguish between emotional intensity and intellectual strength, and uphold the prestige of more independent advisers. She had a sense of mystery, but not of what was secret. By rushing headlong into marriage with Darnley she had wantonly deprived herself of the advice of Moray, her brother, and of Maitland, whose counsel had proved so useful since his return from France. After Darnley's disgrace she turned to Bothwell, seduced or overwhelmed by his furious energy and brutality, and granted him immense political powers unwarranted by his aptitudes.

Mary often translated her emotions into verse, and one of her poems sheds light on the start of this affair:

Pour lui aussi j'ai jeté mainte larme
Premier quand il fut de ce corps possesseur
Duqel alors il n'avait pas le cœur.
[For him, too, I shed many a tear,
when first he was the possessor of this body
whose heart he then had not.]

It is conceivable that Bothwell, who spent a great deal of time alone with Mary, had raped her, and that, having previously been married to two youths, she experienced such a sensual awakening that she desired Bothwell with unbridled ardour from that day forward. Physical passion engulfed her, and sheer impatience and an absolute refusal to be parted from Bothwell, even temporarily, was destined to lose her her kingdom, her son and her reputation. She was perfectly well aware of this, as the conclusion of her sonnet demonstrates:

Pour lui depuis j'ai méprisé l'honneur...
Pour lui j'ai hasardé grandeur et conscience
Pour lui tous mes parents j'ai quitté et amis...
[For him I thereafter spurned reputation...

For him I risked greatness and conscience,
For him I left all my kinsfolk and friends...][10]

What was the lovers' course of action during those first crucial hours on the morning of Darnley's murder? They decided to lay stress on the queen's narrow escape but not on the search for the guilty parties. The same day, Mary wrote to Archbishop Beaton, her ambassador in Paris, that God had preserved her, and that 'the diligence of her Council would permit [her] to punish the cruelty [of the culprits] with a rigour that would serve as an example for centuries to come.'[11] The Council adopted the same line. In announcing the tragedy to Catherine de Médicis, it emphasized that 'the authors of the crime [had] very nearly destroyed the queen and most of the lords in her train' and assured her that an inquiry designed to unmask the murderers had already been set up.

The traditional period of mourning was decreed and Darnley, as befitted a King of Scotland, was laid to rest in the chapel royal. Mary, impassive and almost apathetic, seemed oblivious of the strength of the gathering storm, even though scurrilous posters accusing her and Bothwell of having contrived Darnley's death were already to be seen on walls throughout the capital. She was depicted as a bare-breasted mermaid wearing a crown and he as a hare,* their figures being adorned with an M and a B respectively to make the

---

*A siren or mermaid was synonymous with a prostitute; a hare appeared on Bothwell's coat of arms.

symbolism doubly clear. Far from compelling herself to adopt the low profile incumbent on a widowed queen, and far from protecting her good name by behaving impeccably, Mary left Holyrood a week after the funeral and went to stay at Lord Seton's castle, where Bothwell joined her. When two of her servants were denounced as accomplices, she facilitated their escape by procuring passports for them. Venomous rumours circulated in France, Spain, Venice and above all in England, where they were fostered by the Savoyard ambassador to Scotland, who, on arrival in London, intimated that Queen Mary was probably privy to the conspiracy. 'He does not accuse her, but neither does he acquit her,' reported Guzman da Silva, Philip II's ambassador to England.

Despite all these warning signs, and despite the accusations levelled at Bothwell, which were becoming more and more specific, Mary made no move to keep him at a distance – far from it. As if hypnotized by the man, she favoured him in a way that was shocking under the circumstances. To repeat, the queen's complicity in her husband's murder has never been proved beyond doubt. It is impossible to demonstrate her guilt, but her extravagant behaviour after the event has condemned her without appeal. The facts counted for less than appearances. Her ambassador to the Valois wrote frankly that to spend hours alone with the Earl of Bothwell and then to amuse herself by playing real tennis with him was not only causing talk at court but convincing the public of their complicity. Darnley's father, the Earl of Lennox, took out a suit against Bothwell, but the hearing turned out to be a tragic farce. Bothwell attended court with a sword at his side and a dagger in his belt, accompanied by a thousand henchmen. Lennox dared not come to Edinburgh to press charges, and the intimidated judges returned a meaningless verdict: on the grounds that Lennox's absence nullified the charge, they acquitted Bothwell. Utterly devoid of shame, he rode through Edinburgh in triumph. No one risked voicing any doubts about the outcome of the trial, although the court record stated that it was 'heavily murmured' that he was guilty.[12]

The queen's conduct was hardly calculated to allay suspicion. The day after this verdict she granted Bothwell the privilege of carrying the sceptre and crown at the opening of Parliament. The onlookers, who foresaw his coronation, grumbled that the distance from the hands to the head was short. Moray, forever cautious and at pains to secure his political future, left Scotland for England, where he confirmed to the Spanish ambassador that Bothwell's divorce was imminent, adding in a rather hypocritical tone of respect that he did not, however, believe that his sister would marry him in view of 'her position, her great virtue and recent events'. The news from Scotland was spicier. Bothwell had invited his fellow nobles to dinner and demanded their written consent to his marriage to the queen, who, in the course of a somewhat immodest outburst, had declared that she would gladly exchange France, England and her beautiful Scotland for him, and that she would follow him to the ends of the earth clad in a white petticoat.[13] Astonished at these sudden developments, the English Council was alarmed by the rise to power of a man as irrational as Bothwell. 'Scotland is a quagmire,' Cecil declared. 'Nobody seems to stand still, the most honest desire to go away, the worst tremble with the shaking of their conscience.'[14] But worse was to come.

On 21 April Mary rode off to see her son, who had been taken back to Stirling and was in the custody of Lord Mar. Three days later, as she was returning to Edinburgh, her route was barred by Bothwell and several hundred horsemen. Claiming that some mysterious danger threatened her in the city, he proposed to take her to Dunbar Castle, which he had borrowed for the occasion. The queen's escort, which was commanded by Maitland, took exception to this strange change of plan, but she agreed to go with Bothwell 'rather than be the cause of bloodshed'. Maitland was politely invited to return to Edinburgh on his own, and Mary and Bothwell rode without further incident to Dunbar, where they spent a week closeted alone together. Meanwhile, back in Edinburgh, divorce proceedings were swiftly brought against Bothwell in the Protestant commissary court, which adjudged his adultery with a female servant sufficient grounds for dissolving the marriage. As for the Catholic priesthood, it argued in favour of an annulment because he and his wife were within the fourth degree of consanguinity.

Although no one was deceived by Bothwell's supposed

abduction of the queen, it made her precipitate marriage possible because, if a man forced himself upon a woman, the prevailing code of honour placed him under an obligation to marry her as soon as possible. The only plausible explanation for Mary's impatience was that she knew herself to be pregnant and *had* to marry in short order. But she was plunging headlong into a terrible situation from which there was no escape. Her pregnancy compelled her to hurry, but her haste betrayed complicity in her husband's murder. By April 1567 she was hopelessly embroiled.

At the beginning of May, Bothwell and Mary returned to Edinburgh and rode through the city together, he leading the queen's horse by the bridle. The common folk, formerly so enthusiastic about their young monarch, murmured at the sight. John Craig, a minister of the parish church of Edinburgh, braved Bothwell's threats and expressed his disgust to the Council: 'I laid to his [Bothwell's] charge the law of adultery, the ordinance of the Kirk, the law of ravishing, the suspicion of collusion between him and his wife, the sudden divorcement, and proclaiming within the space of four days, and lastly the suspicion of the King's death which her marriage would confirm.'[15] The French ambassador warned the queen once more that she risked alienating her friends in France. But it was no use. At four o'clock on the morning of 15 May, three months after her husband's murder, Mary Stuart married Bothwell at a hurried ceremony according to the Protestant rite (although she had not converted) in the great hall of Holyrood Palace. There were very few witnesses, all her nobles having chosen to stay away. The French ambassador refused an invitation lest it be thought that his king had been involved in the affair. No balls or banquets were held to mark the occasion. By way of a wedding dress Mary wore an old yellow skirt relined with white taffeta and a long black gown done up with gold braid. Her first wedding had been a dazzling affair and her second far from devoid of promise, but her third was unworthy of her. She had fallen fast in nine years, and her descent was destined to accelerate still further.

Catholic Europe had supported Mary Stuart since her accession. Although foreign courts knew she enjoyed little freedom in the religious domain, she had symbolized a hope for the future. After this cursory wedding to a Protestant divorcé she forfeited all consideration. Charles IX and Catherine de Médicis informed her ambassador that, in view of her unconscionable behaviour, they felt unable to offer her any assistance whatever. The Pope washed his hands of her and she gained no favour in Protestant quarters. In London people declared themselves scandalized, and everyone dreaded the consequences of Mary's three months of folly. The Scots were shocked by her scandalous marriage, which they attributed solely to unbridled lust, and became more and more hostile towards their queen. Her intimates, who were very few in number now that most of the leading lights had left court, were dismayed by her attitude. Du Croc, the French ambassador, was chilled by the relations prevailing between the newly-weds. 'Repentance has already set in,' he reported to Paris. 'On Thursday, when Her Majesty sent for me, I noticed something strange [about the atmosphere] between her and her husband. She sought to excuse herself by saying that, if I found her melancholy, it was because she had wished to banish all joy and desired one thing only: death. Yesterday, when she was with Earl Bothwell, she was heard to call for a knife with which to kill herself.'[16]

Bothwell was no unifier of men. On the contrary, he had a talent for provoking hostility. He knew this and cherished no illusions about it. When a group of lords – Morton, Argyll, Atholl and Mar – met together at Stirling, where the little prince was still residing against the wishes of his mother, who would have preferred to have him at her side, and publicly announced their intention of hunting down Darnley's assassins and attempting to free their queen, Bothwell responded by mustering as many men as possible. For want of any other resources, Mary financed this troop by ordering Elizabeth's christening present, a handsome baptistry, to be melted down. Leaving Edinburgh, which had become unsafe, she accompanied Bothwell to Borthwick Castle, a fortress belonging to one of his allies some twelve miles south of the city. Far from discouraged by this move, the insurgent nobles besieged it. Bothwell, who was too good a soldier to try to sustain a siege under these conditions, slipped away and left the queen to confront them on her own.

Danger reinvigorated her. Mary Stuart was never characterized by a liking for reflection, but action intoxicated her and infused her with courage. Proof against her assailants' threats and insults, she haughtily refused to accompany them to Edinburgh, and they, shaken by her determination, decided to withdraw and await reinforcements. Mary seized her chance without a moment's hesitation: disguising herself as a man, she stole out of the castle by a postern under cover of darkness. Outside the walls a mounted servant was waiting for her with a spare horse. Undeterred by the fact that she was pregnant, she galloped off to join Bothwell at a nearby castle from which they rode on together to Dunbar.

Dunbar Castle was empty, as all castles were in the absence of their owners, so Mary was reduced to borrowing a red petticoat, a blouse with separate sleeves attached with red ribbons in the local fashion, and a black velvet hat. Together with Bothwell, she endeavoured to raise a makeshift army of peasants and mercenaries. Bothwell, convinced that aggression was the key to victory, gave the order to march on Edinburgh and the rebels. On 15 June 1567 the opposing forces met at Carberry Hill. Drawn up on either side of a stream, they confronted each other without moving. Bothwell's men had no wish to charge a body of manifestly well-armed horsemen. Their adversaries were arrayed behind a banner depicting a man's body lying beneath a tree, and beside it a boy child kneeling with his arms raised to heaven, crying: 'Judge and avenge my cause, O Lord.' A miraculous political volte-face had taken place: the rebel lords, all of whom had participated in Darnley's murder, were now proclaiming themselves his avengers. But they hesitated, even now, to move against their queen in broad daylight. The Scots had few scruples when it came to plotting together, but their code of honour forbade them to attack their sovereign openly.

Du Croc, who had turned up as an observer, stepped in and offered to mediate. He crossed the stream on horseback, accompanied by a small escort, and made for the hill on which Mary Stuart, pale and obviously exhausted, was waiting alone at some distance from her men. She had no talent for negotiation and seemed unaware of the weakness of her position. Queenly in manner despite her unmistakable anxiety, she demanded that the rebel lords submit and refused to consider du Croc's suggestion that she abandon Bothwell to his fate. The latter rode up while they were in conversation, bold as brass and oozing self-confidence. The Frenchman, who disliked Bothwell and resented his having placed the queen in such a frightful predicament, was nonetheless impressed by his courage. 'I must acknowledge that I saw in him a great Captain who spoke with undaunted confidence and knew how to lead his men in a vigorous and skilful manner. I could not but admire him, for he knew that his enemies were resolute, whereas he himself could count on barely half his men. Yet he was not dismayed in the least.'[17] Then, being unable rely on his troops, Bothwell suggested settling matters by means of a duel with a nobleman of his own rank. 'Remain here on the hill,' he told du Croc. 'It will be a sight worth seeing.'[18]

In the event, there was no sight to see. The queen rejected the first man to step forward because he was too inferior in rank. The parleying continued. No one took up Bothwell's challenge in the end, not that he had won the day. The queen sent a spokesman to Sir William Kirkcaldy, who commanded the rebel cavalry, requesting him to come to see her on his own. He obeyed – he even bent the knee to her before proposing a compromise: if the queen would return to Edinburgh with the nobles, Bothwell could go wherever he pleased and would not be pursued. Reassured on his behalf, Mary agreed. Bothwell, who had taken no part in this conversation, came forward to say goodbye. Having embraced her, he vaulted into the saddle and galloped off, never to see her again. Mary was left to face her subjects' scorn and anger alone.

Kirkcaldy had promised that she would be escorted back to Edinburgh with all due honour, and it is probable that such was his and his confederates' intention. But he was not in control of the rank and file, who shouted vile abuse at the queen once she was in their midst. Mary's dreadful ordeal began at six o'clock that evening. Still attired in her dirty, borrowed clothes, she rode along behind the banner that demanded vengeance for Darnley's murder. People converged from all the farms and villages on her route to see their humiliated queen. Menacing cries rang out on every side: 'Burn the whore, burn the murderess!' Kirkcaldy tried to part the crowd with the flat of his sword, but he could do nothing about the abusive yells. The cortège entered Edinburgh at ten that night. By then, everyone realized that the dishonoured queen would never reign again. Instead of being taken to the palace, she was escorted to the provost's house under guard.

Fury at having allowed herself to be captured by her nobles imbued Mary with a nervous energy verging on madness. Deaf to reason, she ran to the window to appeal to her subjects. But all they saw behind the bars was a hysterical, dishevelled woman with her bodice ripped and her tear-stained face bespattered with mud.

Disconcerted by an adversary whose only strength was her weakness, in other words, her gender, the confederate lords were uncertain which side to take. Moray was still in England and no one had any authority over Mary in his absence. Moreover, they did not feel on very safe ground because there remained the risk of a genuine inquiry into Darnley's assassination, in which they had all been implicated. Fearing that public opinion might undergo a reversal in Mary's favour, they conferred together and decided to take her back to Holyrood the next day. There, reunited with her women in familiar surroundings, she was at last able to change her clothes and take some food, having refused to eat anything the previous day for fear of poison. This respite was only brief, however. Lord Morton appeared and announced without more ado that she must leave at once. She was not allowed to take any baggage and only two *femmes de chambre* were authorized to accompany her. Did Morton know that she was expecting a child? Probably not, since her marriage was only a month old, but it is doubtful if he would have treated the queen with more consideration had he been aware of her pregnancy. No one wanted a little Bothwell, so a miscarriage would have been welcomed. A 'great wailing' went up from the ladies and servants who gathered in Holyrood's great hall to bid the queen farewell. Realizing that it would have been useless to protest, however, she rose and mounted her horse once more.

Mary believed, wrongly, that she would be taken to Stirling, but the little cavalcade made instead for Leith, to the west of Edinburgh. She tried to slow her horse in the short-lived hope that some loyalists would attempt a rescue, but the men surrounding her whipped it on, and they continued on their way at a breakneck pace. Late that night they reached the shores of Lochleven. There, on an island in the middle of the lake, stood a castle belonging to William Douglas, half-brother of James Stewart, Earl of Moray.* Mary knew the place, having hunted duck and wild geese there in happier days. She was hustled aboard a boat and rowed across the dark waters. No preparations had been made to receive her, so she was lodged in the laird's extremely spartan room on the second floor of the keep. Utterly exhausted and in despair, she sank into a stupor and remained in that state for a fortnight – close to death, it was feared.

---

*James Stewart's mother, Margaret Erskine, had married Robert Douglas, so their son William was his uterine half-brother, nephew of the Earl of Mar and cousin and heir of the Earl of Morton.

7

Lochleven

1567–8

Mary must have had a strong constitution, because she recovered and began to take note of her surroundings. Lochleven Castle had belonged to Lady Douglas, the mother of her half-brother James Stewart. 'The old lady', as she was now known, had in her youth been the mistress of James V and had borne him six bastard sons whom he acknowledged. Subsequently married to Robert Douglas, the robust noblewoman had produced another seven children. Living in the castle when the queen was first imprisoned there were the said Lady Douglas, her eldest son William, the present laird, and her youngest boy, George, a handsome young man who was nicknamed 'pretty Geordie'. The lords who had escorted Mary to Lochleven soon departed, their mission accomplished, leaving two of their number behind to guard her. These were Lord Lindsay and Lord Ruthven, the son of the man who had taken part in Riccio's murder.

Lochleven Castle was a cheerless place. Situated within

its stout granite walls were a large square keep dating from the end of the fourteenth century and a smaller, circular tower that formed a separate building. No fields or woods surrounded this complex, which occupied the entire island.* The loch, one of the shallowest in Scotland, was only three miles across, but the sight of its eternally rain- and wind-lashed waters would have disheartened a person less resolute than the queen.

She was protected by a certain refusal to face the facts. She must have known, in her heart of hearts, that her passion for Bothwell had created an intolerable situation – that she had openly defied both law and convention – but she refused to draw the correct conclusion and admit that her right to wear the crown had been impaired. As she saw it, that divine, inalienable and inviolable right could not be modified – and, in a way, she was right. Therein lies the whole essence of her complex story. To seize the queen and hold her captive constituted a revolutionary act, and it was construed as such on the Continent. No one leapt to the defence of a woman tarnished by her scandalous marriage to a man who had only just got divorced and was accused of having engineered his predecessor's murder. Every court in Europe recognized that she had been dishonoured, that her authority had been irreparably damaged, that it could no longer be exercised in an absolute manner, and that account must be taken of her

---

*The island is bigger today because the level of the lake has fallen considerably.

people's revulsion and anger. Yet the fact remained that a sovereign by divine right could not be overthrown. Assassinated, yes; deposed, certainly not. There was no precedent or machinery that would have enabled Mary to be removed from the throne. In Scotland and Europe at large, Mary's future presented less a political problem than a matter of principle. Her cousin Elizabeth grasped this at once and acted accordingly.

Despite their brutality and the haste with which they had seized her person and, in addition, her silver plate, which they appropriated before leaving Holyrood, the lords would have preferred to reach a compromise with the queen. Their conduct invited criticism. They had acted like boors and they knew it. Mary had agreed to go with them after Bothwell's departure and the abortive battle of Carberry Hill, and they had broken that agreement by imprisoning her.

Moreover, their part in Darnley's murder precluded them from playing the avengers of that crime. Maitland, who had prudently refrained from taking an active part in the intrigues of recent months, was sent to parley with the queen as soon as she was well enough to receive him. He tried to persuade her to agree to divorce Bothwell and mooted the possibility of renouncing the throne in favour of her son, but she flatly refused. Since she was pregnant and had announced her pregnancy, a divorce would condemn her unborn child to illegitimacy. Maitland extracted no concessions whatsoever. Mary refused to be intimidated, even under such distressing circumstances, in part because a letter from Elizabeth had restored her courage.

Although she sharply admonished Mary for her shameful marriage to Bothwell and cast doubt on the legitimacy of the child she was carrying because of its father's questionable divorce, Elizabeth assured her of her sisterly support: 'Now for your estate in such adversity as we hear you should be [...] we are determined to send with all speed one of our own trusty servants, not only to understand your state but also thereupon to deal with your nobility and people as they shall find you not to lack of our friendship and power for the preservation of your honour in quietness.'[1]

Elizabeth gave the clearest instructions to Throckmorton, whom she chose for this mission. He was, first, to strive to obtain Mary's release, it being contrary to divine law to permit subjects to deprive their sovereign of her freedom; then to demand that Darnley's murderers be punished; and, lastly, to endeavour to place young James under English protection by entrusting him to the care of his paternal grandmother. It would have been rash of Elizabeth to neglect a potential heir to the throne in the absence of a successor of her own blood. The little prince's future mattered to her more than ever. This was because, at the very moment when the Scottish drama unfolded, she was finally breaking off negotiations aimed at concluding a marriage with Archduke Charles, which had been resumed in 1566 under pressure from Parliament.

It had been hoped that those negotiations would at last be successful. Although Elizabeth had continued to insist on seeing the candidate before taking an irrevocable decision, she had been reassured by reports of his physical appearance obtained from Cecil's brother-in-law, who was sent to inspect him. Of medium height, he was 'for a man beautiful, and well faced, well shaped, small in the waist, and well and broad breasted', looking in his clothes to be 'well thighed and well legged, the same being a little embowed'.[2] As for his personal qualities, the observer found him to be 'courteous, affable, just, wise, and of great memory'.[3] Furthermore, the archduke had not refused to come to England for a final inspection. Both parties had accepted that an agreement would be reached on the matter of the expense of his household, which had been a bone of contention. There remained the problem of the couple's difference in religion. The emperor's demands were minimal: the prince would agree to accompany the queen to Anglican services on condition that he could hear Mass in private. Although it would have been hard to ask for less, Elizabeth refused to compromise.

This was because the Scottish example had made her think twice, and she thought like a statesman. To bear a child – a hypothetical child, in any case – would resolve the succession, but it would not eliminate the difficulties that might arise from an ill-assorted marriage. On the personal level, the spouses' difference in religion would prevent them from marching in step and exercising a common will – in short, it would render them ineffective. Elizabeth's authority would suffer, especially at a time when religion constituted the main obstacle to national unity, because a Catholic consort, even if he were a model of discretion, could not but reinforce the Papist faction and enrage the Protestants. It was only to be expected that the queen's Catholic subjects would encourage the archduke to demand more and more latitude, first for himself and then for his co-religionists, whose celebration of the Mass exposed them to genuine danger. Thus, far from strengthening the monarchy, such a marriage would shake its foundations. Rent asunder by opposing factions, England would soon fall prey to civil strife. The country would be engulfed in the horrors characteristic of the religious wars that were raging in France and the Netherlands or lapse into the political turmoil that was proving so disastrous to Scotland.

All else apart, the Council was once more split between the advocates of marriage at any price, led by Cecil, and the opposition centred on Robert Dudley. This lack of unanimity reinforced the queen's refusal to embark on a venture of which she herself said that one could err only once. She had declared after the Dudley affair that she would marry as a queen. It was also as a queen that she rejected this proposition. Her standpoint was a valid one.

In 1567, when she declined the most genuine and estimable of her suitors, Elizabeth was thirty-four years old. As her prospects of marriage receded, so she gradually discovered the political and symbolic advantages of virginity. In her youth she had gauged the immensity of the mistake her sister had made by marrying; twenty years later, Mary Stuart's reckless escapades were such as to convince her that a queen cannot win the matrimonial game, whether played for love or politics. She did not yet slam the door for good – the selection of a husband would still raise plenty of dust – but she refused to become obsessed with the desire for a child, hence her added interest in the fate of James, who might some day inherit her crown.

But the Scots had no intention of giving in to Elizabeth, and Throckmorton failed even to obtain permission to see Mary. They did exchange letters, however, and Mary made it abundantly clear that she would never agree to divorce Bothwell while she was expecting his child. Throckmorton, realizing that his efforts were useless, would have preferred to bring his mission to an end, especially as Maitland had bluntly informed him that he was wasting his time.

Although Elizabeth was alive to the weakness of her position and felt no sympathy for Mary Stuart's misfortunes, she persevered. She may even have despised this queen who had twice yielded to passion and twice incurred deplorable consequences – a queen incapable of grasping as she, Elizabeth, had grasped to her cost, that their royal calling demanded personal sacrifices. Her certainty that the Scots were creating a dangerous precedent spurred her on. She feared that her own opponents would be encouraged to follow suit, for, being a thorough realist, she never took the support of all her subjects for granted. Knowing that she had enemies, she did not wish them to be given undesirable ideas by the spectacle of subjects doing violence to their sovereign just beyond her borders.

At the end of July the situation was transformed by an accident: Mary, who had been carrying twins, miscarried. This opened the door to a divorce from Bothwell, or at least to a definite separation from him, which his disappearance from the scene would have rendered all the easier. Despite their undertakings, his enemies had promptly pursued him. He escaped them at first by taking refuge on an island in the Orkneys. The lords responded by surrounding him, but he managed to give them the slip and put to sea in a decrepit fishing boat. He was overtaken by a storm but rescued by a Danish vessel. Recognized on coming ashore, he was briefly detained by the authorities and then released. But not for long. A Danish woman whom he had some years earlier promised to marry took him to court and he was placed under house arrest pending a trial. Meanwhile, the Scots and the English requested his extradition, the former in order to put him to death, the latter to secure him as a hostage and witness. Although the Danes refused to hand him over, they imprisoned him in extremely harsh conditions after his conviction for breach of promise. A keen huntsman and brilliant horseman, Bothwell had always revelled in his freedom of movement. Unable to endure being locked up, he flung himself at the bars of his cell like a raging beast, so he was placed in irons and chained to a post too short to enable him to get to his feet. He lost his mind within a few months, though his body held out for another ten years,* by which time Mary had long ceased to think of him.

In the summer of 1567, in fact, the Scottish nobles were concerned less to lay hands on Bothwell than to depose their queen as quickly as possible. They lost no time. Mary was in a very debilitated condition – exhausted, anaemic and incapable of rising from her bed – when Lord Lindsay presented himself at her door. Lindsay would brook no delay – he was a notoriously brutal man – so she had to admit him and listen to what he had to say. He unceremoniously demanded that she sign a document abdicating in favour of her son and entrusting the regency to Moray, who had at last returned to Scotland. She refused at first, but then, terrified by Lindsay's threats that her throat would be cut (threats confirmed by a secret message from Throckmorton), she gave way. Isolated in a fortress surrounded by the grey-green waters of a lake in which a body could sink without trace, shaken by the fact that her lords had seized a casket containing her letters to Bothwell and some sonnets in her own hand (extremely compromising documents from her own point

---

*His mummified body was displayed in the local church for four centuries. It was finally buried by order of Margaret, the present Queen of Denmark.

of view),* and rightly convinced that a deed of abdication signed under duress had no legal validity, she finally agreed to put her hand to it. Her infant son was crowned on 29 July 1567, becoming King James VI of Scotland at the age of thirteen months. The fireworks that disturbed the silence of Lochleven and the queen's repose were a celebration more of the mother's dethronement than of her son's joyful accession to the throne. Moray was proclaimed regent a month later and calm descended on the country once more.

The queen recovered quickly, thanks to her enforced rest, and life at the castle reorganized itself around her. The violence done to a weak, defenceless woman affected her jailers, who were warmly sympathetic to her from now on. All the women of the Douglas family behaved in a friendly manner. The laird's young wife, who was pregnant herself and, thus, particularly sensitive to Mary's misfortunes, sometimes slept in her room to keep her company and remained at her side throughout the day. The two daughters of the house did their best to entertain her, and even the old dowager soon mellowed towards her. Mary's request that some servants be sent her – a cook, an apothecary and four additional *femmes de chambre* – was granted. The apartment she occupied was furnished as comfortably as possible. When she felt better she asked for her embroidery things, some clothes, some satin sleeves, a cloak of Holland weave and some *chausses,* or

---

*We shall revert to the contents of this casket when dealing with the inquiry into Darnley's murder held at York.

tights. Other items that had to be sent her included wigs, chignons and hairpins. She wanted to look her best.

From now on she spent her evenings with the Douglas family, playing cards and even dancing occasionally. While the ladies plied their needles, Mary made full use of the charm she possessed in such abundance. No longer subject to Bothwell's magnetic personality, she detached herself from the man for whom she had sacrificed her reputation and her kingdom like someone discarding a worn-out garment. She never enquired about his fate and never looked back, intent on her immediate course of action. Her first target was Ruthven, the young nobleman who had treated her so roughly some weeks earlier during the ride back to Edinburgh. This may have been why he had been selected to guard her on the island. Far from displaying any resentment, she made herself so amiable to him and rendered him so amenable to her wishes that his confederates thought it wise to remove him after learning from William Douglas that he had thrown himself at her feet and asked her to marry him. But it would have taken more than Ruthven's departure to discourage Mary. She still had her reluctant hosts, the Douglases, to work on.

She had endeared herself to an orphaned cousin of the family barely out of his teens, 'the little Douglas' or 'Willy', who demonstrated his devotion by carrying her clandestine correspondence. Then she noticed to her satisfaction that young Geordie Douglas, the youngest son of the house, never took his eyes off her — and they were the eyes of a lover, not a jailer. What did she promise him? Everything, or nothing?

Yet again, we do not know. The fact remains that he arranged with a washerwoman who crossed the lake every week with other servants to procure the queen some servant's clothes. It was a propitious moment: the young châtelaine had just given birth and little notice was being taken of Mary's movements. On the morning of 25 March 1568, bundled up in rough clothing with her face concealed by a thick veil, she emerged from the castle and boarded a boat. George Douglas was waiting on the far shore with some horses, but one of the boatmen impudently tried to lift Mary's veil. She fended him off, and her soft hands gave the game away. The men recognized her and promptly rowed her back to the castle.

A full-scale family row ensued. 'Pretty Geordie' received his marching orders, but Mary was not transferred to another prison. After all, what more secure place of confinement could there be than a fortress surrounded by water? A stricter regime was imposed, but nothing more. At the laird's insistence, all the castle's keys were placed on the table after supper. He would then put them in his pocket and take them to his room when retiring for the night. He had not, however, allowed for Mary's ingenuity and the spell she had cast over the young Douglases. George Douglas not only remained in the vicinity but managed to communicate regularly with the queen and her allies, Lord Seton and the Hamilton clan, who were only too happy to put a spoke in Moray's wheel.

Political somersaults being so frequent in Scotland, the confederate lords were unlikely to preserve their cohesion for long. With Bothwell out of it, no one doubted that it would be easy for Mary to obtain an annulment, and this raised the possibility of another royal marriage. George Douglas was in the running, of course. So was one of the Hamiltons and a young Stewart, Lord Methven. Mary hoped that a successful escape could bring about a political turnaround, so George Douglas handled the preparations ashore while little Willy Douglas, completely besotted by the queen, undertook to transport her across the lake less than five weeks after the first attempt. He initially envisaged that she would scale the seven-foot wall at the bottom of the garden and jump down the other side. One of her ladies-in-waiting volunteered to try this feat but sprained her ankle on landing, so the scheme was abandoned. Willy would somehow have to get hold of the keys and enable Mary to walk boldly out of the castle.

The escape was set for 2 May 1568. Taking advantage of the springtime festivities to which the first few days of the month were traditionally devoted, little Willy organized a pageant in which he himself played the Abbot of Unreason and indulged in all manner of tomfoolery. Everyone including the queen took part in this entertainment, it being essential to prevent the castle's inhabitants from noticing that a troop of horsemen was assembling on the lakeshore. That evening, however, someone drew Lady Douglas's attention to this unwonted activity. More serious still, William Douglas was surprised to see little Willy doing something to the boats on the island and made some irate remark about his idiotic behaviour. At this, Mary pretended to faint, compelling the laird to quit his vantage point at the window and fetch her a glass of wine. No one was surprised when she decided to skip supper and retire to bed early.

Willy now went into action. When everyone was seated at table, he 'inadvertently' draped a napkin over the keys and managed to spirit them away. He then gave a prearranged signal to one of the queen's maids, who went upstairs to her room to inform her. Dressed in a countrywoman's kirtle and hood, Mary descended the stairs and walked boldly across the courtyard, where several servants were at work. She went out through the main gate, which Willy locked behind them before tossing the bunch of keys into the lake (they were discovered on the bottom three centuries later). Then they made their unhurried way to the boats, of which Willy had holed all save one to preclude the possibility of pursuit. Waiting for them when they set foot ashore were George Douglas and John Beaton, whose family had always remained loyal to Mary. Ironically enough, the horses they mounted belonged to the Douglases, whose stables were situated on dry land. The grooms had not been surprised when George Douglas chose three of their finest beasts, this being a thoroughly unexceptional request on the part of a son of the family. The fugitives reached Niddry, one of Lord

Seton's castles, in the middle of the night. The next morning Mary appeared on the balcony to cheers from the local inhabitants. Queen once more, she turned to the two Douglases who had engineered her successful escape and graciously expressed her thanks. They were to serve her faithfully until her death. Meanwhile, back at Lochleven, the unfortunate laird tried to kill himself with his own dagger.

He failed, just as Mary failed to regain her throne. For a while she believed she had done so, surprised by the ease with which she rallied a section of the nobility to her cause. Some joined her out of loyalty; others, notably the powerful house of Hamilton, out of hostility to the regent, who had maintained a fragile peace in Scotland by force and thereby irritated many of his peers. The French ambassador called on Mary to present his respects and Elizabeth sent her a congratulatory letter via a special envoy. But Moray was unimpressed by these displays of solidarity, especially as the English government's attitude was ambivalent. On the one hand, Elizabeth rejoiced at her cousin's liberation; on the other, Cecil urged Moray to oppose the full restoration of his sister's regal powers. Having quickly assessed the situation, Moray mustered an army.

Mary would probably have preferred to reach an accommodation with her brother. From Niddry she had moved to a castle owned by the Hamiltons. Although she was not so naive as to believe that their support was disinterested, the surprising influx of men prepared to take up arms on her behalf – her forces outnumbered those of the regent by two to one – encouraged her to join battle on 13 May instead of seeking to regain power by more diplomatic means. She lived to regret this. Her disunited and ill-led troops seemed more inclined to quarrel among themselves than to follow her and attack the enemy. It was a crushing defeat. Moray did not lose a single man, whereas over a hundred of the queen's supporters were killed and three hundred taken prisoner. Mary was compelled to turn and flee to the south of the country, an abidingly Catholic area in which her allies the Herries and Maxwells owned vast estates. She had already made three nocturnal escapes: once with Darnley after Riccio's assassination; next, disguised as a man, to join Bothwell at Dunbar and make their last stand at Carberry Hill; and, ten days earlier, in company with George Douglas. This fourth and last ride was the most arduous, desperate and – ultimately – futile.

The slender young woman had to display extraordinary physical stamina. Wild terrain, primitive amenities, makeshift halts in perilous conditions – there was a nightmarish quality about this breakneck journey as she later described it in a letter to her uncle, the Cardinal of Lorraine: 'I have endured insults, calumnies, imprisonment, hunger, cold, flight without knowing whither, four score and twelve miles across country without stopping or alighting, and then have had to sleep upon the ground and drink sour milk and eat oatmeal without bread, and have lived three nights like the owls, without a woman to attend me in this country where, by way of reward, I am little more than a prisoner.'[4]

As we have already said, Mary had the knack of creating vivid images. How could any novelist fail to be entranced by the vision of a little girl stepping aboard the ship that would carry her to France; of a radiant princess on her wedding day at Notre Dame; of a pregnant young woman riding pillion through the night; or of a captive queen boldly emerging from her place of confinement and boarding a boat under the noses of her captors? How could Sir Walter Scott have failed to fall in love with this intrepid horsewoman who traversed field, forest and moor at a mad gallop? How could he not have been carried away by her – how could he not have hoped that she would prevail? Sadly, reality and romance can be irreconcilable. On this occasion the intrepid horsewoman was hurtling towards an impasse – one that would deprive her of her crown, her freedom and, in the end, her life.

The queen and her retinue ended their headlong ride at Terregles, a Maxwell stronghold. It was impossible for her to go back. She would have to leave the country and take refuge abroad, but where? There were three choices open to her. It would be easy enough to charter a ship bound for France. She could also sail to Flanders and make her way from there to Spain, or simply take a small boat, cross the Solway Firth and place herself in her cousin Elizabeth's hands. Plain common sense should have directed her to France. France was more than her second home; she had lived happily there and been brought up with the king and his brothers. Her mother-in-law was reputed not to like her overmuch, it was true, but as queen dowager Mary would have been dependent on no one, and it is conceivable that she could have lived there in safety, protected by her powerful maternal kinsmen. Spain attracted her less because her recent escapades, notably her Protestant marriage to Bothwell, had alienated Philip II. England presented an even more precarious haven. Mary never disguised the fact that her companions sought to dissuade her, and that the decision to take refuge in England was hers alone, even though she had no close relations, estates or sources of income there. It is true that Elizabeth had backed her unreservedly, despite her critical comments, but supporting Mary in distant Edinburgh was one thing; welcoming a Catholic queen who had never ceased to lay claim to her own throne was quite another. It would have been prudent, at the very least, to seek Elizabeth's opinion and request permission to enter her kingdom.

8

An Unwelcome Visitor

1568–72

Mary Stuart did not wait to be granted the right of asylum by Elizabeth, who may perhaps have had cause to congratulate herself on that account because the Scottish queen's arrival presented her with an insoluble problem. Her immediate response would have been to welcome her cousin with all due honours. As we have already seen, Elizabeth never wavered in her belief that the crown was inalienable. She regarded it as contrary to natural law to imprison, threaten or compel a sovereign to abdicate, and she had unfailingly defended Mary Stuart despite the latter's inept behaviour and the opposition of her own government. This time, however, Mary's irruption into England posed the question in concrete terms. Internal English politics were now involved, for the Scottish queen, whose place in the line of succession made her *de facto* heir to the English throne, had in her youthful impatience claimed it during Elizabeth's lifetime. No member of the Council could forget that Mary had taken the step of proclaiming herself

Queen of England on Mary Tudor's death, and that she had borne the royal arms during her sojourn in France. She could not, therefore, be treated like an ordinary refugee. Her mere presence on English soil threatened to disrupt the equilibrium prevailing between the various political factions.

Mary's misfortunes and her steadfast commitment to her religion would soon have attracted support, especially among English Catholics. A rebellion could easily have been fomented, the more so if France, Spain and Scotland were to favour the plans of the queen in exile. Scottish political life was too unstable to preclude the risk that the clan chieftains, tantalized by the prospect of sowing disorder among their English neighbours, might rally to their sovereign's support. However, some almost insurmountable obstacles made it hard for the English to rid themselves of their untimely visitor.

Putting Mary on a ship bound for France did not appeal to them, for no one doubted that her redoubtable Guise uncles would promote an attempt to regain her original crown and obtain her another. The Council had already heard a rumour that the Guises were contemplating marrying Mary to Duke Henry of Anjou, brother and successor of Charles IX. Given that such a marriage would greatly strengthen Mary's position, Elizabeth's councillors were doubly suspicious of France. To replace her on her throne by force would provoke civil war in Scotland and bring about a resumption of hostilities between the two countries. Moreover, it was inconceivable that a Protestant sovereign should impose a Catholic queen on a people devoted to the Reformation. Sending Mary back to Scotland without the support of an army, on the other hand, would be tantamount to executing her, because there was no way of ensuring that her nobles would not seek to get rid of her. Since Mary had placed herself under Elizabeth's protection of her own free will, the latter could not decently return her to the clutches of such merciless and unpredictable enemies. Guzman da Silva put the problem to Philip II as follows: 'Although these people [the English] are glad enough to have her in their hands, they have many things to consider. If they keep her as in a prison, it will probably scandalize all neighbouring princes, and if she remain free and able to communicate with her friends, great suspicions will be aroused. In any case, it is certain that two women will not agree very long.'[1] Meantime, where exactly was Mary Stuart?

At seven o'clock on the evening of Sunday, 16 May 1568, idlers strolling along the waterfront at Workington, a small port situated on the west coast of England facing the Irish Sea and separated from Scotland by the Solway Firth, sighted a boat approaching. It was laden, not with fisherfolk, but with sixteen obviously well-born passengers, among them a very tall young woman with her face concealed beneath a hood, who stumbled as she stepped ashore. One of her companions, Lord Herries, was acquainted with the local lord of the manor and asked to speak with him as soon as he landed. That worthy was away, but his home was placed at the travellers' disposal. A French servant of his, who recognized the queen at once despite her close-cropped hair, stated that he had seen her before 'in better days'. She spent the next day at the house of a wealthy merchant who, struck by her 'mean' attire, presented her with a length of crimson velvet and had a black gown quickly run up for her. On 18 May the deputy governor of the neighbouring town arranged for her to be transferred to Carlisle Castle. Alive to the potentially explosive consequences of the Scottish queen's arrival, however, he was prudent enough to request instructions from Cecil.

The news reached London on 20 May. As ever in critical situations, Elizabeth opted for a period of reflection. She sent an old friend and cousin by marriage, Sir Francis Knollys,* to Carlisle to take charge and compile a report. An elderly, rather gruff Protestant, Knollys was immediately impressed by the young queen's eloquence, discernment and courage. On 11 June, after spending a fortnight in her company, he still seemed under her spell: 'She seemeth to regard no ceremonious honour beside the acknowledging of her estate regal. [...] She showeth a readiness to expose herself to all perils in hope of victory. [...] It seemeth to be indifferent to her to have her enemies diminished either by the sword of her friends, or by the liberal promises and rewards of her purse, or by divisions and quarrels raised among themselves; so that, for victory's sake, pain and peril seemeth pleasant to

---

*Sir Francis Knollys had married Catherine Carey, the daughter of his aunt Mary Boleyn, elder sister of Anne.

her: and in respect of victory, wealth and all things seemeth to her contemptible and vile. Now what is to be done with such a lady and princess?'[2] Queen Elizabeth took eighteen years to answer that question. In the interim, her foreign policy was turned upside down, her domestic religious policy crystallized, and her succession on the throne by James, the son of Mary and Darnley, paradoxically assured.

Cecil took the immediate precaution of persuading Elizabeth not to allow Mary to come to court. That would have meant coming down firmly on her side against Moray and the lords in power at Edinburgh, thereby creating a hostile junta and prompting them to send the young king to France for safety, just as Mary had been sent as a girl almost twenty years before. Furthermore, the English queen's protection would only have reinforced Mary's personal ambitions. To yield to an initial feeling of compassion, Cecil argued, would be 'to nurse a serpent in her bosom' and lend encouragement to 'factious, murmuring subjects'.[3] Cecil also feared that Mary might try to take refuge in France, so she had to be prevented from escaping yet again. She had demonstrated her ingenuity in that respect – in fact Knollys wrote that all she would need was a sheet attached to her window sill. He was all the more concerned because he himself retired to bed at an early hour, whereas the queen paced her bedchamber until dawn. George Douglas, her admirer and accomplice, never left her side, and Knollys suspected him of hatching audacious escape plans. It was consequently decided to remove the queen and her whole entourage to Bolton, an isolated

Yorkshire castle enclosed by lofty walls. Being in the middle of England, Bolton offered more security than Carlisle, which was so near the coast and the Scottish border.

With infinite patience, Knollys prevailed on Mary to agree to this change of abode, whose drawbacks she fully appreciated, and he valiantly resisted her tears and lamentations. 'Surely,' he wrote to Cecil on 14 July, 'if I should declare the difficulties that we have passed before we could get her to remove, instead of a letter I should write a story, and that somewhat tragical.'[4] She had written her 'good mother', Catherine de Médicis, an imploring missive: 'The king owes me some money, and I do not have a sou. I feel no shame at all in addressing my complaint to you, as to her who nursed me at her breast, for I do not possess so much as the wherewithal to purchase a shift.'[5] Elizabeth had sent Mary some garments of such poor quality that Knollys, ashamed of his queen's parsimony, pretended that they were meant for her servants. She was also sent some skirts, petticoats and accessories from Scotland. Mary not only considered these very poor but noted bitterly that one taffeta dress would never suffice her. She was at last joined by her longtime companion Mary Seton, a skilful hairdresser who used the wig, hairpieces and ribbons she had brought with her to remedy the loss of the tresses the queen had sacrificed. Once she looked decent again, Mary regained her self-confidence and prepared to do battle.

Some hard bargaining began as soon as she was installed at Bolton Castle. Elizabeth had justified her refusal to receive Mary at court by citing her alleged complicity in Darnley's murder. Once her cousin had been cleared by an inquiry conducted by English commissioners, she would be delighted to meet her at last. This, the Scottish queen declared, was an insulting proposal: being a monarch by divine right, she had no judge but God. As to the argument that the inquiry would also examine the role of her lords, she replied that subjects and their sovereign could not be placed on the same footing. Even discounting the divine right of kings, Elizabeth was not on very firm legal ground. A murder committed in Scotland could not be tried in England, nor did she have any legal authority to interfere in a dispute between Mary Stuart and her subjects. Mary was nonetheless compelled to bow to the English queen's wishes. Where the restoration of her freedom was concerned, she could rely neither on Spain, which was embroiled in a costly insurrection in the Netherlands, nor on France, whose ambassador warned her against returning to Scotland, where she would be in even greater danger than under the protection of England.

The inquiry opened at York in October 1568. The English commissioners comprised the Duke of Norfolk, the kingdom's wealthiest and most senior peer, the Earl of Sussex and Sir Ralph Sadler. The latter was the same man who had been sent to Scotland by Henry VIII on the death of James V, and it was in order to satisfy him of Mary's health that her mother had had her swaddling clothes removed in his presence when she was only a few weeks old. The English were joined in their deliberations by Mary's representatives – John Leslie, bishop of Ross, and Lord Herries, who had accompanied her to England – and by some commissioners appointed by the accused Scottish peers. The conference was also attended by Moray and Maitland, both of whom, it may be remembered, had been absent from Edinburgh at the time of the murder and were consequently not under suspicion. Mary herself declined to appear, of course, since she disputed the validity of the proceedings. The English emphasized that the inquiry did not constitute a trial, but a conference charged with shedding light on the queen's role in Darnley's assassination. If Elizabeth thought her envoys would control matters, however, she was mistaken. Mary and her lords promptly engaged in clandestine intrigues.

The paradoxical nature of this inquiry stemmed from the fact that both parties were guilty of the same crime. Darnley's murder had been desired both by his wife and by her lords. Their complicity, cognizance and approval, if not their strict culpability, were beyond dispute. Mary had seen the lords' signatures at the foot of the bond, the agreement concluded between them several days before the murder; they, in their turn, had read her letters to Bothwell and thus possessed a weapon against her. Neither she nor they were interested in revealing the true facts of the matter. According to them, the assassination was Bothwell's responsibility alone, and since he was in a Danish prison there was no danger of him naming his accomplices. The incriminating letters were not officially produced, although Moray, playing a lone hand in the hope that his sister would not return to Scotland and thereby deprive him of his authority as regent, circulated copies of them in the English camp. Mary, realizing that the conference was getting nowhere, decided to play another, hidden card: not a king or a knave but a duke, the premier duke of England.

The Duke of Norfolk, one of the English queen's commissioners, was a widower three times over, immensely rich, and a lukewarm Protestant. Ever since his last marriage to Lady Dacre, a major landowner in the north of England, he had wielded a crucial political influence over that area, which had remained Catholic.[6] He had been predisposed in Mary Stuart's favour by his sister, Lady Scrope, the chatelaine of Bolton Castle, where Mary had been confined, who had given him a moving description of the captive queen. It was true that he had, on his own submission, trembled with disgust at certain documents in the casket Moray had been careful to show him – letters which, as he declared to Queen Elizabeth, revealed 'such inordinate love between her and Bothwell, her loathsomeness and abhorring her husband that was murdered, in such sort as every good and godly man cannot but detest and abhor the same.'[7] Despite this, he constituted himself Mary's defender, abandoned the position recommended by his own queen, and agreed with Mary's representatives not to demand that the notorious letters be read out in public.

He adopted this surprising attitude because of a long conversation with Maitland. And Maitland the diplomat, Mary's former ambassador in London and the most discreet and effective of the Scottish lords, had assured him that the Pope would annul the queen's previous marriage and suggested that Norfolk himself should marry her, thereby opening up the glorious prospect of his becoming King of Scotland – possibly, even, King of England as well. Thus, despite her precarious position, Mary's hand – the little hand whose fingers were clinging to one crown and itching to acquire another – had lost none of its attractions. With one husband dead, one killed and one out of the way, she was back where she started. That Norfolk felt tempted was not surprising. Certain members of Elizabeth's entourage had already speculated that, if Mary returned to Scotland, it would be advantageous to marry her off to a respectable man with England's interests at heart. Furthermore, no one in 1569 had forgotten that, prisoner or not, Mary Stuart was still the undisputed holder of first place in the line of succession. (Catherine Grey had died the year before, leaving only illegitimate sons because her marriage had been annulled.) If she ever succeeded her cousin, the presence of an English consort, a grand seigneur who owned vast estates adjacent to Scotland, might facilitate the transition from one sovereign to the other. Robert Dudley could see no objection; Cecil was informed but, being convinced that Elizabeth would oppose the plan, did not breathe a word to her. However, excluding the queen from these negotiations doomed them to failure and lent them a conspiratorial flavour. Besides, secret conversations did not exist in a world where diplomats and spies were almost indistinguishable. 'Princes have big ears that can hear both far and near,' Elizabeth used to say with pride, and she knew what she was talking about.

Alarmed at the surprising course taken by the York conference, which threatened to end in utter confusion, Elizabeth recalled the Duke of Norfolk. She could often be unfathomable. Although not averse to engaging in intrigue or underhanded diplomatic manoeuvres herself, she came straight to the point where her nobles were concerned. Any other attitude would have betokened a weakness incompatible with the authority of a queen over her subjects, so she asked the duke point-blank if the rumours about his proposed remarriage were well-founded. Poor Norfolk, who was not noted for his courage and cherished an understandable desire to keep his head on his shoulders, knew full well that even to contemplate such an arrangement required his sovereign's approval, and that she would construe a secret plan to marry Mary Stuart as an act of treason. He indignantly denied that he 'ever meant to marry such a person, where he could not be sure of his pillow.'[8]

Elizabeth pretended to be convinced but took the inquiry firmly in hand. She had the proceedings transferred to Westminster, where they could be more closely supervised by herself and attended by Cecil and various members of the

Council. The speed with which a potential marriage between the Scottish queen and the wealthiest and most influential of her subjects had been envisaged without her approval was an indication of how dangerous to her Mary's presence on her soil could be. Abandoning all claim to impartiality, Elizabeth agreed to support Moray. He, for his part, endeavoured to eliminate his sister by producing the contents of the famous casket for inspection. Mary promptly claimed that they were forgeries, but without managing to adduce any firm evidence.* Incapable of countering Moray's attack effectively, her representatives chose to withdraw, though not without having requested the right to defend her before Elizabeth in person – a request that had no chance of being accepted, as everyone knew. They were now in a weak position: the contents of the Scottish queen's correspond-

---

*The question of the documents' authenticity has never been resolved beyond doubt because the originals have been lost, possibly burnt on the orders of James I. Thus the letters are copies translated into Scottish from the original French. The sonnets are also in French. One of the arguments advanced by those who believe Mary to be their author is that no one else in Scotland would have been capable of composing them, and that the letters are far too outspoken, reckless and imprecise to have been written with a view to incriminating the queen. Moreover, it is known that the original letters were written in an Italian script employed by the French court and very rarely found on the other side of the Channel, where a script derived from Gothic was in use. On the other hand, the documents were never shown to Mary Stuart despite her repeated requests. (See the introduction to *Letters and Poems by Mary Stuart, Queen of Scots* (Philosophical Library, New York: 1947); Michel Duchein, *Marie Stuart* (Fayard, Paris: 1987); and Alison Weir, *Mary, Queen of Scots and the Murder of Lord Darnley* (Ballantine, New York: 2003.)

ence precluded her from regaining her authority intact, but negotiations continued on the quiet. Three solutions could be envisaged: either Mary abdicated and remained in England; or she agreed to share sovereignty with her son but entrusted the regency to Moray until the boy came of age; or, a third possibility, she retained her title but did not return to Scotland and left Moray to govern in her stead. Acceptance of the terms of one or another of these arrangements would have required Mary to swallow her pride. Anyone who fancied that she would do so did not know her.

The inquiry was going nowhere fast. It had to be brought to a end, if only to enable Moray to return to Scotland and take up the reins of government again, so Elizabeth resigned herself to a compromise solution. On 10 January 1569 she declared the inquiry closed. She put all her faith in Moray and granted him her support in exercising the regency; at the same time, she acknowledged that Mary's guilt had not been proved. One might have thought that she would permit her to return to Scotland under Moray's authority, but she refused to do this without obtaining the latter's guarantee that Mary's life would be spared. Moray, who wanted to be rid of his sister at all costs, flatly refused to give such an under-taking, pleading that she might be charged with Darnley's murder in Scotland. Elizabeth, who also wanted to be rid of her, threatened to override him and reinstate her on the throne by force, but Mary, instead of displaying a modicum of patience, boasted of her ability to secure the support of France and Spain, not only in recovering her throne but in acquiring Elizabeth's as well. When the Spanish ambassador called on her, she told him that if his master came to her aid 'within three months she would be Queen of England and the Mass celebrated throughout the kingdom'.

This remark was passed on and went the rounds. Its inherent threat could not be ignored, for diplomatic relations with Spain were strained: the Spaniards had seized English ships and merchandise in the Netherlands and Elizabeth had retaliated some weeks earlier by confiscating Spanish property in England. Under these circumstances, a firm alliance with Moray's Protestant government seemed far preferable to any attempt to effect a reconciliation with Mary. For the moment, she remained in England in a legal limbo, neither convicted nor acquitted, deprived of her freedom of movement but not deposed. It was an indeterminate situation in which she wielded no power but, like a time bomb, presented Elizabeth with a potential threat of the utmost gravity.

Mary was placed in the custody of the Earl of Shrewsbury, then a man of about forty. At once weak and pernickety, he was married to the formidable Elizabeth Saintlow, nicknamed Bess of Hardwicke. Ten years his senior and three times widowed, Bess was reputed to be extremely disagreeable in a mannish, authoritarian way. Their life together was divided mainly between Chatsworth, a new and palatial house set in beautiful grounds, Wingfield Manor, and Sheffield Castle, all of which were well to the north of London. For the first time since her arrival in England, Mary became conscious of the gravity of her situation. Her captivity left her a considerable degree of latitude, however. She was deprived of her freedom, it was true, but inside the house she lived like the sovereign of a tiny principality, and a singularly benevolent sovereign at that. The earl and countess never had to put up with any fits of bad temper on her part, and she instinctively exploited her innate charm. Mary could be demanding, but tantrums and sulks were weapons she disdained to use.

She was still assigned a royal canopy over her chair in the great halls of the various residences she occupied, likewise silver tableware. Carpets, a rare luxury at this period, helped to keep her apartments warm. The Earl of Shrewsbury, who showed Mary every consideration, never addressed her without going down on one knee. She did not lack for servants and attendants, physicians and secretaries, dressmakers and tapissers – even a priest. The cost of her suite, which numbered some fifty persons, was defrayed largely by Elizabeth. The earl, to his great displeasure, met the balance of the expense. Mary, who still received an income from France under her marriage contract,* did not contribute to

---

*A widowed queen had an inalienable right to a pension for life, the amount being specified in her marriage contract.

the cost of her upkeep but spent her money conspicuously on almsgiving and more discreetly on funding her clandestine correspondence and paying sundry spies in her employ.

Her days, which were not devoid of entertainment, followed an uneventful course punctuated by visits from neighbouring dignitaries, hunting parties or games of real tennis. She devoted much time to her dogs, some spaniels sent over from France, and her birds and dovecote. In the evenings, musicians played while the ladies plied their needles, embroidery being one of Mary's favourite pastimes. Gossip was rife, and Bess delighted her by indiscreetly relaying a great deal of tittle-tattle about Queen Elizabeth. Her equable temper delighted the earl, who patiently endured the scenes continually provoked by his irascible wife. Young William Douglas, who had been with Mary ever since her escape from Lochleven, offered her the solace of his boundless admiration. The night brought her little rest, however, for the outwardly easy-going guest was an assiduous conspirator.

Her two secretaries, Claude Nau and Gilbert Curle, were given plenty to do. Nau, a protégé of the Guises from Lorraine, had been in her service for a long time, and his excellent knowledge of English enabled him to produce rapid transcriptions, in clear or in cipher, of all Mary's correspondence, which was invariably written in French. She burned the midnight oil composing letters to the French court and the King of Spain, to the Pope and her supporters in Scotland. All her hopes were centred on a Catholic rebellion and the support of Spain. Secret signs and codes were agreed upon and messages concealed in the soles of shoes, in wigs and hollow walking sticks, items of laundry and false lids. Elizabeth's agents, who knew of these clandestine communications, intercepted them on some occasions but deemed it preferable to let them pass on others.

Mary refused to be disheartened. On the contrary, undeterred by Elizabeth's warning to Norfolk, which should have put paid to her marriage plans, she wrote the duke some beguiling letters. He not only answered them but pressed ahead, still hoping, in his incredible naivety, to keep his activities secret. Elizabeth, informed of them as ever, gave him another chance to confide his ambitions. She requested him to call on her at Greenwich and asked what news he brought. None that he knew of, he replied. 'No?' she exclaimed. 'You come from London and can tell no news of a marriage?' She invited the duke to supper and, when dismissing him, gave him a pinch and told him to 'take good heed of his pillow'. Three weeks later, having got wind of some alarming troop movements on the Scottish border, she abandoned her jocular manner. Norfolk was summoned to the palace of Whitehall, the main royal residence in the heart of London, where Elizabeth roundly rebuked him for his disloyalty and demanded that he swear to cease meddling in Scottish affairs. He tried to disarm her by assuring her how little he cared for the Scottish queen. Far from convinced by Norfolk's denials, Elizabeth confided to Cecil that, if she took no action, he would marry Mary and she herself would be in the Tower four months after the ceremony. Norfolk left court without the queen's permission, pleading a fever and letting it be known that he would return within four days. Elizabeth was greatly alarmed by this impertinence: if the duke had taken such an unbecoming liberty, it meant that an even bigger rebellion was in preparation.

She had, in fact, got wind of a storm that was brewing in the Catholic north of England. The growth of royal authority had exasperated the two big regional landowners, Northumberland and Westmorland, 'the northern earls', who had remained Catholic and were disinclined to come and pay court to the queen. Mary Stuart's presence in England prompted them to dream of a change of government: there now seemed a possibility of exchanging an authoritarian monarch for a queen who would owe them her freedom and restore their former grandeur. Mary, from her place of confinement, encouraged the earls with flattering letters and little gifts for their wives. 'The whole of the north is in readiness,' de Spes, the new Spanish ambassador, reported to Philip II, 'and is only awaiting the Queen of Scotland's liberation.'

If Norfolk joined forces with the northern earls, Elizabeth would be in a parlous position. Although she had kept the peace during her eleven years on the throne, she was aware of its fragility. Her sister had had to face two rebellions, one mounted by the supporters of Jane Grey and the other led by Thomas Wyatt. The potential coalition of the Catholic nobles represented a considerably superior force. Elizabeth lost no time. Norfolk was peremptorily commanded to leave his estates and return to London, where he was sent to the Tower forthwith. The queen then took the precaution of having Mary Stuart moved to Tutbury, a Staffordshire castle in Protestant territory, to preclude any possibility of abduction. Perturbed by Elizabeth's resolute attitude, Norfolk sent secret messages to Westmorland and Northumberland putting them on their guard and advising them to call off the whole venture. 'My head is at stake,' he told Westmorland. The two grandees, who had everything to lose, would gladly have curbed their men's ardour. Norfolk's imprisonment was a far from reassuring sign, but to draw back at this stage would destroy their credibility. In high excitement, the assembled Catholic leaders put pressure on Northumberland, and the Countess of Westmorland, Norfolk's own sister, railed at her husband's cowardice: 'We and our country were shamed for ever, that now in the end we should seek holes to creep into.'[9]

On 14 November 1569 the rebels stormed into Durham Cathedral, less than sixty miles from the Scottish border, and tore up the Protestant Bibles there. They then fanned out across the countryside, celebrating the Catholic Mass as they went. But the insurrection was short-lived: the majority of

Catholics failed to rise in revolt. Mary remained a prisoner and the English army's resolute advance soon encountered nothing but a disorganized rabble. Northumberland and Westmorland fled to Scotland, but the former was captured and sent back to England, Moray being uninterested in opposing Elizabeth. As for Westmorland, he succeeded in getting to the Netherlands, where he languished on a very meagre Spanish pension. His wife, whose courage and resolve had won Elizabeth's admiration, was permitted to remain in her castle and lived on a pension awarded her by the queen.

Thanks to popular support and her swift intervention, Elizabeth had proved that the age of big independent fiefs was well and truly over. Her joy and relief are evident from the following autograph postscript to the official letter of congratulations addressed to her general, Lord Hunsdon: 'I doubt much, my dear Harry, whether that the victory were given me more joyed me, or that you were by God appointed the instrument of my glory, and I assure you for my country's good the first might suffice, but for my heart's contentation the second more pleased me.'[10] The queen's spontaneous tone and well-chosen words of gratitude are worthy of note in passing. Her mastery of language enabled her to employ the *mot juste* like an artist. She rewarded Cecil by conferring the title Baron Burghley on him.* The crushing of the conspiracy, followed by a punitive expedition to Scotland, where all the

---

*I shall continue to refer to him as William Cecil.

wanted rebels had taken refuge, reassured the queen to such an extent that she took pity on sick, despondent Norfolk and, in return for a full confession and complete submission, placed him under house arrest in his own castle during the summer of 1570.

In Scotland, however, the violence continued. Moray had been assassinated by a cabal of nobles envious of his authority, and Elizabeth took steps to rid herself of Mary in an honourable manner. The disappearance of the Scottish queen's brother, who had resolutely persisted in his hostility towards her, created a new and, from her point of view, potentially more favourable situation. Once again the two queen's representatives conferred, together with those of the young king, and once again negotiations ground to a halt. The Scots argued among themselves until, in the end, the whole affair was adjourned until Parliament met.

It was at this point that Cecil strove to demonstrate to Elizabeth that the real threat to her stemmed from her spinsterhood and the very existence of Mary Stuart. He succinctly defined the dangers of the situation in a note he drafted on the subject: 'The Queen of Scots is and shall always be a dangerous person to your estate. Yet there are degrees of danger. If you would marry, it should be less; whilst you do not, it will increase. If her person be restrained, here or in Scotland, it will be less; if at liberty, greater. If by law she cannot marry while Bothwell lives, the peril is less; if free to marry, the greater. If found guilty of her husband's murder, she shall be less a person dangerous; if passed over in silence the scare of the murder will wear out and the danger greater.'[11] Although Elizabeth did not always follow Cecil's advice, she always had a perfect grasp of what he told her. Marriage could be the most powerful weapon in her arsenal against Mary – a weapon within her reach, after all, since she was only thirty-seven in 1570. Was it not time to look around her and regain the matrimonial initiative? Now that the international situation had changed, the moment seemed particularly propitious.

During the first part of Elizabeth's reign, England's old alliance with Spain had held firm because economic exigencies outweighed their religious differences: English cloth manu-facturers could not dispense with their Spanish purchasers in the Netherlands and vice versa. Furthermore, England, with its four million inhabitants, was not sufficiently powerful to detach itself from the protection of Spain, which had a population more than twice as numerous and benefited from the immense wealth of its American colonies. Philip II, for his part, did not seek to provoke a conflict that might have imperilled access by sea to his Flemish possessions.

In 1570 or thereabouts, France's policy under Catherine de Médicis became more unpredictable. Her attitude towards

Spain oscillated as she desperately strove to maintain a balance between the warring factions in a France rent by religious strife. When the ultra-Catholics were in the ascendancy she endeavoured to combat Philip II's influence and dreamed of a union with England; when the moderates and the Protestants regained strength she became alarmed, knowing that the King of Spain would not hesitate to invade her country in order to impose the Apostolic and Roman religion and prevent France from interfering in the Netherlands, so she sought to mollify him. In critical situations Catherine always pinned her hopes on personal connections. That was why her fertile brain spawned the idea of making her son Henry, Duke of Anjou, King of England.

A more preposterous scheme can scarcely be imagined. Elizabeth had just refused Archduke Charles for largely religious reasons, yet here was Catherine advancing the candidacy of a prince who was eighteen years younger, a fervent Catholic and heir presumptive to the throne of France.* It was a proposal fraught with every conceivable drawback. Henry's youth and frivolity boded ill for a harmonious personal relationship with the queen, just as his loyalty to the Catholic Church presaged arduous negotiations over the religious freedom to be granted him. An inordinately pleasure-loving young man who dressed with almost ludicrous elegance,

---

*His brother Charles IX, who had just married Elizabeth of Austria, had no legitimate son at this time. He never in fact produced one, so Henry inherited the crown in 1574.

decked out in pearls and diamond earrings, Henry lacked the gravitas of a King of England. Immature and unrealistic, prone to grand passions and untimely declarations, he combined extreme obstinacy with a total lack of experience and attended Council meetings 'having learned or understood little'.[12] Finally, if he ever came to the throne, England would be in dire danger of subordination to France.

The scheme was no less bizarre from the French standpoint, if only because of the potential bridegroom's manifest distaste for it. He adored living in France, which offered him the incessant diversions and advantages provided by his mother Catherine, whose favourite child he was, and he flatly stated that the idea of wedding an old woman horrified him. It must be admitted that there was something absurd about the prospect of marrying a youth of dubious virility and erratic moods to a mature and eminently political woman accustomed to the homage of the distinguished courtiers in her entourage.

So why, in view of all these circumstances, did negotiations begin at all? Because the interested parties were concealing their true interests, hatching dark and often perfidious schemes, and playing to their respective galleries. The final outcome mattered less than the publicity given to the diplomatic effort. In contrast to all her other essays in matrimony, Elizabeth displayed no personal interest in the candidate and no wish to see him in the flesh. It was a case in which the matrimonial project was employed purely as an instrument of politics.

Elizabeth and her councillors were well aware that the Guises and their ultra-Catholic supporters dreamed of freeing Mary Stuart and marrying her to the Duke of Anjou. By announcing that she, Elizabeth, was thinking of marrying him, she put paid to their hopes and banished that danger. (It was quite obvious that Catherine de Médicis would sooner acquire the Queen of England as a daughter-in-law than have Mary Stuart return to France.) Marriage to Anjou seemed the better – perhaps the only – way of holding Mary Stuart in check. It would not only deprive her of French backing but, if the union were blessed with a child, remove her from the succession. What was more, by marrying a French prince Elizabeth would find it easier to send Mary back to Scotland and rid herself of a most unwelcome visitor. The animosity of the Pope, who had excommunicated Elizabeth a year earlier,* would be nullified and the King of Spain highly discomfited if the marriage did, in fact, take place. A further advantage was that the prospect of a defensive alliance with France could not but curb the Spaniards' zeal and check a renewed effort to incite the

---

*The bull of excommunication had no legal validity because it did not conform to canon law. Not only had the Pope failed to give Elizabeth a twelvemonth in which to defend herself, but he referred to her as the 'self-styled queen' of England although Rome had acknowledged her in 1559. The effect of the bull in England was to reinforce popular resentment of the Pope.

English Catholics to rise in revolt. Although Elizabeth had crushed the northern earls' rebellion with ease, she had no wish to repeat the experience. Finally, on the domestic front, it did not displease her to begin matrimonial negotiations on the eve of the reopening of Parliament, thereby sparing herself the customary complaints about her spinsterhood – complaints that always sent her into tantrums from which Cecil, who was forever harping on the subject, suffered more than anyone.

Catherine de Médicis, for her part, wanted this marriage mainly in order to bestow a crown on her favourite son. She also saw it as a means of weakening the ultra-Catholic party, reinforcing France's position vis-à-vis Spain, and banishing all possibility of a marriage between Elizabeth and Henry of Navarre, whom she was reserving for her daughter Margaret.*

King Charles IX of France wished to get rid of this brother whom their mother had always put first and whose flamboyant appearance and way with words he resented. In 1570, moreover, he had it in mind to wrest the Netherlands from Spain and was therefore seeking a rapprochement with England. The time was ripe, politically speaking, because the Huguenots and the Catholics had just reached an accom-

---

*Elizabeth had never shown the slightest interest in Henry of Navarre, who was too young and under-age to be an advantageous match. Catherine de Médicis was alarmed when the French Huguenots floated the idea, however, and kept a careful eye on him. (See N L Rœlker, *Queen of Navarre, Jeanne d'Albret, 1528–72* (Cambridge, Mass.: 1968) p 354.)

modation in France.* An alliance with England could thus be contemplated, even though it remained unlikely that an excommunicated Protestant queen and patroness of the European Huguenots would contract a marriage with the very devout Duke of Anjou, to whom the Pope had sent a sword of honour in recognition of his vigorous defence of French Catholicism.

Acccordingly, serious negotiations began in February 1571 despite the manifest lack of enthusiasm evinced by Anjou, whom no one in France or England took seriously, and despite Queen Elizabeth's prior warnings on the subject of religion. The young duke never ceased to protest at the thought of marrying a woman who could have been his mother, and he put his fingers in his ears whenever his brother and mother intimated that politics, not love, were the order of the day. On the English side, the age difference constituted an inescapable problem: all the marriageable princes in Europe were younger than Elizabeth. Even Charles of Habsburg, whose candidacy had dragged on for ten years, was seven years her junior. All that mattered to the English was her ability to have children. It is worth noting that she authorized her physicians to make public a gynaecological report stating that, in their opinion, there was no reason why she should not conceive and bear a child.

Catherine promoted the venture with the utmost vigour.

---

*The treaty of Saint-Germain, signed on 8 August 1570, sealed this rapprochement.

She refused to allow the Pope's bull of excommunication to be published in France and brushed aside Henry's vehement objections. Elizabeth was no spring chicken, said Catherine, but she still had six or seven years in which to make a child, especially if mated with 'as fine a stallion as the Duke of Anjou'.[13] The latter expressed concern at the rumours of Elizabeth's 'immorality', which were based on reports about the queen's relations with Robert Dudley. Here again, Catherine shrugged her shoulders. In order to attain greatness, she told her son, one must take the bull by the horns. Once the marriage had taken place he could put a stop to such licentious behaviour.[14]

The diplomatic exchanges continued for seven months, which suited both parties because their main objective was to alarm Spain by hinting at a new balance of power in Europe. Without pretending to be attracted by a suitor who did not conceal his aversion to her, Elizabeth played the game and strove to make the French ambassador forget the age difference by looking her best for him. However, she firmly disputed the negotiators' various proposals and eventually rejected all the demands presented by Guido Cavalcanti, Catherine de Médicis' envoy extraordinary, these being that the duke could practise his religion publicly, be crowned on the morrow of the wedding, and receive a permanent allowance of £60,000 per annum. All Elizabeth would grant him was the right not to attend Anglican services, but not the right to hear Mass in his private apartments. Much to Cecil's chagrin, he failed to extract the smallest concession from the queen. Meanwhile, Walsingham, her ambassador in Paris, was marking time in Catherine de Médicis' anteroom. Count de Feria, Philip II's minister, delightedly proclaimed that the marriage had fallen through.

In September 1571, after Anjou had stated yet again that he refused to marry subject to such conditions, everyone went home. Elizabeth, anxious to retain the friendship of France, behaved in a very gracious manner and made the young duke a gift of some superb Chinese vases with silver gilt mountings. She was equally disinclined to court religious problems and complications abroad for the sake of a marriage for which she had no liking.

Elizabeth's intransigence in religious matters was justified. Hitherto, her moderation on the subject had avoided the fanaticism that had marked her sister's reign and ravaged the kingdom of France. Anyone wishing to make a career in government or academia had to swear an oath to the queen in her capacity as head of the Church. Although her subjects were expected to attend Protestant services and could not officially celebrate the Catholic Mass, she did not claim the right to pry into their consciences and deeply-held beliefs. As long as they did not advertise their convictions, English Catholics lived in peace and heard Mass, either privately in the intimacy of their homes, or openly in isolated districts where representatives of the Crown seldom showed their faces. In London the French and Spanish ambassadors flung wide the doors of their private chapels to their English co-religionists with impunity. The policy of 'not liking to make windows into men's hearts and secret thoughts'[15] suited all parties. The papal bull of 1570, which compelled them to take sides, was destined to aggravate the situation and work to the Catholics' ultimate disadvantage. Under these circumstances, it was difficult to accept that the queen's husband could be a practising Catholic. Elizabeth had also shrunk from the military implications of such a marriage.

Charles IX wanted Elizabeth's support for an attack on Spanish possessions in the Netherlands, but she firmly declined to embark on a war against Spain and could discern no advantage in helping the French to supplant the Spanish in the Netherlands. As she saw it, her rapprochement with France was designed to persuade Philip II to discontinue his subversive activities in England, but she was unwilling to commit herself any further than that. Catherine de Médicis was compelled to accept that her son's aversion to marrying Elizabeth was too obdurate to be overcome, but, being an incorrigible matchmaker, she suggested replacing him with the Duke of Alençon, an even younger son. No one took this proposal seriously except Cecil, still desperately in search of a husband for his queen. He tried to interest Elizabeth by telling her – rather pathetically, since their conversation had been limited to the suitor's physical attributes – that Alençon 'hath my stature.' 'Say rather that of your grandson,' she retorted, and went on to remark that, having already rejected so many princes, she would lay herself open to universal derision by marrying an ill-considered youth who was disfigured by smallpox and had three hairs on his chin in lieu of a beard. Catherine did not press her, but neither did she give up. She told an English visitor, Lord North, that evil tongues exaggerated her son's unsightliness.[16] Elizabeth graciously thanked Catherine for having offered her three of her sons in succession. Four months later the atmosphere became less jocular when the St Bartholomew's Day Massacre took place in Paris during the early hours of 24 August 1572.

News of this appalling bloodbath reached London two days later. Henry of Navarre's marriage to Margaret of Valois, celebrated on the parvis of Notre Dame on 18 August, had attracted a large number of Protestants to the capital. This was the moment chosen by Catherine de Médicis for an attempt to eliminate Admiral de Coligny, leader of the Huguenot party, whom she blamed for having removed Charles IX from her influence. The attempt misfired. Anticipating the Protestants' reaction, Henry of Guise sounded the alarm and alerted the Catholics. Spurred on by Guise, Anjou, Catherine and Charles IX, they roamed the streets of the French capital slaughtering any man, woman or child suspected of being a Protestant. Over three thousand people lost their lives. Dead bodies littered the courtyard of the Louvre, and the Seine, full of mutilated corpses, ran red with blood. Charles IX had been seen to fire a harquebus at Protestants attempting to escape. The English reacted with such horror that a rapprochement with France became impossible.

Elizabeth turned her attentions to developments at home, where the machinations of Mary Stuart, the Guises' niece, were beginning to alarm her.

The previous year's diplomatic activity had not prompted Mary Stuart to reflect on her predicament and the little genuine support she could hope to obtain from abroad. If in 1571, after three years of captivity, she had displayed less impatience and more realism – more intelligence, in other words – it is quite probable that she would have regained her throne, albeit with her authority somewhat curtailed. But, despite Elizabeth's stern admonitions, she did not abandon hope of using Norfolk and succeeded in dragging him into a new adventure. She yielded to the temptation to open her mouth too wide – to say one thing to one person and the opposite to another. She schemed, maintained clandestine contacts with Elizabeth's enemies, and exploited her personal charm. It was impossible for her to receive Norfolk in person – it appears that they never actually met – but his ambition contented itself with the queen's reputation for charm and she with her suitor's manifest advantages. She could write to him, however, thanks to those members of her entourage who handled her secret correspondence, and her letters waxed steadily more pressing and personal – indeed, affectionate: 'I am determined that neither good fortune nor ill shall ever part me from you, if you do not reject me. [...] You may find someone better, but none more committed to obeying and loving you, nor more faithful unto death.'[17] A year later, still in the same vein, she became still more explicit and feminine: 'Being at liberty and honourably bound one to the other, we shall do good for our two countries. [...] You have promised not to leave me. But, if you esteem the danger too great, do as you think best. [...] Communicate your orders to me and I shall obey them so as to spare you any danger caused by myself.'[18] In his weakness, Norfolk allowed himself to become entangled once more. It was hard to resist a beautiful young queen who wrote: 'If you do not withdraw, I shall die or live with you.'[19] A new plot – the so-called Ridolfi plot – took shape.

It was certainly ambitious. Roberto Ridolfi, a rather shady Florentine banker living in London, acted as the Pope's secret agent. Prepared to dabble in all manner of intrigues but devoid of consistency and no lover of detail, he was readily dazzled by the great. His initial idea was to persuade Philip II and the Duke of Alva, his representative in the Netherlands, to send a force of between six and ten thousand men to march on London while Norfolk and his friends took up arms, arrested Elizabeth and released Mary. The Duke of Alva, a stern and serious individual, warned his king of the danger of allying himself to a man as garrulous and frivolous as Ridolfi. The plan, he said, did not hold water. Let Norfolk and his allies take up arms. If they managed to hold their own for a month, then would be the time to send them some reinforcements.

Even before the conspirators met, Ridolfi's messenger, a servant belonging to Mary Stuart's representative in London, the Bishop of Ross, was arrested in England. Just to complete the haul, one of Norfolk's servants, who had been entrusted with some bags of gold for Mary's supporters in Scotland, was also detained. Cecil wasted no time: the Spanish ambassador, who had been compromised in a shameful manner, was ignominiously sent home. More serious still, Norfolk was arrested and tried by his peers on 16 January 1572. Doomed by his servants' confessions and, above all, by documentary evidence concealed behind a skirting board in his residence, he was incapable of defending himself against a charge of treason. His judges turned the blade of their axe towards him while the sentence of death was read out.

For Elizabeth, the ensuing weeks were a time of great mental anguish. She knew she could not pardon Norfolk, his offence was too grave and too widely known, but she could not overcome her horror at the thought of putting to death the premier peer in her kingdom. Norfolk was also a kinsman and a friend of long standing, but none of this weighed with her ministers, who feared for her safety. She was urged on all sides to have done with it and punish Norfolk for his unimaginably dastardly crime. Every time she gave the order to proceed she had second thoughts and decreed a reprieve. Her distress was painful to see. Burdened not with doubt but by the weight of her responsibility, she found it impossible to sleep. Her courtiers, ministers and intimates looked on, powerless to help. On 10 April she signed a third death warrant, only to shrink once more from delivering the fatal blow. She rescinded the order in a handwritten note received by Cecil at two in the morning: 'Methinks I am more beholding to the hinder part of my head than well trust the forwards side of the same [i.e. the seat of the intellect].'[20] Her subjects, who failed to comprehend her reluctance, were meanwhile growing restive. There still exists an enormous file containing statements on the subject by everyone of importance in the kingdom: bishops and peers, judges and members of Parliament. Not a single voice was raised in favour of sparing the traitor. The queen received another delegation from the House of Commons and House of Lords entreating her to have done with the matter, but still she procrastinated.

She had no such hesitation about the course to be adopted in the case of Mary Stuart. All negotiations with a view to returning her to Scotland as queen were halted. Once the plot had been discovered, Elizabeth simply accorded formal recognition to King James VI and the new regent, the Earl of Morton. Of more importance to Mary's ultimate fate was the hardening of opinion in England, which found expression in various speeches to the House of Commons. Parliament, which met in 1572, was infuriated by the Scottish queen's intrigues and those of her supporters, and it manifested its collective indignation in the plainest language. The first speaker's advice was 'to cut off her head and make no more ado about her.'[21] The second went further, and the third was just as implacable: 'Warning hath already been given her by statute; and therefore the axe must give the next warning.'[22] Each chamber appointed a committee to study the matter. Their verdict was unanimous. The time to show clemency or leniency was past. It was impossible to safeguard a country and its sovereign if treason went unpunished. 'The example is ill, for men will be afraid to disclose treasons when traitors are not punished, but are suffered to live' and take revenge on 'those true subjects who have betrayed their traitorous attempts. Impunity is a great encouragement to the evil, not to give over, but to proceed in their ill doings.'[23] The twin committees were received by the queen on 28 May. Having thanked them for their concern for her person in the most gracious and well-chosen words, she declined to indict Mary but could delay Norfolk's execution no longer. On the evening of Sunday, 1 June, she went to the Tower to satisfy herself that the arrangements for it were suitably dignified, but she lacked the courage to bid Norfolk farewell. The next morning, after entrusting his children to Cecil's care, he was beheaded.

It is clear that Elizabeth could have had Mary Stuart executed after the Ridolfi plot was discovered. The arguments adduced by her parliamentarians and councillors were irrefutable. Even the King of France, Charles IX, had given up defending Mary: 'The poor, demented woman will not cease until they cut off her head. That will come to pass, and I am well aware that she and her own folly will be to blame. I see no remedy for it.' Unfortunately, Elizabeth herself could see no remedy for the absurd situation created by the imprisonment on her soil of a foreign queen who was guilty of conspiring against her, protected by the concept of divine right, and – most awkward of all – her undeniable heir.

9

A Final Effort

1572–84

A s things stood in 1572, Mary Stuart would have become Queen of England in the event of Elizabeth's death. It is certainly conceivable that a section of the population would have rebelled, outraged at the idea of submitting to the rule of a Catholic queen with such a chequered past. It was also predictable that more distant heirs would assert their claims at the risk of provoking a civil war. What was impossible, however paradoxical the situation, was to prune the Tudors' family tree and, with a stroke of the pen, delete the name of Mary, great-granddaughter of Henry VII by direct line of descent. The cousins of the Suffolk branch had disappeared. Catherine Grey, who had always retained some supporters despite her tribulations, had died in 1568. Her sister Mary was discredited and did not count. A deformed and unintelligent dwarf, she had failed to consult the queen – heedless of her sister's disastrous example – before entering into a bizarre and unfortunate marriage with a man named Thomas Keys, who fulfilled the less than exalted function of Sergeant-Porter at court. On learning of this scandalous misalliance, Elizabeth promptly separated the couple. Keys was imprisoned and Mary entrusted to the care of sundry relations. He died in captivity in 1571 and she disappeared from view soon afterwards.

There remained James, Mary's son and King of Scotland, but he was only six years old at this time. To put one's faith in his succeeding to the English throne meant betting on Elizabeth's longevity. No responsible statesman could have taken such a gamble, but, equally, it was impossible – after the atrocious St Bartholomew's Day massacre of Protestants largely orchestrated by her Guise uncles – to contemplate an England ruled by Mary Stuart. The leading servants of the state refused to accept the very idea of such an eventuality. In that case, what was to be done? The failure of negotiations with the Duke of Anjou had highlighted the genuine difficulty of finding a candidate for Elizabeth's hand. No ideal Protestant prince existed. Finding a Catholic prepared to convert was proving fanciful, and the queen's age – she would turn forty in 1573 – was lending the problem particular urgency. It could not be shelved indefinitely.

Some went so far as to put forward the name of Robert Dudley, who had the advantage of being on such intimate terms with the queen. However, his wife's mysterious death remained an obstacle, and besides, their grand passion had waned. Elizabeth's warm affection for her best friend – she kept a miniature of him in her bedchamber – did not, in her eyes, justify the risk of provoking a fierce spate of jealousy among her nobles. Moreover, as one who was always very alive to popular sentiment, she was discovering the potency of her status as a virgin queen. Painted in 1569, a large portrait of Elizabeth depicts her facing the three goddesses Juno, Minerva and Venus.[1] The symbolic intention is plain to see: Juno, the patroness of marriage, presents an ideal state midway between Minerva, the personification of wisdom, and Venus, the goddess of love. Five years later, the superb royal portrait known as the Pelican Portrait conveyed an entirely different meaning.[2] The pelican, an emblem of charity and self-sacrifice, was appropriate to a sovereign desirous of being perceived as the virgin mother of her nation, as attested by the cherries at her ear ('cherry' being a vernacular word connoting *virgo intacta*). Her sumptuous gown, the extreme profusion of her jewels rendered with a miniaturist's precision by the painter Nicholas Hilliard, and her impassive face, which radiates extreme pallor, denote a wish to appear less like a living, breathing person than an embodiment of majesty and virtue.

Numerous portrayals of the queen circulated in the form of cheap engravings and copies. Her accredited painter had created a standard image of her face that was widely distributed and utilized by all who wished to depict her, whether or not they had ever set eyes on her. But this propaganda was not enough for Elizabeth, who showed herself to her subjects as readily in the provinces as in London. Every summer she would set off, travelling in great state, to stay with one or another of her courtiers. Her visits cost the chosen few dear, because they had to arrange festivities and entertainments for her, if not build on an extra wing to house a large proportion of her court. They also made lavish donations to the queen, who liked to present herself to her people in all her splendour and munificence. She was not content merely to give alms like all the great. More importantly, perhaps, she knew how to accept gifts graciously and express her thanks for the meanest bouquet or sprig of parsley. She would not hesitate to enter a cottage and drink a cup of milk offered her by a farmer's wife, and she would often stop her cortège to listen to a peasant's grievances or alight from her litter to pat the cheek of some foundling from an orphanage. The presence of a royal husband would have cramped her style. A lone star attracts every eye and its fire burns more brightly. Elizabeth thus acquired not only a popularity rare in a monarch but an ability to take the temperature of her public. Fluctuations in public opinion were immediately apparent to her in a way denied to Mary Stuart, whose years of incarceration steadily diminished her sense of reality, and who had no means of gauging the accuracy or credibility of the reports she received from her clandestine correspondents.

More serious still was the captive queen's inability to conceive of the affection Elizabeth's subjects felt for her. Sixteenth-century monarchs were feared but not loved by their people. Elizabeth, who was endowed with a rare talent for public relations, to use an anachronistic term, had engendered a popularity that was quite unprecedented in her kingdom. Her sister Mary Tudor had suffered a resounding defeat in this respect because she lacked the indispensable qualities Elizabeth so naturally displayed: a balance between authority and charm, rigour and encouragement, intellectual self-assurance and a willingness to listen to opposing views. This won her universal respect. In short, the English seemed reconciled to the idea of being governed by a woman, and a woman who defied categorization. That was precisely how she wished to be perceived.

But the political situation continued to develop. The international scene was dominated by agitation in the Netherlands. A union composed of seventeen provinces, this was a possession of the Spanish Crown, but a possession whose population was split between Protestants and Catholics. Cruelly treated by their Spanish rulers, notably the Duke of Alva, and angered by the re-establishment of the Inquisition and the flouting of their civil rights, the Protestants were constantly in revolt. In 1572, after a wholesale insurrection, Zealand and Holland seceded under the leadership of William the Silent. Elizabeth could not do otherwise than take a stand.

Her sympathy for the Protestant cause did not extend to giving the rebels open and unconditional backing. She had adopted a very clear-cut principle exemplified by the support she had given to Mary Stuart during her disputes with her nobles: that subjects should not take up arms against their sovereign. She also deemed it inappropriate to intervene in a conflict that did not directly affect her. The Netherlands belonged to Philip II, so it was up to him to resolve the problem. Embroiling herself in a religious crusade struck her as dangerous and absurd. The protection of England's interests, on the other hand, was a matter that concerned her in the highest degree. She was therefore precluded from total inactivity, especially as, however the political conflict turned out, the threat of Spanish aggression would persist.

If Philip II crushed the rebellion, increased security in the Netherlands would enable him to use it as a base for an attack on England. Elizabeth feared his religious fanaticism. The Spanish king had never accepted the defeat of Catholicism in England, and she was well aware that he aspired to re-establish it, if need be by force. But if Spain lost the Netherlands, France would advance to fill the vacuum and threaten England all the more seriously because the Franco-Scottish alliance could then be revived. Elizabeth's only solution was to maintain a state of rebellion in the Netherlands sufficient to keep Spain occupied and uneasy but not effective enough to bring about a change of regime. This entailed acting in secret, which suited her perfectly, so she confined herself to granting the Protestant rebels some meagre financial support, sending her subjects to play at pirates in the Channel and the North Sea – unbeknown to her, as it were – and sheltering refugees.

In 1576, however, exasperated by this costly guerrilla war, Philip II appointed a new governor-general of the Netherlands in the person of his young half-brother, Don John of Austria, a romantic condottiere who had defeated the Turks at Lepanto* and had at one time considered marrying Mary Stuart. The threat to Elizabeth was manifest. Don John had the drive and military skill needed to crush the rebels at last. The temptation to invade England, free Mary Stuart and, at a stroke, acquire a queen and a kingdom would then be irresistible. Don John succeeded at all he did, and the English ministers did not minimize the threat he represented. The situation called for swift and vigorous action.

In 1578 the entire Council urged Elizabeth to finance the rebels more generously and send them some soldiers as well. They failed to convince her. She resisted their advice, unwilling to tempt fate by hazarding men and substantial sums of money. Although Cecil prevailed on her to underwrite the pay of some German mercenaries, she declined to do more. Her councillors tore their hair and consoled themselves with philosophical musings. As one of them wrote to Cecil, who despaired of the situation: 'You must be contented and make a virtue of necessity, and say with yourselves that this world is not governed by wisdom and policy, but by a

---

*In October 1571 the Turks and the combined fleet of the Holy League (Spain, Venice and Rome) fought a naval battle off Lepanto, a Greek town fortified by the Venetians. It had immense repercussions throughout Christendom. Don John, the illegitimate son of Charles V and Barbara Blomberg of Regensburg, was acknowledged as his half-brother by Philip II.

secret purpose or rather fatal destiny.'[3] Even Robert Dudley, the only one of Elizabeth's intimates who dared to tell her the truth to her face, admitted that he could do nothing. He referred to her as 'Our only queen, whom God alone, I see, must now defend and uphold by miracle.'[4] God – or blind fate – did, in fact, spare Elizabeth the terrible consequences of a Spanish invasion when Don John of Austria died of a pernicious fever in August 1578. Walsingham's conclusion: 'God dealeth most lovingly with her Majesty, in taking away her enemies.'[5]

But the queen did not leave her luckless ministers in peace. Having shown little enthusiasm for marriage throughout her adult life, she chose this moment, just as she was reaching an age when the odds against a royal pregnancy were lengthening fast, to evince genuine interest in an unexpected suitor. This was Francis, Duke of Alençon,* who had returned to the fray with a few more hairs on his chin than before. Still as feather-brained and unsightly as ever, he had become a pawn in the politics of the Netherlands by taking the Protestant rebels'

---

*Like all princes, the fourth son of Henry II and Catherine de Médicis changed his name in the course of his life. Born Hercule de Valois, he became Francis, Duke of Alençon, then Duke of Anjou on the accession of his brother Henry III. I shall continue to call him Alençon for greater clarity. He also bore the title 'Monsieur', which was always accorded to the eldest of the king's brothers.

side. A Catholic prince, the brother and heir presumptive of the King of France, a leader of Protestants? It seemed fanciful in the extreme. Alençon took initiatives on his own authority, however, heedless of the interests of the French Crown and guided solely by personal ambition. Unlike his brothers and sisters, he scoffed at his mother's orders and advice. Armed with the title Protector of the Netherlands, he pitted himself against the Spanish governor, Alexander Farnese, Duke of Parma, whom Philip II had appointed to replace Don John. The political justification for Alençon's overtures to Elizabeth was their common interest in the Netherlands. Sir Thomas Smith, sent by the queen to Paris to gauge the French court's state of mind, reported back in measured terms.

Elizabeth's erstwhile suitor, the Duke of Anjou, had come to the throne in 1574 and was now King Henry III. Just as his brother Charles IX had once dreamed of unloading him, so now, in 1578, Henry yearned to rid himself of his younger brother, who was engaging in clumsy but persistent political opposition to him. It was only natural, therefore, that he favoured an English marriage.

Catherine de Médicis, who had lost none of her unshakeable aplomb and incurable optimism, could not contain her joy at the thought that this project, stillborn in 1572, had come to life again. She considered that six years had done wonders for the physical appearance of her son Alençon, who 'was far from as ugly and misshapen as had been reported [to Elizabeth]',[6] especially now that his beard concealed the ugly scars left by smallpox. Furthermore, the fact that Alençon disregarded his brother's religious fanaticism and blithely pursued his personal interests rather than being guided by his faith reassured Catherine that the inevitable negotiations about freedom of worship would present no obstacle. Finally, the queen mother added – somewhat enigmatically – that Anjou seemed more likely to sire some children than his elder brother.* There remained the vexed question of the personal relationship between the parties concerned.

Sir Francis Walsingham, a protégé of Cecil's who was English ambassador in Paris and destined to become one of the queen's principal advisers, shuddered at the thought of a woman in her forty-sixth year yielding to a disreputable little runt whose main activity consisted in opposing the French king and queen mother, rallying dissidents around him and betraying them as soon as he detected a change in the prevailing wind. He had never given evidence of the least military skill or intellectual ability.

Cecil, whose dearest wish during the previous twenty years had been to see his queen married, was the only one

---

*Henry III never managed to procreate despite countless visits to various shrines specializing in the relevant field.

of her ministers to perceive more advantages than dangers in the situation. It was true that Alençon was young, scatterbrained, ill-educated and, if the French were to be believed, not overly attractive (although Cecil hoped that English physicians would be able to obliterate some of the traces of his regrettable smallpox), but at least he was not devout. He had sided with the Dutch Protestants and, even though he could not abandon the Catholic faith as heir to his brother Henry III, he would at least not offend any English Protestants by practising his religion in public. Addressing himself to the crucial problem of the queen's fertility, the elderly minister sought reassurance from her physicians and female attendants by questioning them once more.

Apart from obsessing Elizabeth's ministers, her subjects and foreign monarchs, this problem has exercised her numerous biographers. According to one theory, she never married because she knew she was incapable of conceiving, but this has never been established. Elizabeth was a robust, active woman who long retained her youthful looks. That does not, of course, prove that she would have been capable of bearing children, but the espionage to which she was subjected by various foreign ambassadors, who paid her laundresses good money for information about the regularity of her menses, must have indicated that they were normal. Why else would Philip II, Ferdinand I of the Holy Roman Empire and Catherine de Médicis have been so eager for their respective candidates to prevail? Why should William Cecil, the queen's closest associate, have so often incurred her wrath by urging her to marry, had he not been reasonably sure of her capabilities? Never one to shrink from questioning her attendants regularly, he recorded the conclusion he drew from these investigations in a note dated 27 March 1579, in other words, when the queen was well over forty. She had 'no impediment or smallnesss of stature, of largeness in body, nor no sickness, nor lack of natural functions in those things that properly belong to the procreation of children, but contrary wise, by judgement of physicians that know her estate in those things, and by the opinion of women being most acquainted with her Majesty's body in such things as properly appertain, to show probability of her aptness to have children, even at this day. So as for anything that can be gathered from argument [investigation], all other things, saving the numbering of her years, do manifestly prove her Majesty to be very apt for the procreation of children. [...] It may be by good reasons maintained that by forbearing from marriage her Majesty's own person shall daily be subject to such dolours and infirmities as all physicians do usually impute to womankind for lack of marriage... .'[7] .

The Duke of Alençon's impetuosity, coupled with his lack of scruple, created an unexpected situation. Deciding to gamble on emotion, he declared himself madly in love with the queen. Far from being surprised by this *coup de foudre,* Elizabeth greeted his declarations of love with pleasure, and they exchanged letters whose contents were not disclosed to anyone.

This suitor who spoke more of love than of politics had materialized at the right moment, for the queen had just learned of the marriage of Robert Dudley, Earl of Leicester. Her onetime suitor had been having a surreptitious affair with Lettice Knollys,* Essex's widow and a cousin of the queen. When Lettice told him she was expecting a child he married her in secret. Elizabeth is said to have been told the news by the French ambassador, who hoped that it would further his country's interests. Although she permitted Dudley to resume his place at court after some unpleasant scenes, her animosity towards the new countess never waned. She went so far as to slap Lettice in public, enraged because she had appeared in her presence regally attired. Just as there was only one sun in the sky, Elizabeth exclaimed angrily, so she wanted only one queen in England. However, her wounds were somewhat salved by Alençon's ardent courtship, which consoled her with the belief that she could still attract the opposite sex. What followed was a distasteful charade in which one party trifled with the other. The question was, which?

In November 1578 Alençon sent one of his favourite companions, Jean de Simier, his Master of the Wardrobe, to woo the

---

*Lettice was the daughter of Sir Francis Knollys, Mary Stuart's first custodian, and the mother of young Essex, who was destined to be Elizabeth's last flame.

queen by proxy. Simier, a great favourite with the ladies, was reputed to be versed in all the arts of love. He was also a cruel and unscrupulous member of the band of minions that populated the court of Henry III and helped to create a depraved and dangerous atmosphere there. Accused of having murdered his brother after catching him *in flagrante* with his wife, who poisoned herself to avoid an even more unpleasant fate, Simier tackled his mission with great enthusiasm. On his arrival in London escorted by sixty gentlemen, he distributed handfuls of jewels among the courtiers to avert their potential hostility – an infallible method. Above all, however, he bewitched Elizabeth with his charm and eloquence. Catherine de Médicis was informed by her ambassador, La Mothe-Fénelon, that 'his words are rejuvenating her'.[8]

Overblown compliments and flattering remarks, avowals, protestations and jests that verged on the risqué – all were grist to Simier's mill. The queen, still upset by Dudley's marriage, listened enthralled. A ball was held in the visitor's honour. Elizabeth, who had never lost her love of late nights, kept Simier constantly at her side and christened him 'the Monkey', a not overly ingenious play on his 'simian' name. He roared with laughter at this, and his subsequent missives to her were signed: 'Ever your Monkey, the most faithful of your beasts.'

Elizabeth never tired of showing off the book of miniatures in a jewelled binding which Simier had brought her as a gift from the duke. The letter in which Alençon assured her that only the sight of 'the most perfect goddess of the heavens' would 'restore a languishing life'[9] never left her hand. Her entourage, aware that she was quite capable of deluding her visitor, rejoiced at her high spirits. However, on learning that Simier had, with her permission, entered her bedchamber to purloin a handkerchief and nightcap as 'trophies' for his master, her councillors were shocked by his effrontery and condemned it as 'an unmanlike, unprincelike, French kind of wooing'.[10]

Paris congratulated itself, and Catherine de Médicis, abandoning her customary subtlety, wrote to Elizabeth that she would not be content until she saw the couple in bed together.[11] The new French ambassador, M. de Mauvissière, went so far as to inform Catherine that 'The Queen of England has never been more pretty or more beautiful. There is nothing old about her except her years. [...] I myself will be as old on the twentieth of this month, and we are of the same age and not similarly fortunate. Those who are born under this sign* are never barren and seldom die without heirs.'[12] London ridiculed these methods. The problems occasioned by the queen's age were openly discussed, the

---

*Paradoxically, the sign of Virgo is considered propitious to fecundity. This letter was destined for the eyes of Catherine de Médicis, a devotee of astrology.

odds against a marriage being quoted at three to one. But the charade, far from coming to a sudden end, dragged on. The public did not approve, and no one relished the prospect of acquiring a French king who was a papist into the bargain. One Anglican minister was courageous enough to declare from the pulpit, and in the queen's presence, that 'marriages with foreigners would only result in ruin to the country'. Elizabeth ostentatiously rose and stalked out in the middle of his sermon, making a great clatter.

In March 1579, however, the two sides got down to business. Simier drafted a marriage treaty and submitted it to the Council. He was brought down to earth with a bump when he learned that his basic demands had been rejected. These were that the duke should be crowned King of England once the marriage had been celebrated, that he and the queen would share the right to distribute ecclesiastical posts, and that he would receive an annual allowance of £60,000 until his children came of age. Simier hurried to the queen to complain of her ministers' obduracy. Elizabeth greeted him with her usual affability, albeit in a melancholy mood, and advised him to be patient. She had not lost all her pride, because she declared: 'If they [the French] had to deal with a princess that either had some defect of body or nature, or lacking mental gifts, such a kind of strainable proceeding might in some sort have been tolerated. But considering how otherwise – our good fortune laid aside – it hath pleased God to lay His gifts upon us in good measure, which we do ascribe to the giver and not glory in as proceeding from ourselves (being no fit trumpet to set out our own praises), we may in true course of modesty think ourself worthy of as great a prince as Monsieur is without yielding to such hard conditions.'[13]

Alençon proceeded to demonstrate the flexibility vaunted by advocates of the marriage. He instructed Simier not to insist, but to await his arrival in England before undertaking further negotiations. Unlike Archduke Charles, who had always refused to submit to a visual inspection, Alençon disregarded his royal brother's advice, disguised himself and paid an incognito visit to England in August 1579. Officially, only the queen and Simier were warned of his coming, but his visit soon became an open secret. According to Mendoza, the Spanish ambassador, who always delighted in passing on spiteful tittle-tattle, the queen was 'afire with impatience' and congratulating herself that 'her talents and beauty are so great that they have sufficed to cause him to come and visit her without any assurance that he will be her husband'.[14]

The duke, who got to Greenwich very early on the morning of 17 August, was immediately conducted to a house in the palace grounds, where he was to stay with Simier. He woke his envoy and demanded to be taken to the queen at once.

Simier curbed his impatience, telling him that she disliked rising early, and that it would be better not to take her by surprise. By now, elaborate preparations were required to render Elizabeth presentable. The big red wigs she used to conceal her hair, which had become very sparse, took a long time to adjust. She then had to select a gown from among the three thousand that cluttered the wardrobes in her palaces, don her huge lace collar and detachable sleeves, perfume the ornately embroidered gloves she liked to wear, and, last of all, adorn her hair and deep décolleté, hands and waistband with an assortment of jewels. A message from Simier announcing her suitor's arrival stated that he had persuaded him to rest awhile between the sheets and added: 'Would to God you were at his side.' This set the tone for what was to come.

Alençon benefited from the disastrous reputation for ugliness that had preceded him. Elizabeth told him at their first meeting, which took place the same day, that he was not as unsightly as people said. And indeed, if a portrait by Clouet is to be believed, far from being repulsive, he had a rather proud demeanour. At nightfall the queen stole out of her palace to dine with Simier and his royal lodger.

There followed thirteen days of secret assignations and childish subterfuges, frivolity and silliness, ardent sighs and exchanges of gifts. The incognito charade was maintained, lending a certain piquancy to the proceedings. The pair would meet, as if by chance, at the bend in a path or in the depths of a copse. The queen was enraptured by the whole performance. For the first time in her life, she was behaving like a hare-brained old maid.

Although her courtiers affected to notice nothing, rumours were rife. Elizabeth did not practise discretion. She concealed her suitor behind an arras during a court ball and flashed repeated smiles in his direction while dancing a surprising number of sprightly galliards. The unthinkable seemed to be happening: the young duke – her 'Frog', as Elizabeth nicknamed him – had taken the queen's fancy. The diplomatic couriers were run off their feet. According to Mauvissière, Elizabeth was captivated. Mendoza wrote to Philip II that the queen and her visitor seemed enchanted with one another, and that she had stated that she would gladly marry him.

When Alençon departed on 29 August, after less than two weeks, Elizabeth put one of her ships at his disposal. Simier was left behind to keep an eye on his interests, which he did with his customary flamboyance. He gave the queen a touching account of the duke's last night in England. Unable to sleep, Alençon had allegedly spent it sighing, lamenting, and waking Simier again and again to speak of the queen's 'divine beauties and his extreme regret at being separated from your Majesty, the jailer of his heart and mistress of his liberty.'[15] The duke's contribution was to write her four letters from Dover and three from Boulogne, moistening them with his tears but taking care not to obliterate his protestations of love and sorrow. He also sent her a miniature of himself, a pearl, and a little gold flower with a frog perched on top.

For her part, Elizabeth expressed her feelings in a heart-rending sonnet. The infatuated teenager had given way to a mature woman torn between passion, propriety and sadness at the passing of time:

> *I grieve and dare not show my discontent;*
> *I love, and yet am forced to seem to hate;*
> *I do, yet dare not say I ever meant;*
> *I seem stark mute, but inwardly do prate.*
> *I am, and not; I freeze and yet am burned*
> *since from myself another self I turned.*[16]

She seemed genuinely smitten with a rather contempt-ible little man who was unworthy of her and respected by no one in France or the Netherlands. The hostile wind that was blowing in London quickly gained strength. The English tended to observe their queen's matrimonial manoeuvres with a touch of amusement as long as she played the game to their advantage, but they were taken aback by the situation prevailing in 1579.

If Elizabeth was really thinking of marrying Alençon, she was placing herself in a ridiculous position; if she was making fun of him, what she did hope to gain? The common folk found it as incomprehensible as her ministers. It may even be that she had succumbed to the complex emotions of a woman on the point of losing the divine self-assurance of youth, abruptly aware that her future would be limited by the irreparable ravages of time and obliged to acknowledge the ineluctable passing of the years. Robbed of some of her composure by the Frenchman's exaggerated but flattering attentions, she may have fallen prey to conflicting desires.

It is, perhaps, surprising that Elizabeth's forty-six years seem to have sat so lightly on her hitherto, but the great of this world are plied with extravagant flattery. Those who are told that they look young and beautiful end by believing it. What also helped to explain her insensitivity to the ageing process was her rude health, her stamina on horseback, her energy, and her capacity for hard work and concentrated mental exertion. There were many ladies younger than the queen who found it exhausting to keep up with her. Finally, her childlessness had not only exempted her from physical stress but deprived her of a mirror whose message could not be disputed. If she had had a child she would, like it or not, have been more conscious of her age. Not having had one, she still considered herself a young woman with her life ahead of her. She invariably dressed like one, her plunging necklines tactfully concealed by innumerable collars.

She received a rude awakening. English Puritans were not in the habit of mincing their words. John Stubbs, a Norfolk squire whose brother-in-law was a leading Puritan theologian, circulated a fiercely-worded pamphlet in which he warned the country of the perils of being governed by a French prince: the Catholic Mass would spread like wildfire, inextinguishable by all the water in the seven seas. Adding insult to injury, Stubbs fulminated that the House of Valois was riddled with the pox, and that Alençon bore the traces of divine wrath. That such a man had been unleashed upon their queen was an atrocious ruse on the part of the French. She should listen to her physicians and command them to speak their mind, and they would tell her that she was exposing herself to a frightful death. Elizabeth, infuriated by what she perceived as incitement to sedition, ordered the arrest of John Stubbs and the printer of the pamphlet. Despite the protests of two judges, they were sentenced to have their right hands cut off. It was the first time Henry VIII's cruelty had manifested itself in his daughter.

The scene became imprinted on the public mind. Stubbs proffered his hand to the man wielding the cleaver. When the deed had been done and the wound cauterized with a red-hot iron, he held up his left hand and, before losing consciousness, cried 'God save the Queen!' The printer, who refused his guards' help and walked off unaided, found the strength to shout: 'I have left there a true Englishman's hand!' The hostile crowd, chilled by the spectacle, murmured angrily.

Thanks to her unerring political instinct, Elizabeth realized at once that she had taken the wrong tack. Her people's respect and affection, which she had never lacked hitherto, were essential to her. The easy-going relationship she enjoyed with her subjects warmed her heart, constituted the source of her authority over her Council, and justified her solitary existence.

She summoned a meeting of the Council for the purpose of learning its views on the Alençon marriage. Her ministers conferred at great length, deliberating from eight in the morning until seven at night. Opinions were still divided, but Cecil, although in favour of the marriage, conceded that opposition to it was well-founded. Walsingham feared that, in the improbable event of the queen's conceiving a child, she would die giving birth, and this argument could not be lightly dismissed. He also pointed out that if Henry III had no heir, the Duke of Alençon would remain his direct successor. One could not, therefore, discount the possibility that he would become King of France while married to the Queen of England. If Elizabeth died, what then? The ministers very wisely resolved to consult her own opinion before going any further. The queen construed this as proof of their want of enthusiasm. Her councillors been exhorting her to marry ever since her accession; if they refused to encourage her now, it could only mean that they considered the project dangerous or, worse still, that she was past it.

She wept and raged and loudly protested her desire to have a child. Refusing, like them, to commit herself, she gave them no answer. They had no need of any. Everyone knew that the marriage would not take place, and the witnesses of this scene were all convinced that her womanly despair was sincere. She was seeing her last chance of personal happiness disappear – seeing her youth give way to old age without the solace of a warm and intimate relationship. Whether she would have derived any satisfaction from life with so debauched, thoughtless, ignorant and vain a youngster is more than doubtful, but she had temporarily lost her sense of reality. To her credit, she quickly pulled herself together. Although her distress was no less intense, it did not prevent her from using this potential match as a potent political argument. She privately resolved not to marry Alençon, but she did not reveal her hand because he could still be useful to her. Elizabeth now demonstrated her ability to employ feminine emotionalism to blind people to the fact that she thought like a man.

England was in an extremely dangerous position because the Catholic menace had revived on all fronts. English interests were gravely threatened by Spain's activities in the Netherlands, as we have already seen, but that was not all. On Elizabeth's accession, the most ardent and militant English Catholics had fled to Jesuit-run seminaries in Douai, Rheims and Rome. There they trained for the priesthood and prepared to reconquer England at the risk of martyrdom. Having infiltrated the country, they fomented dangerous agitation and greatly strengthened the morale of their more lukewarm co-religionists. In Scotland, a cousin of the young king, Esmé Stuart, Seigneur d'Aubigny, was dispatched to Edinburgh by the Pope and the Guises. He acquired so much influence over James VI, who at twelve already took a very close interest in his government, that the English party was temporarily eclipsed. The Pope and Philip II took concerted action in Ireland, where a group of English Catholic exiles and some thirty Spaniards landed on the coast and called on the Irish to take up arms. Although they were driven back into the sea, it had been a close call. These concrete dangers were allied with a climate of nervousness promoted by incessant conspiracies aimed at invading England and crowning Mary Stuart. All these threats were mutually reinforcing. Exposed to them on every side, Elizabeth had a vital interest in an alliance with France.

Catherine de Médicis not only distrusted the Guises and Catholic fanatics but feared the consequences of the Portuguese succession, which had fallen to Philip II, thereby giving Spain access to the immense wealth of Portugal's possessions in South America. It so happened, therefore, that Catherine herself could not dispense with English support. The two queens' interests being divergent but connected, it was advantageous to them both that matrimonial negotiations should continue, if only to keep Philip II in a state of suspense. Unlike Elizabeth, however, Catherine persisted in believing that the Alençon marriage would actually take place.

Although Elizabeth was in no hurry to break with her suitor, therefore, she wrote him a firm but affectionate letter explaining how impossible it was for her to commit herself more frankly. 'You must be aware, my beloved, that the delays [I impose on you] stem from the fact that our actions must rejoice our people and be greeted with acclamation [...] and the public exercise of the Catholic religion so sticks in their craw that I shall never consent to let you to come and confront a band of malcontents. [...] I entreat you to give great consideration to a subject which weighs so heavily on the English that it would defy your imagination were I not to inform you of it. [...] For my part, I own that there is not a prince in the world [...] with whom I would more gladly spend the years of my life, on account of your rare virtues and sweetness of nature [...] but I doubt that we shall agree, and, [...] in conclusion, trust that we shall remain faithful friends unless you inform me that you have renounced the public exercise of your religion.'[17]

Cecil, finally compelled to acknowledge that Henry VIII's line would become extinct, advised Elizabeth to be blunt, or she would irritate the French instead of making allies of them. Walsingham worked to the same end. The queen's artifice and procrastination were making her hated abroad, he wrote from Paris.[18] Elizabeth listened, sometimes ill-humouredly, sometimes patiently, but she never opened her heart altogether, even to her ministers. Although perfectly capable of grasping the need to continue to negotiate with France, they disapproved of the intrusion of sentiment. Imperturbable as ever, Elizabeth disregarded their expostulations and continued to exploit her gender, impart an air of candour to her political initiatives, and use the exit whenever it suited her to withdraw. The woman stood the queen in good stead. She was not going to deprive herself of a correspondence that flattered her and alarmed Philip II, especially as her own ministers did not always know whether they were dealing with their sovereign or a woman in love. Her jeweller made an earring out of a little emerald frog Alençon had sent her embedded in the seal on one of his letters. She was never without it, just as she kissed a pair of gloves he had given her a dozen times a day. This behaviour exasperated her ministers but failed to deceive Simier. He did not underestimate the queen's 'admirable wit'[19] and continued to warn Catherine de Médicis, who was mistakenly convinced that she had hooked the old maid, and that she could 'win the game' by refusing to 'temporize'.[20]

There still remained the question of the Netherlands, so vital to England's trade and economy. Cecil urged the queen to lend more vigorous support to the Protestant rebels, who were being mauled by Alexander Farnese's ruthless military campaign. Alençon, for his part, had not abandoned his ambitions and aspired to become sovereign of the Low Countries. Having more and more need for an English marriage and English gold,[21] he pestered Elizabeth relentlessly, but she still refused to commit herself.

The indispensable diplomatic negotiations were conducted by Walsingham and Catherine de Médicis. Walsingham, rightly fearing that his queen would repudiate him, refused to take any decision without referring to London. Catherine, all-powerful *de facto* but devoid of authority *de jure,* played her role like an artist in imprecision. Her son Henry III, who was often paralysed by melancholia, willingly allowed her to take the helm. This gave the queen mother scope for gaining time, whenever she deemed it useful, by pretending that it was essential to consult him. The situation was made to measure for two women who rivalled each other in caution and subterfuge.

They were both agreed on the advantages of creating an alliance against Philip II, each hoping that, in the event of war, the other would send the requisite troops into the fray. Negotiations hung fire, needless to say, and the marriage question refused to die. In default of a marriage, the French rejected any proposal to form an Anglo-French league against Spain. The English, through Walsingham, rejected the matrimonial precondition – 'although the queen's affections are not opposed to it, on the contrary'[22] – because Elizabeth could not afford to risk her subjects' animosity in order to satisfy her personal inclinations. Walsingham and Alençon eventually had a conversation during which the latter came clean at last.[23]

He justified his demand that marriage should precede an alliance by citing his fear that Elizabeth would confine herself to watching the inevitable war between France and Spain without taking an active part in it. Walsingham, for his part, did not drop his diplomatic guard, being well aware that such was his queen's real intention. He did, however, declare that she would never adopt a course of action so incompatible with her honour and interests. Far from convinced, Alençon suggested that, in default of marriage, Elizabeth should undertake to support him financially in the Netherlands. Walsingham, who knew how jealously she husbanded her resources, had no authority to agree without consulting her.

He went to London to obtain clear-cut instructions. Which would she prefer, an alliance plus marriage, or an alliance sans marriage but with financial expenditure? The queen was not prepared to give him a definite response. Meanwhile, Ivan the Terrible had sent an envoy to sound her out on the possibility of a marriage between them. This time, she was too well acquainted with the Muscovite's reputation even to consent to begin negotiations, but she delightedly broadcast the news to Europe. Walsingham felt he was going mad. 'I should repute it a greater favour to be committed to the Tower,' he confided to Cecil, 'unless her Majesty may grow more certain her resolutions there. Instead of amity, I fear her Highness shall receive enmity... .' The King of France had spent over 60,000 crowns to cover his, Walsingham's, expenses and those of the envoys he had sent to negotiate in England. If he obtained neither marriage nor an honourable friendship, he might conclude that his money had been ill spent.[24]

Elizabeth, who did not heed his advice, persisted in her enigmatic methods. It would have been imprudent to attack Spain supported by an ally as shaky as Catherine de Médicis when Catholics were engaging in dangerous agitation at home and Ireland and Scotland were in ferment. Better to keep Alençon on tenterhooks and encourage him to distract Spain with his machinations in the Netherlands.

But on learning that Catherine de Médicis, whose duplicity equalled her own, was advising her son to abandon his ambitions in the Netherlands and marry an Infanta, Elizabeth reacted with surprising speed. She promptly sent Alençon £15,000 and promised him a like sum the following month, thereby guaranteeing the continuation of her policy. Alençon, delighted to have regained a measure of independence thanks to Catherine's approaches to Philip II with a view to obtaining his daughter's hand, expressed his grateful thanks to Elizabeth and assured her that the magic power in of one of her garters would grant him victory.

The situation suited Elizabeth admirably: Alençon was furthering her plans and the chances of their marrying were just sufficient to exert pressure on Philip II. But £30,000 was not enough for Alençon, who was now wholly dependent on Elizabeth, so he decided to pay another visit to England, less to renew his suit than to obtain more funds.

He was preceded in April 1581 by a huge French delegation of over five hundred gentlemen, who were lavishly entertained. The queen, Cecil and Dudley took it in turns to stage some magnificent festivities. There were parties, balls and a mock battle in the course of which the attackers, under the banner of 'Desire', mounted a vain assault on the 'Castle of Perfect Beauty' to symbolize Alençon's designs on Elizabeth's virginity. Alençon himself arrived in November and was greeted by the queen with numerous tokens of affection. The amorous atmosphere revived to such an extent that it undermined her dignity. Was she allowing herself to be swept off her feet, or had she deliberately decided to sow confusion in those around her?

Whatever the truth, the scene that occurred on 22 November was not only startling but disconcertingly vulgar. The queen and Alençon were strolling along one of the galleries in the palace of Whitehall when the French ambassador came up and, on his royal master's behalf, enquired if Elizabeth had come to decision regarding her marriage. Her response: 'You may write this to the king: that the Duke of Alençon shall be my husband.' So saying, she turned to the duke and 'kissed him on the mouth, drawing a ring from her hand and giving it to him as a pledge.'[25] Ambassador Mendoza of Spain was so surprised by this incident that he reported it in great detail, although he was not entirely convinced by it.

The English ministers, who were not unduly worried, told themselves that the queen was merely amusing herself. Only a few weeks later, in fact, she somewhat unceremoniously got rid of her suitor. Encouraged by her behaviour, Alençon had rather forgotten that his activities in the Netherlands were all that lent him importance in her eyes. Having tasted the pleasures of life at the English court, he showed no eagerness to return to the fray, whereupon Elizabeth came down to earth and began to find his presence irksome.

His departure was an expensive business: it took £60,000

to persuade him to leave. Although Elizabeth accompanied him as far as Canterbury, assured him how sorely she would miss him and swore that she would gladly give a million pounds if 'her Frog could swim in the Thames once more', she was so relieved by his departure, like all her entourage, that she danced for joy on returning to her palace.[26]

Alençon soon gave another demonstration of his political and military incompetence. Defeated by Alexander Farnese's forces and crippled by a dispute with the adherents of William of Orange, who should really have constituted his support, he was compelled to abandon all claim to power and died in May 1584. Elizabeth wrote Catherine de Médicis a letter of condolence in the extravagant style she sometimes affected: 'For, inasmuch as you are his mother, so it is that there remain to you several other children. But, for my part, I find no consolation save death, which I hope will soon reunite us. Madame, if you were to see the image of my heart, you would see the portrait of a body without a soul.'[27]

Curiously enough, Henry III of France and Elizabeth of England were in the same position. Neither of them had a direct heir, and the religion of their successors – the Protestant Henry of Navarre and the Catholic Mary Stuart – presented them with an almost insoluble problem. This was the moment when Elizabeth turned her attention to James,

King of Scotland, who was now fifteen, and began to write to him regularly.

It was then, too, that she finally abandoned marriage as an instrument of diplomacy, though not without regret. It had served her well and enabled her to avoid an open conflict with Spain for several years, but from now on she was denied its use by her age.

However, she still possessed the magical power of virginity. At the time when the Alençon marriage project stalled, one of her courtiers, Christopher Hatton, commissioned the painter George Gower to produce a portrait of her holding a sieve, the first in a long series. It shows her sumptuously attired, with a smooth, impassive, ageless face. The sieve in her hand had been an emblem of chastity ever since Tuccia, a Vestal Virgin, demonstrated her virginity by crossing the Roman Forum holding a sieve full of water without losing a drop. Also used to separate wheat from chaff, the sieve additionally symbolized unerring judgement. Elizabeth's relationship with her subjects regained its serenity, but she never lost a bitter-sweet recollection of this last essay in matrimony. 'Melancholy doth so possess us,' wrote Walsingham, 'as both public and private causes are at a stay for a season.'[28] But the lull was only temporary, and her private melancholy would soon be dispelled by the exigencies of public affairs.

10

The Execution

1587

Although the queen had sometimes courted public ridicule by engaging in her interminable flirtation with Alençon – Catherine had floated the idea in 1571 and Elizabeth had finally sent the duke packing in 1582 – uncertainty as to its outcome had had the welcome effect of keeping Philip II in a state of painful indecision. Obsessed by his desire to regain England for Catholicism, Philip had it in mind to conquer the country, depose Elizabeth and crown Mary Stuart in her place. This grandiose venture, which was christened the *Empresa*, the enterprise or undertaking, could not be brought to a successful conclusion without the acquiescence, if not the active support, of France, the papacy and Scotland. For as long as he was threatened by the prospect of a matrimonial alliance between France and England, the Spanish king's hands were tied. One can picture the frenzy of excitement that erupted in the Escorial when it was announced that Elizabeth had finally decided to break it off. The espionage and counterespionage services seethed with activity. And, once again, Mary Stuart found herself the hub of every conspiracy.

She had remained in the custody of the Earl of Shrewsbury throughout these years, moving from one castle or mansion to another and leading the cramped and monotonous life of a provincial *grande dame*, deprived of her freedom of movement but treated with invariable respect and consideration by the earl and her own entourage. To a woman who had experienced extreme situations, tasted the fierce excitement of the unforeseen, known the raptures of love and been exposed to transports of rage, the eternal sameness of those empty days was torture of an unendurably gentle kind. She was exasperated by the feigned consideration of her jailers and their immutable, insincere courtesy, but how could she complain of it? The Earl of Shrewsbury also laboured under the contradiction inherent in the situation: he did not wish to displease Elizabeth, but he was loath to be strict with a woman who might some day be his queen. Moreover, he appreciated the calmer atmosphere prevailing in his household since Mary Stuart's arrival, enjoyed his conversations with her and welcomed them as respites from his nagging wife. To the Council, therefore, Shrewsbury too often seemed to be championing the Scottish queen's interests, and he was regularly criticized on that account.

Elizabeth's ministers were indignant at the concessions

he granted his captive, her visits to Buxton spa to relieve her rheumatism, the number of visitors she received and her free-and-easy outings on horseback – even though soldiers stationed around the castle and in the neighbouring villages made an uprising improbable. The expense incurred by the proliferation of the royal retinue was another bone of contention. When the Ridolfi plot was discovered, Mary had had to content herself with a suite of thirty including her childhood friend Mary Seton, a kinswoman, Agnes Fleming, and her husband Lord Livingston, her favourite *femme de chambre* Jane Kennedy, her master of the household John Beaton, two secretaries, a physician, an apothecary, a cook, a potager, and sundry laundresses, grooms and coachmen. Little by little, her servants increased in number once more. Shrewsbury, incapable of resisting her demands, shut his eyes to this. He often interceded with London to obtain some alleviation of her lot, censored her correspondence with only half an eye and failed to subject her regular visitors to serious surveillance. Important letters escaped his censorship altogether. The queen's women passed them to his own servants, who had been generously bribed, and they reached the outside world by that means.

Mary could freely dispose of her income as a queen dowager of France and spent nothing on the upkeep of her household. She thus had money enough to purchase these intermediaries and, more important still, to finance English Catholic exiles in France and the clandestine missionaries who returned to preach and foment unrest among the English population.

The incorrigible prisoner persisted in establishing secret channels of communication – regularly detected by Elizabeth's counterespionage services – with all the monarchs of Europe. This was the period at which Mary signalled the revival of her hopes by requesting Pope Gregory XIII to annul her marriage to Bothwell, which he speedily did. She then considered marrying Don John of Austria, Philip's illegitimate son, who was waging war against Alençon in the Low Countries. But, as we have seen, Don John died in 1578.

The time hung heavy despite all this furtive activity. Mary would soon be forty and had aged faster than Elizabeth, if only because she was bored. She succumbed to frequent fits of depression, was often prevented from riding by rheumatism and pains in her side, and found it claustrophobic to be confined within four walls. The slim horsewoman had become a rather stout middle-aged lady who walked with difficulty and spent her evenings stitching elaborate embroideries in which she incorporated poems, her motto, *En ma fin est mon commencement* (In my end is my beginning), and semi-anagrams inspired by the French version of her name. *Tu est martyre* (Thou art [a] martyr), *Tu te marieras* (Thou shalt marry) and *Sa vertu m'attire* (Her virtue attracts me) recur in all her compositions. She also liked to depict plants and animals. One proof of her exceptional skill is a piece based on an illustration in a natural history book: a little monkey embroidered in fine silk cross-stitch and mounted on a square of sumptuous velvet.[1] She worked with almost manic enthusiasm, embroidering handkerchiefs and shawls, the curtains around her bed and the tapestry-covered seats of her chairs, but reserved enough of her attention for the scurrilous gossip about Queen Elizabeth recounted with gusto by her formidable 'hostess', Bess of Hardwicke, who bitterly resented her own enforced exile to the provinces.

In 1584, possibly in revenge for Bess's accusation that she had seduced her husband, Mary wrote Elizabeth a letter detailing all the slanderous allegations Bess had made about her. The Countess of Shrewsbury had assured her that the queen 'had lain innumerable times with the Earl of Leicester, with all the licence and liberties that can be practised between husband and wife'; that she would never marry the Duke of Alençon lest she lose 'the freedom to make love and take her pleasure with some new lover'; and that she had 'met with the duke clad only in her shift and night cloak'. Moreover, Mary concluded, 'the countess advised me, laughing exceedingly, to offer my son to make love to you, the which would be greatly to my advantage.'[2]

This is such an extraordinary letter that one would be tempted to think it apocryphal, were it not for the existence of the original, which never left the archives of the Cecil family. It is certain, however, that Elizabeth never read the letter, either because it was intercepted by Cecil or found unsent among Mary's papers, which were confiscated at

Chartley in 1586, at the time of the Babington plot, of which more anon.

Mary Stuart's importance to France had diminished for as long as Elizabeth's marriage to the Duke of Alençon remained on the cards. In 1582, when the project was abandoned, Philip II regained the freedom to take more vigorous action against England and consolidate his links with the most fanatical of the French Catholics led by the Guises. The English, well aware of this growing threat and the genuine risk to Elizabeth's person, reinforced their spy rings and stepped up their surveillance.

The difficulty of protecting the queen was greatly aggravated by her refusal to submit to security measures that would isolate her and prevent her from being seen by her subjects. She would never have agreed to live like a recluse in the manner of Philip II, shut up in his Escorial. Her sister, her brother or even her father had never stopped their coach or litter to speak to a man of the people or, better still, listen to what he had to say. Elizabeth, by contrast, was forever interrupting her progresses to do so. A crowd-pleaser *par excellence*, she needed to demonstrate her benevolence and prove that her authority derived its 'chiefest strength and safeguard' from 'the loyal hearts and goodwill of my subjects'.[3] Her spontaneous walkabouts among the spectators who lined her route enabled her to refresh her ideas and receive the tokens of affection she refused to forgo. However, it is impossible to exaggerate the disquiet and anxiety felt by her Council at a time when Pope Gregory XIII and the Duke of Guise were openly advocating her murder.

Early in 1583 Walsingham got wind of a suspicious incident. A messenger from the Spanish embassy had been arrested at the Scottish border. He managed to bribe his guards and escape but dropped a mirror, concealed in the back of which some letters were found. This was how Walsingham discovered the existence of the *Empresa*. In order to learn more, he began by concentrating on the correspondence between Mary and the French ambassador. He made no spectacular finds apart from some recipes Mary gave for invisible writing: soak the paper or a very fine cloth in a solution of ammonia and alum twenty-four hours before use; the invisible writing would reappear when moistened. Alternatively, she suggested writing between the lines of a book, but only on every fourth page, the doctored volume being identified by a green thread or ribbon inserted between the pages. Another ruse was to hollow out the heel of a boot or fit a casket with a false lid or sides.

None of this was very important, but surveillance of the embassy alerted the English to the suspicious activities of one Francis Throckmorton,* an English Catholic employed as a spy by Mary Stuart. Walsingham had him tailed for

---

*His uncle, Sir Nicholas Throckmorton, had served Elizabeth at the beginning of her reign.

six months until, in November 1583, he had amassed enough evidence to have the man arrested and seize his papers. Although all they yielded were lists of Catholics and foreigners favourable to a Spanish invasion, Throckmorton was tortured into making a full confession and ended by informing Walsingham about the conspiracy's international ramifications: the Pope, the Duke of Guise, Philip II and the English Jesuit missions were all implicated. Throckmorton named a number of accomplices who had no time to escape and were thrown into prison. Mendoza, the Spanish ambassador, was requested to leave the country within two weeks and Throckmorton himself was executed. Elizabeth still refused to have Mary indicted, however. She limited herself to removing her from the custody of the Earl of Shrewsbury, whose incompetence could no longer be ignored, and to reinforcing her control over the prisoner's activities.

Paradoxically, given these difficult circumstances, a definite agreement was reached with Scotland, and Elizabeth was finally reassured by the restoration of peace on her northern border. What accounted for this unwonted stability was the arrival on the scene of a new player: none other than James VI, Mary Stuart's son. The influence temporarily exerted on the young king by the French party led by Esmé Stuart did not endure for long. Reacting with their habitual violence, the Protestant lords ousted his Francophile entourage and re-established the English alliance. An exceptionally serious and precocious youth, James now realized that his future depended on friendship with England. He abandoned the

Catholic cause just when, at sixteen, he began to wield power in his own right. Wisely, he evinced no desire to intercede on his mother's behalf and never sought to obtain her release, nor even to improve the conditions of her imprisonment. It should here be pointed out that there had been no contact between mother and son in all these years. Although Mary had written to James from time to time and sent him gifts, notably a little monkey, she persisted in addressing him as Prince of Scotland, not King, so the Scottish lords had returned all her communications. Their principled stance had thus precluded any relationship between them, however formal.

Like his mother before him, James tried to persuade Elizabeth to recognize him as her successor, but he did not press the point when she proved reluctant. His prime concern was to maintain good relations with her. In July 1586 he unhesitatingly ratified the Treaty of Berwick, which sanctioned the English alliance and marked the beginning of a relationship with Elizabeth which, if not devoid of complexity, was at least peaceful. They corresponded regularly, and always in their own hand. She called him her 'dear brother'; he addressed her as 'madam and mother' and often signed himself 'your brother and son'.[4] Like a kindly parent who knew of her youthful offspring's love for the chase, Elizabeth sent him the finest horses and hounds. It should be added, more prosaically, that he also received a generous annual allowance, and that the most Anglophile of his advisers were judiciously rewarded.

The two cousins had many things in common despite the

thirty-three years that separated them. Elizabeth's memory of the ordeals she had undergone lent her an intuitive understanding of James's psychology denied to his mother and their respective ministers. James's childhood and adolescence had been those of an orphan; Elizabeth had been subject first to a cruel, capricious father and then to a hostile sister. Ever since his boyhood, James had displayed a circumspection and tenacity equalled only by Elizabeth's. They had both found the prospect of inheriting a kingdom likely but, at the same time, never a foregone conclusion: Elizabeth because she was at her sister's mercy and uncertain of her own fate until the latter's death; James because the abstract certainty of being best placed to succeed Elizabeth did not blind him to the unforeseen obstacles that might bar his path.

On a more personal level, their intellectual tastes and love of language facilitated exchanges of letters. Elizabeth was an avid reader, as we have already mentioned, and enjoyed translating from Greek and Latin. She never stopped learning, and in 1585 she engaged the services of a classical scholar, Sir Henry Savile, the Provost of Eton, whom James commissioned some years later to help carry out his admirable plan to translate the Bible into English.* Thus the two cousins established a genuine understanding that resulted in the smoothest of relationships.

James's position was somewhat confusing. The Scots

---

*The King James Bible was translated by royal command. The king's close interest in the project reflected his belief in the unrivalled power of words.

regarded him as their crowned king, the Lord's Anointed, yet his mother had never abdicated. On the contrary, she never ceased to claim her throne, and her pathetic insistence on protocol during her captivity only underlined the fact that she still considered herself queen, and queen by divine right. Thus the mother's very existence undermined the authority of the son, who would never truly be king until the day of her death. Although Elizabeth had no designs on James's throne, she held the key to his future, for it was up to her whether he eventually enjoyed the immense advantage of reigning over two united kingdoms. Only her death would open the door to that great future, but their difference in age encouraged him to bide his time patiently. So his interests lay closer to Elizabeth's than to his mother's. Both had a great deal to gain from Mary Stuart's death, to be blunt, but they were inhibited from showing their hand by personal respect and, even more so, by respect for the institution of monarchy by divine right.

Mary was now confined under more rigorous conditions. The indulgent Earl of Shrewsbury, who so disliked regarding himself as her jailer, was replaced by Sir Amyas Paulet, a strict and fussy Puritan immune to his prisoner's charm. In January 1585 Mary was transferred to Tutbury Castle in Staffordshire. She already knew the huge, dilapidated fortress, having stayed there before, and she thoroughly detested it.

Appallingly damp and exposed to the elements, its lath and plaster walls were so riddled with gaps that the wind came whistling into every room.

Her physician, having experienced 'the incredible chill' that prevailed in the queen's bedchamber at night, washed his hands of her care unless she was accommodated in greater comfort,[5] nor did she have any gallery or chamber to retire to, just 'two small holes' from which all she could see were the castle's gloomy, encircling walls.[6] The English, who remained adamant, congratulated themselves that Tutbury, which was situated on a hill, was easy to defend and almost impregnable. The members of the Council derived additional reassurance from the measures taken by Mary's new jailer.

Paulet, a man of integrity but no *grand seigneur,* was quite unimpressed by the combination of relaxed familiarity and great respect that had prevailed between the queen and his predecessors. An incorruptible Puritan, he was solely concerned to carry out his mission to the best of his ability. And his mission consisted in treating Mary as a prisoner, not as a royal guest detained against her will. Paulet introduced a draconian regime. He forbade the queen to go out, even to take the air, and clandestine correspondence was precluded by stricter supervision on the part of his servants. No communication between the latter and members of the queen's household was permitted except in Paulet's presence. The queen's servants had to be accompanied by a guard whenever they left the building, and the comings and goings of laundresses and coachmen were supervised with redoubled vigilance. Coachmen in particular had considerable scope for passing messages thanks to the parcels with which they were regularly entrusted. Paulet performed his duties so well that the only letters Mary was permitted to receive were from the French ambassador. However, Walsingham reserved the right to read the letters they exchanged. He had hitherto read Mary's official correspondence – that is to say, such letters as did not go through secret channels – by having them opened without breaking the seals, thanks to one of his employees who specialized in that technique. In May 1585 he removed his kid gloves and instructed Paulet to return them to his prisoner opened.

After a year of this treatment Mary's health gave rise to genuine concern and the French court requested that she be transferred to a more salubrious abode. Paulet himself conceded that the stench of the middens around the castle was becoming unbearable. The whole of the little community was eventually transplanted to Chartley Hall, a manor house belonging to the young Earl of Essex, the son of Lettice Knollys and, thus, Dudley's stepson. This was a more modern and comfortable establishment, but one with a wide moat that discouraged all hope of attempts at rescue or escape. Mary retired to her bed on arrival and remained there for several weeks. Walsingham took advantage of this interlude to set a trap whose treachery matched its efficacy.

Francis Walsingham's main responsibility was national security. He came of a modest background, like his patron William Cecil, and owed his advancement to sheer force of intellect. The lawyer son of a lawyer, he had been elected to Parliament in 1563, at the age of thirty. Cecil, who very soon singled him out for promotion, put him in charge of the government espionage network. His excellent knowledge of French, Spanish and Italian, coupled with his love of detail and knack of recruiting the boldest and most skilful agents, worked wonders. His men operated as efficiently in London's waterfront taverns as they did in the drawing rooms of the French and Spanish embassies. He was rewarded with the post of ambassador to France in 1570, at the time of the queen's matrimonial negotiations with the Duke of Anjou, and became one of her most influential ministers on his return in 1573.

Walsingham's relations with Elizabeth were never cordial. He was too pessimistic and inflexible; in other words, too puritanical to endear himself to her. He did not stoop to flattering her or lauding her beauty and intelligence in the high-flown language customary at court. On the contrary, he was blunt and outspoken with her, never hesitating to draw her attention to the limits of her power. For her part, Elizabeth respected the man she nicknamed 'the Moor' and was too appreciative of his intelligence and unflagging diligence not to accord him a position of great influence. She knew that her survival was more dependent on the protection of this stern, modest, discreet man in black than on all the handsome officials who adorned her court. Walsingham was convinced that all his efforts would be in vain if the Scottish queen remained alive, hence his determination to incriminate her in so flagrant a manner that her execution would become inevitable.

Gilbert Gifford, the son of a Staffordshire family from the vicinity of Chartley, had completed his education at a seminary in France, like many English Catholic exiles. He was contacted there by one of Mary's agents, who persuaded him to go to England and try to organize some means of communicating with her. On landing he was arrested and interrogated by Walsingham's men, who spotted that he was unscrupulous enough to make a good double agent. In the event, Gifford agreed to help set up a channel of communication to which the government would be privy. All that remained was to devise one.

Walsingham then sent for Thomas Phelippes, whose insignificant appearance and pock-marked face concealed the fertile brain of a first-class cipher expert and vital cog in the spymaster's machine. Walsingham introduced Gifford to him and sent him off to Chartley to assess the situation. On his return, Phelippes came up with the following scheme. The brewer who supplied Chartley with beer would insert a waterproof packet containing letters addressed to Mary in a cask of ale. The packet would be removed by the cellarer and handed to Nau, the queen's secretary. Her replies would travel back by the same route.

The queen's friends had still to be convinced that this

system was secure. Accordingly, Gifford got in touch with Châteauneuf, the new French ambassador, and informed him that he had discovered a means of access to the Queen of Scotland. The ambassador decided to entrust him with some innocuous letters as an experiment. Mary, who received this first packet on 16 January 1586,[7] had been deprived of news for a year. The renewed ability to write freely to her friends and receive uncensored letters gave her a *raison d'être,* so she set to work with a will. Two weeks later Châteauneuf received a whole sheaf of correspondence. The delay was unsurprising: Mary's letters continued to be written in code, an elementary precaution that was never abandoned despite the time it consumed.

The final operation took the following form. Letters from abroad travelled to England in the French diplomatic bag. The ambassador passed them to Gifford, who took them straight to Walsingham. Gifford then made for Chartley without waiting for Phelippes to complete the difficult task of transcribing them in clear. Mary employed over a hundred different codes. Either the letters of the alphabet were not used in the customary order, or the secretary replaced them with numbers, symbols, or even signs of the zodiac. Some codes had to be deciphered with the aid of a grid, a sheet of paper perforated with holes in such a way that only the relevant characters showed through. The persons and places most often referred to were represented by various symbols: a cross and a circle for Queen Elizabeth; an X with a loop at the top left corner for the king of France; an X with a loop on the right for the Pope; a π for Spain; and a heart for the month of July.[8]

Once read and copied, the documents were dispatched to Paulet, who handed them to Gifford, who took them to the brewer. For increased security, the latter sent them back to Paulet, who was anxious to ensure that nothing had been surreptitiously added to the packet and that Gifford was not playing the triple agent. Finally, after a brief sojourn in the barrel, the papers were surreptitiously conveyed to Mary. The brewer passed her outgoing mail to Gifford, who handed it over to Paulet for forwarding to Walsingham. Once Phelippes had finished deciphering the letters, Walsingham managed to get them dropped at the French embassy without arousing suspicion. Gifford never touched them again, such was Walsingham's extreme distrust of him. The brewer was onto a good thing. Although royally rewarded by Mary and generously paid by Paulet, he kept increasing the price of his beer, which had become indispensable to all concerned.

Mary recovered her vitality. Her aches and pains vanished, and she even expressed a wish to go riding again. The letters she received and the news they contained, together with an endless succession of conspiracies, seemed to prove that the outside world had not forgotten her. She requested the ambassador to send her all the correspondence that had accumulated – twenty-one packets of it – since the Throckmorton conspiracy was unmasked. The game became so exciting that Elizabeth indulged in a piece of bravado whose very audacity deprived it of serious consequences. *'Monsieur l'Ambassadeur,'* she told the French ambassador suavely, 'you exchange great and secret intelligence with the Queen of Scotland, but believe me, I am apprised of all that passes in my kingdom. I myself was a prisoner in the time of the queen my sister, and I know what devices prisoners employ in order to acquire servitors and secret intelligence.'[9] One might have hoped, for Mary's sake, that the diplomat would take note of this.

One might also have hoped that Mary would not cast all caution and discretion to the winds, but she did. On 20 May 1586 she incriminated herself by writing to Charles Paget, one of her English supporters in Paris, and to Mendoza, the Spanish ambassador who had been expelled from England and was now *en poste* in France. She informed them that she favoured the Spanish invasion plan. She also demonstrated her political and parental naivety by telling them that she would endeavour to interest her son in it. Instead of contenting himself with such incriminating documents, Walsingham allowed Mary to continue corresponding. Thus, he learned of the arrival in London of an English Jesuit, Father Ballard, who was very close to Mendoza. Ballard proceeded to get in touch with a young Englishman, Anthony Babington, who had some years earlier fallen under Mary's spell as a page in the home of the Earl of Shrewsbury. The French ambassador judged him to be 'very young, beardless and rather simple-minded'.[10] Nevertheless, Ballard informed Babington of a new conspiracy based on the same expectations: a Spanish invasion supported by an uprising on the part of Queen Elizabeth's Catholic subjects. This time, however, Walsingham could closely follow all developments by reading Mary Stuart's correspondence and the reports of the spies employed to shadow Ballard and Babington. He watched their movements like a hawk, well aware that Elizabeth's assassination formed part of the conspirators' plan. It should be remembered that in 1583 the Duke of Guise had offered a large reward to anyone who succeeded in killing her, and that the Pope had given his apostolic blessing to any person who would rid the world of this heretical monarch. In the course of his conversations with Ballard, Babington stated that he saw little chance of success 'while her Majesty is alive', and Ballard replied that 'this difficulty has been foreseen and resolved'.[11]

Young, reckless and extremely susceptible – like many Catholics – to the romantic image of an innocent princess imprisoned at the behest of an evil queen, Babington lacked the most elementary discretion. He dealt the whole enterprise a fatal blow by writing the Scottish queen a letter giving precise details of the attempt to be made on Elizabeth's life, of her replacement by Mary herself, and of the foreign invasion. He also asked her to provide an 'honourable' recompense for the heroes who were going to accomplish the 'tragic execution'.

For Walsingham, the end was now in sight. Anxious not to waste a moment, he sent Phelippes to Chartley to decipher Mary's reply on the spot. It was not long in coming and surpassed all his hopes. Mary not only signified her approval of the whole plan, Elizabeth's murder included, but added some advice of her own. She ended by asking Babington to burn her letter once he had read it.[12] Phelippes sent Walsingham his transcription without delay and, to emphasize that it ought to 'inspire the queen with the heroic courage required to avenge this attack on her safety and that of the state',[13] drew a gallows on the outside of the letter. Armed with this evidence, Walsingham felt strong enough to act. Father Ballard was the first to be arrested in London on 4 August 1586. On hearing the news, Babington fled to St John's Wood on the northern outskirts of the capital. Discovered there on 14 August, he was conveyed to the Tower to the sound of bells pealing in celebration of the capture of 'traitors who had made a dastardly plot to assassinate the sovereign'.[14] The pace of events was also accelerating at Chartley.

On 11 August Paulet suggested that Mary might care to go hunting. She agreed with pleasure, this being a treat she was rarely granted. Having dressed with care, she rode out into the countryside accompanied by her two secretaries and her personal physician with Paulet bringing up the rear. All at once she sighted a band of horsemen galloping towards her. For a moment she thought they had come to rescue her, but she was speedily disabused of that idea by the leader of the little party, Sir Thomas Gorges. 'Madame,' he told her, 'the

Queen, my mistress, finds it very strange that you, contrary to the pact and engagement made between you, should have conspired against her and her State, a thing which she could not have believed had she not seen proofs of it with her own eyes and known it for certain.' Mary, taken unawares, denied that she had acted contrary to the interests of 'her good sister' Elizabeth, but to no avail. Terrified, she saw her secretaries dragged away. Paulet announced that she could not return to Chartley but would be taken instead to Tixall, a country house not far away. Her physician would be permitted to accompany her.

Mary tried to resist. She dismounted and sat on the ground, refusing to budge, but Paulet was unmoved. If she persisted in refusing to mount her horse, he told her, he would have her put into a coach by force. At last she gave way and was conveyed to Tixall, where she never left her room throughout the fortnight she spent there. Two of her women and her equerry joined her there, bringing a change of clothes and her indispensable embroidery case. Meanwhile, her apartments at Chartley were methodically searched and her letters and various ciphers sent to London.[15]

Babington and his accomplices were executed in short order. Popular sentiment was not conducive to leniency. Peals of bells, bonfires, ballads swiftly composed and no less swiftly taken up by people in the streets, pamphlets passed from hand to hand – all these testified to the joy and relief of a population enamoured of its queen. Elizabeth thanked Paulet in the warmest terms: 'Amyas, my most careful and faithful servant, God reward thee treblefold in the double for thy most troublesome charge.' She referred to Mary as 'your wicked mistress' and bade him tell her to 'ask God forgiveness for her treacherous dealing'.[16]

Her kingdom was overcome by a strange mood of panic. Had Frenchmen been seen coming ashore? Was it true that a Spanish fleet had dropped anchor off the coast of France? Troops were mustered everywhere for safety's sake while Elizabeth and her ministers made preparations for Mary's trial. To be more precise, her ministers and councillors steeled themselves to counter the objections the queen threatened to raise, for the fundamental problem persisted: on the one hand, Mary's part in the plan to assassinate her was beyond doubt and should attract the death penalty in accordance with the Act of Association passed by Parliament in 1585; on the other, there remained the argument according to which a sovereign by divine right was answerable to God alone and not subject to the law of man. The ministers espoused the rule of law and the primacy of political expediency; Elizabeth was utterly opposed to subjecting a queen to the law of man and refused to be the instrument of such justice.

This difference of opinion manifested itself as soon as discussion turned to the question of where Mary should be held in custody. The Council wanted her brought to the Tower. Elizabeth decided in favour of Fotheringay Castle in Northamptonshire, some 120 miles north of London, a less demeaning place and less likely to strike terror into Mary's heart. Preparations for the trial proceeded at a snail's pace.

Every word had to be weighed because Elizabeth proved finicky in the extreme. Walsingham expressed a heartfelt wish that she would, like other princes, leave matters to those best qualified to handle them successfully.[17] The trial opened at last, however, and after two days of argument Mary consented to appear before the judges – thirty-six commissioners appointed by Queen Elizabeth – while refusing to recognize their legitimacy.

She defended herself with courage and eloquence, firmly insisting that the celebrated letter addressed to Babington had been forged by Walsingham. The latter rose to defend himself against this accusation. He called on God to witness that he had done nothing unbefitting an honest man or unworthy of the public office he held, but only what was necessary to safeguard the queen and her realm.[18] In face of the evidence, Mary did not press the point. The depositions obtained from her secretaries, Claude Nau and Gilbert Curle, who were forced to admit that the letters produced in evidence were authentic, rendered any denial nugatory. The two men made no attempt to put up a futile defence and were released in exchange for their cooperation. The court could have delivered its verdict without delay, but the queen summoned it to London for a meticulous re-examination of the entire case. Nau and Curle were recalled and questioned anew before being granted permission to return to France. It was not until 25 October that the members of the court were called upon to deliver their verdict. It was unanimous with one exception. The Queen of Scots was pronounced guilty of the 'compassing, practising and imagining of her Majesty's death'.[19] At Queen Elizabeth's request, the judges stated that the verdict did not prejudice James's claims to succeed her.

The punishment – death – was in no doubt because the Act of 1585 had provided for that penalty, but the queen had still to authorize promulgation of the sentence and sign the death warrant. Parliament had been convened 'to lighten her burden' and 'reassure foreign nations' about the validity of the proceedings. Foreign nations may have been satisfied but the queen's doubts persisted. She was nonetheless obliged to acknowledge the danger that threatened her. 'I am not so void of judgment as not to see mine own peril; nor yet so ignorant as not to know it were in nature a foolish course to cherish a sword to cut mine own throat; nor so careless as not to weigh that my life daily is in hazard,'[20] she declared to Parliament in November, but she still delayed signing the warrant.

Her foremost argument related to foreign policy: Mary's execution would prompt Philip II to open hostilities against England at once, supported – as he would be – by the whole of the Catholic world. She attributed her reluctance to concern for her reputation. 'What will they not now say when it shall be spread that, for the safety of her life, a maiden queen could be content to spill the blood even of her own kinswoman?' This convinced no one but gained her some time. The sentence was finally promulgated in December notwithstanding the French ambassador's efforts. The streets of London rang with rejoicing – premature rejoicing, because Elizabeth was still loath to sign the fatal death warrant. In January rumours of a plot hatched by the French ambassador intensified. It was said in the provinces that London was ablaze, that thousands of Spaniards had landed in Wales and that the Queen of Scots had escaped. Men stood to arms and set up roadblocks. The situation was becoming impossible.

What rendered it even more awkward and distressing was that the Scots, confronted by Elizabeth's imminent decision, waxed so indignant that James felt obliged to intercede on his mother's behalf – *in extremis*, as it were – and plead that it was unacceptable for men to judge a queen whose crown had been bestowed on her by God. 'What monstrous thing is it that sovereign princes themselves should be the example-givers of their own sacred diadems' profaning!',[21] he wrote to Elizabeth. The queen needed no reminding. She was so torn between conflicting emotions, she yielded to an ignoble temptation and suggested that Paulet have Mary murdered. He rejected this proposal in horror: 'God forbid I should make so foul a shipwreck of my conscience, or leave so great a blot to my poor posterity, to shed blood without law or warrant.'[22] Elizabeth made a few sarcastic remarks about gentlemen who bayed for blood but were reluctant to soil their hands, leaving that terrible responsibility to their sovereign.[23] She was experiencing the absolute solitude of a monarch confronted by her conscience, her personal feelings and the cruelty inseparable from her status. Her dread at the thought of having to execute Mary sprang from the very depths of her being. Putting one of the Lord's Anointed to death struck her as inconceivable. Elizabeth was too much of a queen, and too alive to the mystique of monarchy by divine right, not to balk at shouldering such a crushing moral burden at the risk of seeming irrational, hysterical and hypocritical.

Under mounting and irresistible pressure from Parliament and the streets, she finally decided to sign the warrant on 1 February. Walsingham, who was ill, had been replaced by one of Cecil's protégés, William Davison. Either the latter did not appreciate the queen's propensity for mood swings and changes of heart, or he was complying with Cecil's and Walsingham's advice, because he wasted little time. Having consulted the Council and obtained its agreement, he dispatched the document to Fotheringay on 4 February.

Mary Stuart had demonstrated a disastrous lack of realism throughout her captivity. What ultimately doomed her was a refusal either to abdicate in her son's favour or at least to desist from all the futile conspiracies whose sole effect had been to bring about the death of the Duke of Norfolk and many of her young supporters. In her final hours, however, she conducted herself with such courage and dignity that she redeemed her reputation and covered herself in legendary glory. If she had agreed to abdicate and end her days in peaceful retirement she would now be forgotten, but she resolved that her death should vindicate her devotion to her religion and the principle of royalty by divine right; in other words, that she would die a Catholic martyr. It was the most intelligent act ever performed by a queen entirely devoid of political discernment. She had not lost her 'diamond heart' and was determined not to present the world with the spectacle of a defeated or, worse still, frightened woman. When Parliament delivered its verdict, Paulet had removed the royal cloth of state beneath which her chair had always stood. Instead of protesting, Mary replaced it with a crucifix and a painting of Christ's Passion. Her *mise en scène* was taking shape: she intended to die so heroic a death that, in the words of one of her mottoes, her end would be her beginning. Paradoxically, Mary was less afraid of dying than Elizabeth of giving the order to kill her.

At eight o'clock on the evening of 7 February 1587, Mary received a visit from the Earl of Shrewsbury, her kindly jailer during most of her imprisonment, and Lord Kent. Shrewsbury, going down on one knee, informed her that Queen Elizabeth had commanded that sentence be carried out the next morning. Mary, surrounded by her women, remained impassive. 'I thank you for such welcome news,' she replied. 'You will do me great good in withdrawing me from this world, out of which I am very glad to go.' She added that 'all my life I have had only sorrow' and expressed her joy at being able to die for the greater glory of God's name and his

Catholic Church. Her only fear in the preceding months had been that she would be poisoned or done away with in secret. What she aspired to was a public death that would enable her to regain all her majesty. She was assisted in doing so by her captors' petty efforts to deprive her, on the threshold of death, of the last rites.

They rejected all Mary's last requests. When she asked to see her chaplain they offered her the services of the Protestant dean of the nearest town, Peterborough. Needless to say, she declared that she would not betray her faith in the very hour of her death. Next she asked that her body be buried in France, either at Rheims or at Saint-Denis. This request, too, was denied. Finally, when informed that the execution would take place at eight the next morning, she remarked that they were giving her little enough time in which to prepare herself. Her servants wept and protested, but she herself remained unruffled and tried to calm them. Left alone with her women and her physician, she had some supper and asked those who served it to drink to her. Then she proceeded to dispose of her personal effects.

She divided such money as she had into little packets on which she wrote the names of her various servants. Certain objects were reserved for her French relations: King Henry III, Catherine de Médicis and the Duke of Guise. To her physician, Bourgouin, she bequeathed her music book and some rings; to her female attendant Elizabeth Curle two miniatures, one of Francis II and the other of her son James. She also made some very detailed alterations to her will, going so far as to specify that her servants were to have the use of her coach and horses to convey them to London after her death, and that the proceeds from the sale of the horses should be given them to defray their expenses. Having attended to her temporal affairs, she turned to spiritual matters and wrote her chaplain a long letter in the form of a confession. Her last letter, written at two in the morning and thus dated the day of her death, was addressed to Henry III, King of France. She informed him that she was to be 'executed at eight o'clock in the morning, like a criminal', asked him to ensure that her servants were rewarded, and commended her son to him – 'insofar as he deserves it, for I cannot answer for him'.[24] She then lay down for several hours, well within earshot of the sentries pacing up and down outside her chamber and of the sinister din made by workmen erecting a scaffold in the great hall of Fotheringay Castle.

At six o'clock she rose and dressed with the utmost care in a black satin dress with black velvet embroidery, full sleeves slashed to reveal the violet inner sleeves beneath, a full petticoat of crimson velvet, and a high neckline. Her black stockings were clocked with silver thread and her shoes were of fine Spanish leather. A white veil festooned with lace and pinned to her collar fell almost to her feet, and her auburn hair could just be glimpsed beneath an openwork bonnet. Two rosaries hung from her waist and her collar was held in place by an amber brooch in the shape of an apple. She asked Jane Kennedy, one of her attendants, to hold a large white handkerchief embroidered with gold thread. Her physician brought her a piece of bread and a glass of wine to fortify her for what was to come. She kissed her women and then withdrew to her little oratory. They came for her just after eight. The sun was rising on an exceptionally fine February day.*

Before entering the great hall she was dealt an unexpected blow. The sheriff of Northampton, who had been detailed to escort her, stopped those who were preparing to follow and informed Mary that Queen Elizabeth had ordained that she should die alone. She thereupon turned to Paulet and the other lords and asked if she might at least be accompanied by her closest servants, so that they could bear witness to the manner of her death. Impossible, Paulet replied, because their tears and lamentations would upset those present and the queen herself. Moreover, they would dip their handkerchiefs in her blood and make relics of them. Mary replied that she would vouch for their behaviour, adding that she could not believe that the queen, her kinswoman, had given an order so cruel and contrary to custom. 'You know that I am cousin to your Queen and descended from the blood of Henry VII, a married Queen of France and the anointed Queen of

---

*This account of Mary's death is based on Bourgoing's journal, Henry III's report from his ambassador Châteauneuf, and a letter from Richard Wingfield, Cecil's special envoy.

Scotland.' The lords quickly conferred, then permitted her to choose six persons to be present at her death. Of those who remained with her to the end, four were men: James Melville, her old ambassador, Bourgouin, her physician, Gervais, an old retainer, and Didier, her porter. The two women were Elizabeth Curle and Jane Kennedy, who had served her all her life.

A fire was blazing in the huge fireplace of the hall, where three hundred people stood waiting in a horseshoe around a stage on which three stools had been placed, two reserved for Shrewsbury and Kent and a smaller, cushioned one for the queen herself. At the back of the stage were two men dressed in black velvet, masked and wearing big white aprons. Lying on the ground was a large axe 'like those used for felling trees', as Bourgouin described it.* Although she stooped a little from rheumatism and walked with difficulty, carrying her crucifix and missal, Mary's bearing was dignified in the extreme. All present were struck by her remarkably serene expression.

Having ascended the three steps that led up to the platform, she listened with detachment to the sentence being read out but vigorously protested when the dean of Peterborough proposed to harangue her according to the Protestant rite. 'Mr Dean,' she told him, 'I am settled in the ancient Catholic Roman religion, and mind to spend my blood in

---

*A clerk of the Council left a very detailed drawing of the execution scene, now preserved in the British Library.

defence of it.' She then addressed herself to the two earls: 'If you will pray with me, my lords, I will thank you, but to join in prayer I will not, for that you and I are not of one religion.'

An absurd scene ensued: the dean knelt and proceeded to pray loudly in English while the queen just as loudly invoked the Almighty in Latin. When the dean finally fell silent she prayed in English for the English Catholic Church, for her son, and for Elizabeth. Then she kissed her crucifix and made the sign of the cross. The executioner and his assistant stepped forward and asked her, in the customary manner, to pardon them. 'I forgive you with all my heart,' she told them, 'for now I hope you shall make an end of all my troubles.' Her women proceeded to help her out of her dress and put on some long red gloves. The executioners held out their hands for her ornaments, which were their perquisites by right. When they made to take her gold rosary, however, Jane Kennedy protested and the queen herself intervened, assuring them that they would be compensated with money instead. Mindful of her promise that the women would not weep if admitted to the hall, she was heard to silence their sobs by saying: '*Ne pleurez point pour moi. J'ai promis pour vous... .*' Jane covered her eyes with the big white handkerchief and wrapped it around her head, leaving the neck entirely bare. Mary knelt, recited a psalm in Latin, and rested her head on the block, adjusting her chin with both hands. Having moved her hands aside so as not to cut them, the chief executioner brought the axe down. He missed her neck and only cut into the back of her head. The second blow decapitated her. When the executioner raised the head by the hair, according to custom, it came away in his hand. The head itself – that of an ageing woman with cropped grey hair – fell to the ground, lips still quivering. The queen had been wearing a wig.

When they came to pick up the lifeless corpse and carry it into the room next door, the blood almost indistinguishable from the queen's crimson garments, something stirred beneath them. Her little dog, a Skye terrier, had followed her in unobserved, concealed by her skirts, and was nestling against her. It refused to leave its mistress and had to be removed. The queen's body, which was embalmed and placed in a lead coffin, remained for the time being at Fotheringay Castle.

Late that day a courier left for London. The inhabitants of the capital celebrated the tidings of Mary Stuart's death with bonfires. Bells rang in every church and people danced in the streets. Elizabeth was not of the same mind. On hearing the news, which reached her at nine in the morning, she collapsed in hysterics. She had always intended to review her fatal decision, she sobbed. She wept unceasingly, would not eat, lay awake all night and refused to see her ministers for several days. It was her way of demonstrating her absolute refusal to take responsibility for having beheaded her 'dear sister'. Davison, the minister guilty of excessive zeal, was arrested, tried, sentenced to pay a substantial fine and promptly imprisoned in the Tower. She lost her temper with William Cecil and subjected him to fierce tirades, accusing him of treachery, mendacity and hypocrisy, calling him a wretch and forbidding him to appear in her sight.[25]

The old minister braved the storm philosophically. He was convinced, doubtless correctly, that it suited the queen to fly in the face of the evidence and deny her part in implementing the sentence, that her fury was not a hundred per cent genuine, and that there was a substantial element of play-acting in the whole performance. It was obviously convenient to her to have a scapegoat to offer James VI and Henry III before she could gauge reactions abroad.

James VI had certainly never tried to challenge the alliance with England, as witness a remarkably frank letter he wrote to Robert Dudley: 'How fond [foolish] and inconstant I were if I should prefer my mother to the title, let all men judge. My religion ever moved me to hate her course, although my honour constrains me to insist for her life.'[26] Nevertheless, Elizabeth was quick to write James a pathetic letter in her own hand, its purpose being to convince him of her innocence: 'I would you knew though not felt the extreme dolour that overwhelms my mind for that miserable accident, which far contrary to my meaning hath befallen. [...] I beseech you that – as God and many more know – how innocent I am in this case. [...] I am not so base minded that fear of any living creature or prince should make me afraid to do that were just or, done, to deny the same.' Duplicity, she added, did not befit a monarch.[27]

The Scottish king was in an awkward position. It would have been hard for him not to react to his mother's execution, even if he could not remember ever having seen her, and tactless of him not to join in his subjects' vehement protests. The fact remained, Mary's death would make his life easier. He correctly guessed that the Scots would soon calm down again. The thorn that was poisoning relations between England and Scotland had been extracted at last. By virtue of his lineage and the elimination of all other valid candidates, he, James, was Elizabeth's indisputable successor. His position was greatly strengthened by the fact that he was a man, and a Protestant into the bargain, and he welcomed it that Elizabeth's excuses and outward dismay absolved him from any obligation to defend his filial honour. Thus he willingly acquiesced in the notion of an 'accident' and had the queen's letter circulated among all the European courts.

In Notre Dame on 3 March 1587 a Requiem Mass for Mary Stuart was attended by the whole of the French court and parliament. But so tense was the political situation in France, which was threatened once more by civil war, and so fragile was the position of the king, who was having to contend with simultaneous attacks by Protestant Huguenots and Catholic fanatics rallying behind the Duke of Guise, that Mary Stuart's death did not constitute a decisive political factor. Paradoxically, this blow that directly affected the Guises served Henry III's purposes inasmuch as he was desperately striving to blight their ambitions. The Scottish queen's fate had long ceased to matter in France, and the Parisians' reaction to the news of her death was as short-lived as Walsingham had foreseen.

Mary Stuart's death did, in fact, have momentous consequences, but only in the long term. As Elizabeth realized, her execution demonstrated that a sovereign was answerable to man, not merely to God. The concept of royalty by divine right, whose corollary was that kings and queens could not be called to account for their actions, had been undermined: the people were destined to exchange subservience for sovereignty. Mary Stuart's death set a precedent that would justify the execution of her grandson Charles I, which would in turn justify those of Louis XVI and Marie Antoinette. Elizabeth could not foresee the future, of course, but she was too thoughtful and intelligent not to grasp that her decision had changed the rules of the game. Relieved by the muted reaction abroad, however, she recovered her poise.

Although one could attack her decision on the moral plane and argue that the legal grounds for Mary Stuart's imprisonment and execution were highly debatable, it is impossible not to recognize, on the political plane, that Elizabeth was right to get rid of her. The agitation that had been fomented by persistent conspiracies and constant threats was succeeded by tranquillity. In June the queen made it up with Cecil and paid him a long visit at Theobalds, his handsome country house; on 29 July Mary Stuart's remains were laid to rest in Peterborough Cathedral, where Catherine of Aragon had been buried, and the threat of civil war subsided. English Catholics would have had no compunction in accepting Mary Stuart as Elizabeth's successor. Some of them – the activist minority – had been in favour of a *coup d'état* to put her on the throne and the rest were prepared to await the natural course of events. With Mary dead, however, no Catholic pretender remained. Philip II claimed the succession on the grounds that Mary Tudor had bequeathed him her kingdom, but no Englishman could have contemplated such an eventuality. When the Armada sailed up the Channel the following year, Catholics and Protestants rallied to their queen's colours and united against the aggressor without a second thought.

11

Elizabeth Triumphant

1587–9

In 1587 Elizabeth had been on the throne for twenty-eight years, during which time she had been confronted by two nagging and almost insoluble problems: the fate of Mary Stuart and the question of her marriage. The first had been finally disposed of by the headsman's axe. The second was resolved in a less dramatic fashion, simply by the passage of time. Elizabeth was now fifty-three years old, so the question had become redundant.

Freed at last from these twin causes for concern, she proceeded to prove her mettle. Despite the intensity of her reaction to Mary's death, she did not give way to remorse or melancholy. On the contrary, she savoured her popularity, which increased with every passing year and owed nothing to chance.

Unlike her father and grandfather, Elizabeth had never left her island. A prince might have gone to the Continent, if only in a military capacity; a girl, even a royal princess, had no such opportunity. Moreover, Elizabeth's difficult childhood had not been conducive to travelling. She had no reason to regret this because she very soon seized the opportunity to present herself as a pure-bred Englishwoman motivated by an exclusive passion for her own kingdom, which she never tired of traversing. It has been established that she spent at least one night in no less than 241 different places.[1] She moved around primarily because contemporary hygiene demanded that a palace not be occupied for more than two months at a time, but also to gratify the humble folk who craved her presence and that of her entourage, because a visit from the court was of great financial benefit to local merchants and tradesmen. Last, and most importantly, the queen was anxious to be seen as often as possible, and not only by the inhabitants of London. Accordingly, she established a circular route which she travelled every year. She had a choice of fourteen royal residences set aside for her own use, but she never hesitated to invite herself to stay with one or another of her subjects.

She always spent the last two months of the year in London, staying at Whitehall Palace for judicial or parliamentary sittings and in order to preside over the November festivities that commemorated her accession, which acquired an importance comparable to that of Christmas as the years went by. Her birthday and the anniversary of her accession were marked by elaborate tournaments that brought thousands of spectators crowding into the spacious palace courtyard. The queen, who was far from averse to blood sports, gladly attended the entertainments arranged for the occasion, which included bullfights and bear-baiting (a cruel sport in which mastiffs were unleashed on a bear chained to a stake). Then, as if to emphasize the diversity of her interests, she would retire to her library, which was arrayed with hundreds of volumes bound in velvet and encrusted with precious stones, or discourse on philosophy with the most erudite of her courtiers. The Christmas festivities, accompanied by a series of very popular theatrical presentations, took place either at Whitehall or at one of her other palaces nearby: Hampton Court, Windsor or Greenwich, which stood beside the Thames and were easy to reach by river. Elizabeth was passionately concerned to preserve the dramatic art from attack by the Puritans who would have liked to close every theatre in London. A royal troupe called 'the Queen's Men' was formed and played not only at court but in the provinces. Lord Howard followed Elizabeth's example, as did Lord Hunsdon, and it was they who respectively enabled Marlowe and Shakespeare to make a name for themselves.

As winter drew to a close the court settled down at Nonesuch or Oatlands in Surrey, south-west of London, until the queen had to return to her capital for Easter. She spent the spring visiting palaces in the vicinity and devoted the summer to more extensive tours known as 'progresses'. These required an immense amount of organization, for Elizabeth travelled with a train of five hundred persons, all of whom had to be fed, lodged and entertained. Her courtiers, especially the older ones, detested the whole business. This was because, instead of spending the summer months on their country estates, they were obliged to travel rutted roads in convoy and had sometimes to sleep under canvas. But the queen liked to be accompanied by her most glamorous courtiers because these progresses served a dual purpose: for one thing, to impress provincials with the splendour of her court, and, for another, to provide her with an opportunity to display her benevolence to the crowds who flocked to see her. She always lodged with some member of the gentry or nobility, sometimes at a manor house but preferably at castles or country mansions where her hosts would court financial ruin by offering her the choicest entertainments. Since they received a year's notice, the skinflints would invent pretexts for forgoing such an expensive honour. The ambitious welcomed these visits and vied with one another in devising ways to impress her. Some dug manmade lakes, others created artificial grottoes in which to conceal musicians, and a few built on extra wings to accommodate her in style. Sir Francis Carew tented his cherry trees in order to provide her with fresh fruit out of season. It went without saying that her hosts had also to organize large-scale hunting parties and firework displays and commission occasional works from poets. The festivities devised by Dudley during a fortnight's royal visit to Kenilworth Castle became legendary.

Although stops were pleasurable occasions, the intervening journeys were devoted to the hard work of public relations. Elizabeth enjoyed travelling on horseback, but on coming to a town she would create a glamorous image by donning a white gown and making her entrance in a coach or gilded litter. Her patience was inexhaustible. If local residents staged a display of singing and dancing to mark her passage she would stop the whole convoy and express her cordial thanks to the mayor and his officials, sometimes with tears in her eyes. She listened assiduously to anyone who approached her, believing that it was 'the duty of a prince to hold an equal hand over the highest and the lowest', and that she was 'queen of the meanest subjects as well as of the greatest.'[2] In an address to Parliament towards the end of her reign, she defined her role in maternal terms that laid greater emphasis on a queen's concern for her people than on her power: 'There will never Queen sit in my seat with more zeal to my country, care for my subjects, and that will sooner with willingness venture her life for your good and safety, than myself... . And though you have had, and may have, many princes more mighty and wise sitting in this seat, yet you never had, nor shall have, any that will be more careful and loving.'[3] Nor would they ever have a queen more intent on charming them and better at devising ways to impress them.

For instance, she never attended a play or a concert without ensuring that the audience could see and watch her with ease. An inconspicuous box would not do. At Christ Church, Oxford, a doorway was cut in the wall between the auditorium and her lodgings in college so that she could enter directly. It was rightly considered that to have her enter with the rest of the audience would have detracted from her personal impact. Elizabeth had always been something of an actress, and one who never neglected her appearance. Her hair was washed with lye, a solution of wood ash and water. She had it dyed when the first grey strands appeared and soon made use of wigs and postiches. She devoted the greatest care to her cosmetics. A face cream compounded of white of egg, powdered eggshell, crushed poppy seeds, alum and sodium borate lent her skin an exceptional pallor. In an attempt to preserve the whiteness of her teeth, she rubbed them with a mixture of white wine and vinegar boiled in honey. She never ceased to improve her performance and dazzle her public with pomp and ceremony. The ceremonial at Versailles would have struck her as irksomely unpretentious.

At the end of her reign she attended divine worship every Sunday, not only on feast days, surrounded by her entire court and watched by a crowd for whom the doors of the palace were thrown open for the occasion. The big procession that assembled in her antechamber was led by the knights of the Order of the Garter, the Chancellor holding the Great Seal, and the bearers of Her Majesty's sword of state and sceptre. Then came the queen herself, dressed in a ceremonial gown of white to underline her virginity. Fifty gentlemen armed with gilded battleaxes escorted her, followed by a gaggle of maids of honour and ladies-in-waiting. The procession set off in the direction of the chapel, all present kneeling as the queen passed by. She would sometimes pause to exchange a few words with a foreign ambassador, either in his own tongue or in Latin, or address some subject who had caught her eye. On reaching the door of the chapel she occasionally deigned to receive a petition. Her benevolence always drew loud cheers, which she acknowledged with 'I thank you, my good people' before continuing on her way. The service, admirably accompanied by fifty choristers and forty musicians, was never to last longer than half an hour. Elizabeth made no secret of her dislike of long sermons. Although she could be the soul of affability, she could also fulminate when bored or angry. To quote her godson, Sir John Harington: 'When she smiles, it was a pure sunshine, that everyone did choose to bask in; but anon came a storm from a sudden gathering of clouds, and the thunder fell in wondrous manner on all alike.'[4]

Her indiscretions with Alençon were forgotten and her power had won the respect of all Europe. Even Pope Sixtus V, who had succeeded her old enemy Gregory XIII, recognized her merits and expressed his reluctant admiration: 'She certainly is a great queen, and were she only a Catholic she would be our dearly beloved. Just look how well she governs! She is only a woman, only mistress of half an island, and yet she makes herself feared by Spain, by France, by the [Holy Roman] Empire, by all.'[5] Strangely enough, she was not feared for her heroic virtues. On the contrary, what perturbed people was her dissimulation, her changes of heart, and the fact that her total rejection of fanaticism made her unpredictable.

Unusually for a sixteenth-century monarch, Elizabeth never gave military considerations precedence over political ones. When Don John of Austria presented a threat in the Netherlands, she demonstrated this by her refusal to come in on the French side and provoke a war with Spain. Her sex exempted her from having to lead her soldiers in battle and made it easy for her to save face. She never minded appearing indecisive when she had to play for time. No man could have vacillated as she did without seeming unequal to his task. If people attributed her indecision to her femininity, so much the better; her self-confidence remained unshaken. Elizabeth felt no obligation to affect a knowledge of matters beyond her ken, so she delegated her authority widely, nor did she aspire to play the general or admiral, being well aware of her lack of military expertise. On the other hand, she forced herself to master the subject of public finance.

Her own financial resources had been limited ever since her youth, and she would never have asked help from her sister or brother. Cecil had impressed on her the need to tailor her expenditure to her income. As queen she continued to apply that principle at the risk of seeming miserly. One year there was an inexplicable increase of £12,000 in court expenditure on bread, ale and firewood alone. She asked the official in charge for his accounts, saying that she wanted them clearly set out so that she could understand them. The patent dishonesty of her household officials annoyed her all the more because she knew that purveyors to the court purchased their wares at a discount. She took a very close interest in the management of her affairs, knowing that they were one and the same as those of England. It was the queen's personal responsibility to fund the court and her government. In an emergency she could ask Parliament to come to her aid by imposing additional taxes, but this expedient had to remain the exception, and Elizabeth, who appreciated the importance of personal popularity, was loath to avail herself of it too often. One source of expenditure difficult to control was the army, because the system of payment, which dated from the mercenary armies of the Middle Ages, was an invitation to embezzlement.

In the old days the commander of a body of men rented them out to the highest bidder. It was then up to him to pay and feed them. Elizabeth did not employ mercenaries, but she paid the captain of a company a fixed sum on condition that he fed, clothed and armed them. Needless to say, he endeavoured to do as well out of it as possible by making economies at the poor wretches' expense, either faking their numbers or discharging them without pay heedless of the depredations committed by bands of starving ex-soldiers let loose on the countryside. Outraged by the men's pitiful condition and appalled at this waste of her resources, Elizabeth demanded that officers render accounts and refused to give any money to those who failed to comply. Feeding and paying her soldiers and sailors was one of the queen's constant preoccupations. As a woman she was far more sensitive to the horrors of war than a man inured to them by service in the army. Her soldiers were duly grateful to her and the word got round, a well-lined belly being a great guarantee of popularity.

And then the inevitable happened: this queen who was so tight-fisted with her troops, so jealous of her resources, so distrustful of long-term commitments and concerned for her people's welfare, found herself confronted by war with Spain. Not a vicarious war, as in the Netherlands, but a genuine naval conflict accompanied by a very real risk of invasion. Relations between the two countries had deteriorated considerably since 1585. While refusing to engage in open hostilities, Elizabeth had inflicted two pinpricks on her brother-in-law. The first was delivered by Dudley, whom she dispatched to the United Provinces* at the head of an army, the second by a gentleman pirate of remarkable courage and audacity. Renowned for his voyages of exploration, his daring raids and reckless offensives, followed if necessary by rapid withdrawals, Sir Francis Drake had operated all over the world: the South Seas, the Sunda Islands, the coasts of Chile and Peru. He attacked Spanish vessels at every opportunity and seized their cargoes of precious metals. Elizabeth, who admired his courage, welcomed the booty he brought her. Above all, however, she appreciated the fact that she could, depending on circumstances, shower him with honours or publicly disown him. Drake, for his part, appreciated the exigencies of political life.

---

*The United Provinces, a Protestant power, comprised Holland, Zealand and several independent cities that had seceded with William of Orange in 1572 and were in constant opposition to the Catholic provinces forming the Low Countries.

In April 1587, still obsessed with a desire to eradicate heresy in England, Philip II made no further secret of his intention to attack Elizabeth by sea and concentrated all his efforts on strengthening the Armada. The queen did not react, outwardly at least, preferring to use Drake discreetly. Their plan, a singularly bold one, consisted in destroying the Spanish fleet in its home ports before it could assemble at Lisbon, the Armada's prearranged point of departure.

Drake unobtrusively set sail for Portugal in command of a small flotilla. Having escaped observation by keeping well clear of land, he turned east. Once off Cadiz, he boldly entered the harbour and captured, sank or burned a hundred-odd vessels lying at anchor there. Then he crossed the Bay of Cadiz and made for Cape St Vincent, destroyed every Spanish ship within range and headed north again. He sailed up the estuary of the Tagus and tried to engage the Marquis of Santa Cruz, the Spanish admiral, who declined to do battle. Drake then made for the Azores in search of vessels laden with the riches of the New World. Having captured a big Spanish merchantman whose cargo was worth the equivalent of half the queen's annual budget, he decided to head for home.

Thanks to Drake, England had acquired a substantial war chest, delayed the Armada by a year and humiliated Spain. The discomfited Spaniards accused him of sorcery. It was claimed in the streets of Cadiz that a mysterious mirror had enabled him to survey the Spanish fleet and all that went on aboard its ships. Poor Philip II, by now an elderly man so tormented by gout that he walked with the greatest difficulty, was hidebound by routine, fussy in the extreme and incapable of delegating authority. He continued his laborious preparations, refusing to be discouraged by this enemy who had struck with such diabolical speed and paralysed his naval commanders by scorning traditional methods of warfare. He gave orders that the fleet should be re-formed. For a year he toiled away at his desk, seldom leaving it except to limp into his oratory and kneel in prayer. When summer came round again in 1588 he prepared to attack, determined to rob his heretical sister-in-law of her triumph.

The Spaniards were putting all their faith in God. The king now spent whole hours at a time in prayer and his people devoted themselves to religious processions, fasting and divine worship. The Pope had sent Philip a ceremonial sword to symbolize his support for this new crusade. Unfortunately, neither God nor his saints had prompted the king and his ministers to study the differences between the Mediterranean, the Atlantic Ocean and the North Sea. The Spanish fleet was ill-suited to the rough seas off the English coast. It was true that Philip II had at his disposal the Portuguese fleet,* which included some ships better suited to the Atlantic, and that a number of the ships destroyed had been replaced by Portuguese merchantmen, but Spanish tactics were obsolete. The Spaniards had always tried to lay alongside enemy vessels and board them, in other words, to fight a

---

*In 1580, on the death of Henry the Cardinal, the successor of his grand-nephew Sebastian, Portugal had passed to Philip II.

hand-to-hand land battle at sea. They could not conceive of any other method, whereas the English technique was altogether different. Henry VIII had promoted the revolutionary idea of arming his ships with cannon mounted along the sides, not on the towering sterncastles of yore, which destabilized them in heavy seas. Thus the new ships were faster and more manoeuvrable – murderously so. The object was to sink enemy vessels in battle, not capture them. This tactic was so effective that English ship's captains could dispense with the costly and cumbersome presence of numerous soldiers on board.

Wisely, Elizabeth refrained from putting her entire faith either in God or in her ships. She did not underestimate the genuine danger of an invasion. It should not be forgotten that the Spanish forces in the Netherlands commanded by Alexander Farnese, Duke of Parma, were not only formidable but just across the English Channel. In the spring of 1588 Drake learned that the Spanish fleet had left Lisbon but had been forced to take shelter at La Coruña, in the extreme north-west corner of Spain, to repair the damage inflicted by a violent storm. He planned a raid on it, hoping to repeat his success of the previous year, but encountered adverse winds and turned back. The queen preferred to regroup her forces in any case, and the ships' absence would have left her coasts vulnerable to a surprise attack.

Her government attended to the country's land defences as well. For safety's sake, all Catholic gentlemen owning estates near the coast were placed under arrest and the local inhabitants alerted in readiness to resist a landing. A series of beacons was quickly set up at regular intervals along the coast to warn of the enemy's approach. In addition, two special armies were formed: one stationed around St James's Palace to protect the queen's person and the other at Tilbury, east of London in the Thames Estuary, to repel an attack on the capital.

On 21 July 1588,* under the command of the Duke of Medina Sidonia, the Armada finally set sail. The religious nature of the enterprise was underlined once more. All the soldiers and sailors had been shriven, blessed and issued with a medallion bearing the image of Christ on one side and that of the Virgin on the other. The Spanish plan was to sail north along the French coast, enter the English Channel, pass Calais, and get to the Netherlands, where a link-up would take place with the Duke of Parma's forces just north of Dunkirk. Then, protected by the Spanish fleet, Parma would send an army across to England. Medina Sidonia's orders were extremely precise, having been vetted and approved by Philip II, and left him no scope for initiative.

---

*This date and those that follow it accord with the Gregorian calendar, which superseded the Julian calendar in 1582 and advanced the date by ten days. The English long persisted in adhering to the former, hence the apparent chronological discrepancy between some accounts of the Armada's progress and others.

The Armada entered the Channel on 30 July, and the sight of those three hundred vessels spread out over a distance of two miles made a deep impression on the watching English. 'We never thought,' wrote one eye-witness, 'that they could ever have found, gathered and joined so great a force of puissant ships together and so well appointed them with their cannon, culverin and other great pieces of brass ordnance.'[6] The largest vessels weighed over two hundred tons, the smallest only sixty; some were armed with forty-eight cannon, others carried four. The English, who appreciated the difficulty of keeping such a large number of ships in formation, given their great difference in size and spread of canvas, concluded that such skilful and well-disciplined crews would prove formidable foes.

However, the Spanish fleet's formation was disrupted by two accidents. An explosion shattered two decks and the superstructure of one of the best-armed vessels, the *San Salvador,* killing half her crew of four hundred men. Then came a collision that dismasted a big galleon, the *Rosario.* Drake promptly seized the opportunity to attack her. Unable to manoeuvre, the Spanish captain was forced to surrender his ship and her rich cargo. Medina Sidonia reorganized his still formidable force as quickly as possible and ordered it to make for Calais, sending the Duke of Parma a messenger by pinnace to make arrangements for their link-up.

The Duke of Parma had always insisted that he would need six days' notice before launching an invasion. This was because he could not afford to concentrate his troops and boats openly at Dunkirk, where they would be vulnerable to attack by Protestant rebels from Holland and Zealand. Accordingly, he had divided his forces between four different ports and concealed the flat-bottomed barges required for a landing in various canals. It should also be borne in mind that he had to transport horses, supplies and munitions as well as men. All this required lengthy preparation. Finally, in order to deceive the enemy about his dispositions, he himself kept shuttling between Antwerp, Ghent and Bruges. Needless to say, it could take several days or a messenger to reach him. Although the news that the Armada had got to Calais took him by surprise, however, he informed Medina Sidonia that he would be ready by 12 August. The Spanish fleet would simply have to wait until then.

Their preliminary skirmishes with the Spaniards had convinced the English that their guns were not powerful enough to sink the big Spanish vessels in a pitched battle, especially as they could not engage at very close quarters for fear of being boarded. At a council of war held on board the flagship at dawn on 7 August, they adopted a simple but effective plan. The wind and current being favourable, they converted eight ships into incendiary bombs. Laden with gunpowder and equipped with pre-loaded, double-shotted cannon that would go off automatically when subjected to extreme heat, these fire-ships were towed into the darkness.

Then, as soon as the tide permitted, they were released and drifted towards the Spanish ships.

Utter panic broke out. The strength of the current had compelled the Spanish captains to use two or three anchors to keep station in the turbulent waters of the Channel, and there was not enough time to hoist them. Their only means of making a quick getaway was to cut the cables, which most of the captains did. This decision had disastrous consequences, quite apart from the financial loss incurred – an anchor cost hundreds of ducats, as all the chroniclers pointed out. Worst of all, the ships could no longer lie at anchor while waiting for the Duke of Parma to be ready, nor could they approach any coast in safety.

The English proceeded to attack in full strength, and battle was joined. The confused fighting lasted for nine hours. Medina Sidonia managed to regroup enough of his ships to resist the English bombardment, but despite the number and size of his vessels he failed to regain the advantage in an engagement dominated by artillery. The English could reload very rapidly thanks to their wheeled gun carriages and well-trained crews. The Spaniards, by contrast, were accustomed to fire once and then board the enemy at speed. It was impossible for them to reload in a hurry, their heavy gun mounts being hard to manhandle.

The Spaniards' gunfire was inaccurate, too, because their cannon balls varied in diameter according to their place of manufacture, and great care was needed to ensure the compatibility of guns and ammunition. The overcrowded decks, which were cluttered with soldiers as well as sailors, proved an additional handicap. The English kept up a regular barrage which, although not powerful enough to destroy the Spanish ships, demoralized the men aboard. Last but not least, there were the elements. The Spaniards could not contend with wind, wave, tide and the English as well. Harried but not annihilated, their fleet could only escape to the north and abandon all hope of covering an invasion by the Duke of Parma.

This respite, however welcome, did not dispel Elizabeth's fears entirely. On the contrary, although her ships had sustained very little damage, the fighting had exhausted their stocks of ammunition. These could not be replenished at once, so England would have been unable to cope with a renewal of hostilities. Moreover, there was still a risk that the Duke of Parma might attempt a landing after all, and that the Armada might find shelter in Scandinavia, heal its wounds and return to finish the job.

Elizabeth, whose remarkable fortitude throughout this ordeal had greatly heartened those around her, did not wish her forces' morale to be impaired by a false sense of security. She decided to go to Tilbury to review and encourage her troops. This was the occasion of one of her most memorable speeches: 'Wherefore I am come among you not for my recreation and pleasure, but being resolved in the midst and heat of the battle to live and die amongst you all, to lay down for my God, and for my kingdom and for my people, mine honour and my blood, even in the dust. I know I have the body of a weak and feeble woman, but I have the heart and stomach of a king, and of a king of England too; and I take foul scorn that Parma or any prince of Europe should dare to invade the borders of my realm. To the which, rather than any dishonour shall grow by me, I myself will venter my royal blood; I myself will be your general, judge and rewarder of your virtue in the field. I know that already for your forwardness you have deserved rewards and crowns, and I assure you in the word of a prince you shall not fail of them.'[7]

The men cheered her enthusiastically, after which she went off to dine with her old friend Dudley. It was then learned that Medina Sidonia had decided to sail round Scotland and return to Spain via the western coast of Ireland – an immense detour. All Philip II's prayers had been to no avail: a terrible storm put paid to the whole venture without the English having to intervene. Spain had lost over half its fleet, whereas Elizabeth's navy was still intact. Rather than ruin herself by continuing to pay her men, she economized by rapidly demobilizing them. Cheers greeted her in London and bonfires were lit in the streets. Meanwhile, far across the sea, Philip II remained closeted in the Escorial, incommunicado to all save his father confessor. In France the Spanish brought about a resolution of the conflict between Henry III and the Guises, who were dependent on Philip's gold and protection. The French king had regained his self-confidence. In December 1588, before the year was out, he lured Henry of Guise into a trap and had him stabbed to death by his henchmen. Catherine de Médicis died in January 1589.

Henry III did not savour his enemy's assassination for long. In May 1589 he himself was murdered by a knife-wielding monk. Henry of Navarre, the Protestant who had always been supported by England, became King Henry IV of France. Elizabeth's triumph was complete.

In the midst of all this public rejoicing, however, the queen had cause to weep. Robert Dudley, her youthful flame and lifelong friend, died in September. On 29 August he had written her a note inquiring after her health, 'the chiefest thing in the world I pray for'. She folded it carefully and put it in the jewel box she kept on a table beside her bed. This was the first in a long series of bereavements. Although Elizabeth herself remained robust and active, her own generation – and, more importantly, that of her earliest advisers – was beginning to flag. The queen was extremely loyal to her ministers, some of whom had served her ever since her accession. Their frequent disagreements resulted in heated arguments but not, thanks to the strength of their mutual respect, in any dismissals or removals from office. Cecil and Knollys were growing old. In 1589 Elizabeth lost Walsingham and, at the same time, his extensive network of spies. 'Good news,' Philip II scrawled in the margin of the diplomatic dispatch announcing his death. The circle of courtiers that dated from the queen's youth, when they had danced and gone riding together, was shrinking fast. The favourites who had earned affectionate nicknames were disappearing, some carried off by death, others by disgrace.

Christopher Hatton, a friend of twenty years' standing nicknamed 'My Lids' or sometimes 'Mutton', died in 1591. Malicious gossip claimed that the queen's eye had been drawn to this 'mere vegetable of the court that sprang up at night' solely by his talent for dancing. Hatton was sustained by his looks, charm, wit and absolute devotion to her. In 1589, by which time his greater seriousness and genuine political acumen had gained him advancement at court, he was appointed Lord Chancellor. Alone among the queen's male circle, he refused to marry. As he saw it, that would have been a betrayal of his love for her, which he never tired of expressing in letters whose fervent language sometimes takes the modern reader aback. At the height of a smallpox epidemic, for instance, he sent her a hollow ring containing a prophylactic potion and recommended her to wear it around her neck 'betwixt the sweet dugs, the chaste nest of most pure constancy'.[8]

Hatton was extremely jealous of Walter Raleigh, and one can understand why. Raleigh was ten years his junior and seventeen years younger than the queen. A tall, handsome, strapping man with a dark beard and sparkling eyes, Raleigh was not only an efficient soldier and adventurous seaman but a poet with a very inquiring mind. He charmed Elizabeth, who found it highly amusing to favour one or another of the young men around her at the risk of tormenting the others. Royal favour was always accompanied by great financial advantages and marks of distinction. Walter Raleigh – the queen called him 'Water' in a play on his forename and seamanship – was knighted and rewarded with large estates in England and Ireland. Elizabeth also bullied the Bishop of Durham into relinquishing his big London mansion to Raleigh, who was always asking for more for himself and his friends, among them the poet Edmund Spenser. The queen tapped him on the cheek one day and asked him when he was going to stop playing the beggar. His response: 'When Her Majesty ceases to be my benefactress.'

Raleigh was not content to sit back with his hand held out. He mounted numerous piratical expeditions against Spain and invested in voyages to the New World. Inveterately parsimonious, the queen saw to it that his various activities benefited her exchequer. When he seized a large tract of land on the North American coast and christened it Virginia in her honour, she received a substantial share of the profits and was delighted to see the seed potatoes he brought back growing in her vegetable gardens.

Unlike Hatton, however, Raleigh did not sacrifice his manhood on the virgin queen's altar. He had the effrontery to court Elizabeth Throckmorton, one of the queen's maids of honour and the daughter of her former ambassador to Paris. She soon became pregnant, and a hurried marriage took place without the queen's knowledge or consent. Her fury was unbounded. Disgusted by what she considered a treasonable act, she sent the couple to the Tower. Raleigh wrote her the most charming letters of entreaty in which he recalled beholding her 'walking like Venus, the gentle wind blowing her fair hair about her pure cheeks like a nymph', but it was no use. He eventually regained access to the court, if not to the queen's favour, but he never obtained permission to appear there with his wife. This episode illustrates Queen Elizabeth's complex demands upon men – young and handsome ones, of course.

Steeped in the rules of courtly love, Elizabeth took no account of differences in age. That she should arouse amorous feelings seemed quite normal to her. That she should not yield to a young man was in accordance with chivalresque conventions; that she expected absolute and palpable fidelity was less so; and that she should inflict undue punishment for a misdemeanour, an urge for independence, was less so still. In the Middle Ages a knight's love for his lady was meant to be platonic; it left him free to marry and raise a family. This did not suit Elizabeth. Although she refused herself, she was too conscious of the indeterminate, delightful zone between the platonic and the carnal to be content with a disembodied love and refrain from demanding total devotion and constant attendance.

Age had not subdued her emotional temperament. She needed the excitement of a passion, the warmth of a male presence, the impetuosity of an admiring gesture, the surprise engendered by an unexpected gift, the shared pleasure of dancing or the chase, the certainty of having inspired genuine love. She herself, however, retained her freedom. Amused, entertained and charmed, yes; conquered, never. She did not allow her feelings to influence her judgement. Her intellect remained as steely as ever. And, to the surprise of the naive, the romantic old lady's emotions did not prevent her from doing her job. Just as she never lost her head, so she was never tempted to sacrifice the interests of the state to her admirers' vanity or ambition. Personal charm was no passport to the Council.

Only men of genuine intellectual ability sat round the table at which England's destinies were decided. In the closing years of the century, however, gaps had appeared in their ranks: Walsingham, Dudley, Shrewsbury and Hatton were dead. William Cecil continued to soldier on despite the gout that often kept him away from meetings. Although his son Robert proved a competent replacement, the queen could not resign herself to dispensing with her old minister. She consulted him ceaselessly, sending him files and awaiting his replies. For him, and him alone, she reserved the solicitude worthy of a daughter. Once, during a lengthy ceremony at Oxford, she interrupted her address in Latin to ask, in English, that a chair be brought to spare Cecil the discomfort of standing, then resumed her speech without faltering. She had relied on his advice for so long, it seemed impossible to her to do without it, and she told him one day that she hoped she would not outlive him. This brought tears to the old man's eyes. Elizabeth, too, wept for her lost youth and the loneliness of her latter years.

Already within her orbit, however, was a man who would enable her to savour once more the pleasures of an ardent friendship – short-lived pleasures only, for she soon felt threatened yet again by the dangers latent in an affair of the heart.

12

Essex, or the Irresistible Appeal of Youth

1590–8

The death or retirement of her old advisers did not prompt Elizabeth to change her mode of government. She had always had two types of men in her service: the respectable, reliable, conscientious pen-pushers of whom William Cecil, nicknamed 'the Queen's mind', had been the prime example; and the more glamorous, aristocratic and amusing young blades – men of the Renaissance devoted as much to the art of poetry as to military exploits. Of these the closest to her heart had been Robert Dudley. In 1590 the pen-pushers acquired a new chief in the person of Cecil's son. Not the elder, who lacked sufficient intelligence for the job, but the younger, Robert, who was born to be a pen-pusher. He was hunchbacked, having been dropped by his nursemaid and left with permanent curvature of the spine. Unfit to bear arms and engage in athletic pursuits, he received a wholly academic education centred on politics. His father, who had recognized his intellectual ability, groomed him to become his successor.

Robert Cecil was also interested in the arts and enjoyed socializing, in fact he liked to gamble heavily. But, although wittier and more light-hearted than old William, he was just as assiduous. 'Pygmy', as the queen called him (affectionately, one hopes), took to working at his father's side and gradually replaced him. His physical appearance exempted him from those flirtatious games which Elizabeth found so necessary, and which required such perseverance on the part of suitable candidates. Instead of wasting his time on dancing attendance on her, he got through a prodigious amount of work, and the queen, in her wisdom, fully appreciated this. His father had instilled a basic principle in him: a minister must never fail to form an opinion but must not change it in order to please the queen, that being an offence against God. On the other hand, he owed his sovereign absolute obedience. Elizabeth required her ministers to take an independent view of things. She was not afraid to argue if differences arose, but if she held to her decision she wanted it unhesitatingly respected.

On Walsingham's death, Robert Cecil inherited his responsibilities but not his post and emoluments. Although he had to wait another six years before obtaining the title of Secretary, he was appointed to the Council in 1591 and rapidly acquired a preponderant influence. He was described in 1594 as walking through the Presence Chamber on his way to the queen 'like a blind man, his hands full of papers and head full of matter'.[1] By the end of her reign he was 'the greatest councillor of England…without whose favour little good is done here.' He was 'in the greatest credit, the Queen passing the most of the day in private and secret conference with him'.[2]

To counterbalance Cecil, Elizabeth needed a glamorous 'blade', a man capable of acquitting himself as brilliantly at social functions as at the head of his troops. In an attempt to reconstitute the William Cecil-Robert Dudley duo, she turned to the Earl of Essex, Dudley's stepson and Lettice Knollys's son by her first marriage. Although Elizabeth had hated Lettice ever since she married her beloved Robert, she did not extend that antipathy to her son. Being the grandson of Sir Francis Knollys, a member of the queen's very first government, and of her cousin Catherine Carey, young Essex was, as Dudley used to say in jest, a member of the tribe of Daniel, in other words, of the queen's own family. His paternal line, star-studded with numerous marriages to Plantagenets, glittered with antiquity. His father had ruined himself in Ireland in Elizabeth's service, and she had not forgotten her debt to him. When the latter died at Dublin in 1576, he entrusted his nine-year-old son to her and William Cecil. The boy was brought up in Cecil's home in company with his son Robert, who was four years older. The two youngsters, so dissimilar in their tastes and talents, had never been close, but William Cecil's affection for Essex and the latter's respect for the old man were never disputed.

Robert Dudley brought his stepson to court in 1584, then took him over to the United Provinces to instruct him in the arts of war and practical diplomacy. On returning to England the young man made a promising debut at court. The queen's memory of his father stood him in good stead, and Dudley introduced him into her immediate circle. His personal charm and urbane ease of manner did the rest. He won the approval of Elizabeth's courtiers and the friendship of the queen herself.

Captivated within a few weeks by his gaiety, wit and high spirits, she became besotted with him. They were soon inseparable. She demanded his constant attendance everywhere, in her royal apartments, in garden and forest. He went hunting with her. They galloped to the same rhythm, for she still rode with remarkable vigour for a woman in her fifties. She would dance with no one else, having retained the love for energetic galliards that had so impressed Melville, Mary Stuart's ambassador, during his first sojourn in London. Finally, she discovered to her great delight that Essex was not averse to spending whole nights gaming and gossiping with her. Elizabeth's dislike of retiring to bed before dawn exhausted her entourage, but the young earl tirelessly kept her company. After an evening at the theatre they would return to the palace and play interminable hands of cards. According to a manservant of his, Essex used to return home 'at the hour when the birds were beginning to sing'. His youth, coupled with the charm of a new face, helped Elizabeth to overcome her melancholy at the tragic death of Mary Stuart. Before long she could not do without him. Six months after the young man's arrival in London she assigned him an official apartment in the palace of Whitehall* and appointed him Master of the Horse like Robert Dudley thirty years before. There, analogies between the two men end.

Robert Dudley had always played the part of a chivalrous devotee, a role whose vocabulary and manner he had mastered perfectly. Submission to his royal mistress came naturally to him because he acknowledged her intellectual superiority and never questioned her political pre-eminence. He knew that, like his father and grandfather before him, he owed his advancement entirely to the Tudors. It is also conceivable that the memory of their execution had infused him with greater than usual respect for sovereign authority. Last but not least, he and the queen had been linked since their youth by a genuine, loving friendship. He had no doubt that, in happier circumstances, she would very probably have married him, and that certainty made it easier for him to pay her compliments and tributes without the smallest reservation. Never in the course of their long relationship had the queen suspected him of pursuing a political agenda of his own. 'He is my creature,' she had said of him in the old days, and she was right.

---

*A royal favour that did not exempt Essex from maintaining a large house in London.

The situation with Essex was altogether different. The product of another generation, the self-assured, triumphant generation that had defeated the Spaniards, he had no memory of the instability and uncertainty that had prevailed at the beginning of Elizabeth's reign. With the reckless confidence of youth, he believed that, whatever he did, he would always persuade the queen to forgive him. He very soon discovered that he had only to threaten to leave court for her to yield to his whims and importunities.

The queen's youthful courtier, who failed to appreciate her complex personality, regarded her merely as an ageing, rather pathetic coquette. He was adept at flattering her in his letters and in the sonnets he dedicated to her. To cite only one example of his prose style: 'If my horse could run as my thoughts do fly, I would as often make mine eyes rich in beholding the treasure of my love as my desires do triumph when I seem to myself in a strong imagination to conquer your resisting will.'[3] He also exploited the effect of the paintings he commissioned as gifts for her. One of them depicted a young man wearing the black and white of Elizabeth's tiltyard colours and the doleful expression of a jilted lover, leaning against a tree garlanded with wild roses. To those who knew how to interpret such symbols, and no one was better at this than Elizabeth, the tree represented constancy and the wild roses, her favourite flowers, were an attribute of Venus. But, although Essex excelled at this game, he rather despised the queen for enjoying it and failed to discern that the pleasure the old lady derived from his badinage and ridiculous compliments belied her remarkable intelligence and experience, her prudence, perseverance and unshakeable authority.

At the end of her reign Elizabeth governed a country where internal peace had established order and the rule of law, generated increasing wealth and enabled England to set its sights on the outside world. A reckless and wildly ambitious young man like Essex failed to realize how much he owed to the condition of his country, and thus to his sovereign's policy. Nor did he appreciate her immense prestige in Europe. She continued to work hard, and Noël de Caron, the ambassador of the United Provinces (whom Elizabeth nicknamed 'Charon' because he was forever asking her to sacrifice the lives of more English soldiers), reported that her conversation, which dealt with economic conditions in the Netherlands, problems in Ireland and the likelihood of Henry IV's conversion to Catholicism, was still diverse and interesting.[4]

Elizabeth scored a personal triumph during an audience she granted to the Polish ambassador, a magnificent personage attired in a long black velvet robe with gold and diamond buttons. Addressing the queen in Latin, the ambassador subjected her to a thoroughly undiplomatic tirade in which he fiercely accused her of dealings contrary to his country's commercial interests. She listened to him in astonishment.

Then, when he had ended his diatribe, she drew herself up to her full height. '*Expectavi orationem mihi vero querelam adduxisti*,'* she said ironically, and went on to extemporize a voluble and vehement Latin response laced with sarcasm. The diplomat withdrew in confusion, and the queen, turning to her courtiers with a broad smile, observed that she was still capable of resurrecting her Latin, which had become somewhat rusty over the years.

Hurault de Maisse, Henry IV's ambassador, confessed to being surprised by the scope of Elizabeth's knowledge and, more especially, by the intelligent use she made of it.[5] He had, however, been taken aback by the ageing queen's appearance: 'Her white dress, embroidered with silver, had big slashed sleeves lined with red taffeta. Attached to it were other, narrower little sleeves that hung down to the ground. The queen kept removing and replacing them, forever talking and twisting them. Her dress was cut very low and left her breasts bare. The front of the dress was unbuttoned, and one could see the whole of her bosom. She held the cleavage open with both hands, as if she were too warm, so that one could see her whole midriff down to the navel.'

On another occasion she received him in a dress open like a coat to reveal her withered bosom and some vestiges of her past beauty, which she blithely exposed to her visitor's

---

*'I expected you to treat me to a truly disputatious speech.'

curious and startled gaze.* 'On her head she wore a garland of the same material, and beneath it a great reddish-coloured wig with a great number of spangles of gold and silver, and hanging down over her forehead some pearls, but of no great worth. On either side of her ears hung two great curls of hair, almost down to her shoulders and within the collar of her robe, spangled like the top of her head. Her bosom is somewhat wrinkled. [...] As for her face, it is and appears to be very aged. It is long and thin, and her teeth are very yellow and uneven...and on the left side less than on the right. Many of them are missing, so that one cannot understand her easily when she speaks apace.'[6]

Thus, and thus alone, was how Essex and his youthful companions saw their sovereign. They could not have been more mistaken. To smirk at the queen's appearance was an understandable shortcoming; to underestimate her keen intelligence and political acumen was a fatal error. Elizabeth wisely refused to contemplate an all-out war because England could not have sustained the requisite effort. Despite the opposition of her dashing blades – Raleigh, Drake and

---

* It was customary at the Tudor court for young women to wear dresses which we would consider indecently low-cut. Not being married, Elizabeth felt she still belonged to their number. Paul Hentzner, a German visitor, noted with surprise that 'her bosom was uncovered, as all the English ladies have it before their marriage'.

Essex among others – she imposed a policy that was more defensive than offensive in character. Her aim was to erode Spain's naval power so as to prevent a reappearance of the Armada, maintain a Protestant presence in the Netherlands without necessarily driving the Spaniards out, and obtain a share of the West India trade. These limited ambitions were justified by equally limited resources, both of money and of manpower. Although opposed to open aggression, however, Elizabeth gladly authorized swift, clandestine, piratical raids that were easy to disown.

Her subjects now excelled in this field. The regular voyages made by Spain's colonial fleet, which was laden with gold and silver from the Americas or spices and precious stones from the East Indies, presented an easy target to fast English ships operating on behalf of syndicates financed by various partners. Elizabeth often participated in these ventures on her own account. The government never intervened, and she was careful not to notify her councillors in order to preserve the unofficial nature of this activity. All the English freebooters had to do was to lie in wait for their prey in the waters around the Azores archipelago, through which the Spanish ships had to pass.

In 1589 ninety-one prizes were taken, substantially swelling the queen's coffers. Philip II was so incensed that in 1590 he cancelled the annual crossing and brought about a series of disastrous bankruptcies in Spain. In 1591 he protected his convoy with an armed escort. Undeterred by this, the queen's pirates assembled at the rendezvous in time to pick off the stragglers. Essex took an enthusiastic part in these expeditions. Elizabeth reluctantly permitted him to go, but the truth was, he forced her hand. One year he had the effrontery to join Drake without telling her in advance, but his real ambition was to command an army.

Despite her unwillingness to commit troops on the Continent, the queen could not refuse to support Henry IV, who was desperately striving to occupy the throne that had fallen to his lot.* Essex, intoxicated by the prospect of taking part in a military campaign, begged her to have faith in him. She remained unconvinced. He returned to the attack three times, pleading his case on his knees. She considered him too impetuous to be entrusted with the command and maintained her refusal until persuaded by Cecil that Essex would make an effective commander if accompanied by a good staff.

So he left for France at the head of four thousand men. In communicating her decision to Henry IV, Elizabeth stated that the young man had 'more need of reins than spurs'. That the campaign was not a success was less the fault of Essex than of King Henry, who tried to mollify her with the gift of a baby elephant, which was ill received; it would grow big and cost her dear, she complained. But, although Essex

---

*Henry III had been murdered in 1589. In the absence of any direct male heir, he was succeeded by his cousin Henry of Navarre, who took the name Henry IV. Being a Protestant, he was unacceptable to many of his French subjects. After four years of civil war he embraced the Catholic faith and the gates of Paris were finally opened to him in 1593.

had not displayed the qualities of a superior strategist, he had endeared himself to his officers and men. Traditionally, a commander had the right to reward an officer for prowess in action by knighting him on the spot – a privilege seldom exercised because Elizabeth was anxious not to debase such an honour. Essex dubbed no less than twenty-four of his companions, not for gaining a glorious victory, but because they had displayed alacrity. This pretext was so ludicrous, it conveyed the impression that his motive had been to create a personal following. Infuriated by her protégé's irresponsible and profligate behaviour, Elizabeth peremptorily commanded him to return forthwith.

She made no attempt to ruin him, however. Unwilling to risk an impulsive outburst on his part, she treated him with unwonted forbearance. To attribute her indulgent attitude to amorous sentiment seems absurd. The queen was no longer a woman prepared to surrender to sensuality, but she continued to be an enthusiastic proponent of courtly love, that is to say, an exquisite blend of devotion, respect and admiration. It is unlikely that Essex aroused her sexually as Seymour had aroused her as an adolescent or Dudley as a young woman. Her response to his unauthorized marriage to Walsingham's daughter is an indication of this. She had reacted with fury to Dudley's marriage, which she considered treason; Essex's independent action earned him a scolding, nothing more. Her attitude towards her rebellious young favourite was more like that of a mother aware of her child's potential, fearful of his petulance and tantrums, eager for him to succeed, and torn between severity and leniency. Although Essex could make her melt with tenderness, she was conscious of his shortcomings and did not abandon hope of remedying them. Elizabeth was never maternally affectionate to the young women in her entourage, but the young man who had irrupted into her life on the threshold of old age touched her heart and enlivened her fundamentally lonely existence. Consequently, she decided to put her faith in Essex despite his dangerous tendency to indiscipline, of which she was only too well aware, and appointed him to the Council in 1593. Given that he was only twenty-seven, why did she accord him such an honour?

His reluctance to follow orders, coupled with a certain recklessness and lack of perseverance, betokened an immaturity that could sometimes lead him astray. On the other hand, his courage and powers of leadership worked in his favour, as did his undeniable intellectual brilliance and family connections. What was more, he represented the party of the future, the aggressive and adventurous spirits in opposition to the older, more level-headed men ranged behind Robert Cecil. The queen had no objection to arguments and lack of unanimity in Council. She would listen to both sides, then make her decision. Besides, Essex did his best to justify her faith in him by becoming more serious. She was not alone in having taken a gamble on him. Essex had acquired an adviser of the highest quality in Francis Bacon, a maternal cousin of Robert Cecil's and son of Sir Nicholas Bacon, Elizabeth's erstwhile Lord Keeper of the Great Seal.

In 1576, at the age of fifteen, Francis Bacon had accompanied Sir Amyas Paulet during his ambassadorship in France and remained at his side for two-and-a-half years, a productive period that afforded him an opportunity to observe a foreign court at first hand, sit in on diplomatic negotiations and complete his education. This was when he became friendly with Thomas Phelippes, the master cryptographer who had entered Walsingham's service during Mary Stuart's latter years. Having become initiated into the subtleties of espionage at the highest level, he began by sending some much appreciated reports to his uncle, old William Cecil. Recalled to England on the death of his father, he decided to study law and was then elected to Parliament. He broadened his knowledge, but his career hung fire despite the intellectual brilliance that was destined to make him one of the greatest Renaissance philosophers. The queen bore him a grudge for having delivered a speech opposing some taxation she deemed necessary, and his uncle was more concerned to further his son's career than that of his nephew, so he had to make his own way in life.

Bacon's observation of Essex had convinced him that the young earl possessed great promise, and that if he managed to curb his natural impetuosity he could occupy a predominant position in the realm. The favourite's career was not all plain sailing. He had to be constantly in attendance and ready to thwart the intrigues of envious rivals. It took time, knowledge and imagination to prepare himself for meetings of the Council, come up with novel solutions and present a more martial, muscular policy than that of the Cecils, father and son. This meant that Essex needed friends, advisers and supporters – in short, a faction, since people did not speak of political parties at this period. To be well-informed on every level was the prime necessity, not only from a personal point of view but in order to gain the ear of the queen.

Bacon correctly estimated that, if Essex managed to acquire a network of personal informants, he would greatly strengthen his position. Walsingham had held his own for so many years because nothing that happened in England and Europe escaped him. In order to match him, Francis employed a trump card in the person of his brother. Anthony Bacon had lived in Europe for many years, during which time he had made many contacts and formed close friendships, not only with Protestants – he remained in constant touch with Henry IV and the great theologian Théodore de Bèze – but with Catholics as well. Montaigne thought so highly of Anthony that he corresponded regularly with him and his mother, Lady Bacon. Hitherto, Cecil and Walsingham had fed on this inexhaustible source of intelligence. When Francis introduced his brother to the earl, they took to each other at once. Quite capable of appreciating the Bacon brothers' formidable intellects, Essex offered them his friendship. From now on the stream of information, facilitated by a brisk correspondence, was diverted from the Cecils to Essex. The queen appreciated the quality of the information she received. Intelligence lay at the very heart of her policy, so she welcomed the fact that, thanks to Essex, she learned things that not even the Cecils knew. One of the secrets of her authority was an ability to boast of being the best-informed person in her realm. She could not, therefore, depend on a single source and was quite happy to encourage competition in this sphere.

Francis stated that Essex's affairs then became 'In a sort my vocation. I did nothing but devise and ruminate with myself...of anything that might concern his Lordship's honour, fortune or service.'[7] He drafted the earl's correspondence, composed the occasional verses required for the entertainments he staged for the queen's delectation and gave him well-weighed advice, drawing on his knowledge of parliamentary custom, his familiarity with problems of foreign policy, and, above all, his knowledge of the queen's psychological make-up. Among leading servants of the Crown – Francis Bacon's milieu, in other words – an understanding of Elizabeth's *modus operandi* was absolutely essential. Bacon strove to convince Essex of this.

He kept telling the earl that he was impetuous by nature and enjoyed a measure of popularity thanks to his spells in the army. To a monarch, and especially to a queen of Elizabeth's temperament, there could be no more dangerous combination. He urged Essex to try to admire her opinions sincerely and request favours for the pleasure of yielding with good grace if she denied him – to renounce all outward marks of military authority and seek civilian posts unconnected with the army, which were more remunerative in any case. Last but not least, said Bacon, Essex must reduce his expenditure. Unless he was seen to be more economical, the queen would expect him to ask her to subsidize him more heavily and suspect that he cherished wider ambitions.

But Essex lacked discipline. He ran up debts. In his defence, it must be said that maintaining one's position as a royal favourite cost a great deal of money. The queen's insistence on sartorial elegance was no joking matter, and her male courtiers had to renew their wardrobes annually at vast expense. Gaming, an unavoidable pastime at court, consumed whole fortunes. Finally, Essex had to keep up his large London residence, on which all petitioners for places and pensions converged. A favourite was honour-bound to demonstrate his influence by obtaining favours for his friends, his kinsmen and dependents. Although the queen had been generous to the young earl, no one who knew her would have failed to realize that she kept a strict account of her disbursements. Elizabeth's affection for Essex did not make her unmindful of her frugal principles. When she eventually asked him to repay a loan he resigned himself to giving her one of his manor houses in lieu. Touched by this gesture, she granted him the right to collect the duty payable on sweet wines imported from the Mediterranean area: the muscats,

Frontignacs and lachryma Christis so popular at this period. This post was of substantial benefit to him, not only because of the sums it yielded but because it constituted a guarantee of further loans. Relieved and flushed with success, Essex forgot that the farm of sweet wines was bestowed for a term of only ten years and continued to push his luck.

He not only sought positions for all his friends but pestered the queen relentlessly when she would not accede to his demands. He wanted Francis Bacon to have the post of attorney general, which she was reserving for a more experienced and suitable man. One night, when he had raised the subject for the umpteenth time, she sent him home and told him to go to bed if he could talk of nothing else. 'Wherefore in a passion I went away,' he wrote to Bacon. 'Tomorrow I will go hence of purpose, and on Thursday I will write an expostulating letter to her.'[8] He was behaving like a spoilt child, and the more he raged the more Robert Cecil's influence grew.

One of his gravest errors was to fail to appreciate the queen's spirit of independence and accept that no one wielded a decisive influence over her. Whenever she refused him a favour – an appointment for one of his clients, say – he persuaded himself that this setback was the work of some enemy, Robert Cecil being the person he most often held responsible. He was wrong, in fact. In vain did old William Cecil explain to Essex that his own authority and that of his son derived solely from their ease of access to the queen and the opportunity it gave them to present their arguments. Essex refused to believe this and made enemies to no purpose. Worse still, he construed every royal rebuff as a personal insult and would leave court swearing never to return. The queen would then recall him and they would make it up, only to start all over again. 'By God's death!' she exclaimed one day. 'It was fit that some one or other should take him down and teach him better manners, otherwise there would be no ruling of him.'⁹

Essex's vagaries and tantrums led to a polarization at court: some were for him, others against, and the divisions he created had political repercussions. Until now, political disagreement had not implied personal animosity. 'Among councillors there may and must rise, by way of argument, divisions in opinion ... and oft doth without causes of mislike at all.'¹⁰ The tensions engendered in Council impaired the government's efficiency because personal feuds precluded rational discussion. At one meeting, during which some extremely delicate negotiations with France and Spain were being debated, Essex cast reason and moderation to the winds and advocated all-out war, whereas most of his fellow councillors favoured an accommodation. Old William Cecil, though deaf and crippled with rheumatism, had lost none of his intellectual acuity. Incapable of smoothing his former ward's ruffled feathers, he ended by holding a psalter under his nose, pointing to the last verse of Psalm 55 and enjoining him to read it: 'The blood-thirsty and deceitful men shall not live out half their days.' Elizabeth did not intervene or lose her temper, merely looked on in silence, convinced that Essex would eventually quieten down and justify her faith in him.

In the ensuing years he obtained command of various naval expeditions. In 1596 he jointly commanded an English flotilla charged with reproducing Drake's success of 1587 and attacking the Spaniards in Cadiz itself. He accomplished the first part of his mission. The English took the port by surprise, paralysed its defenders by setting fire to the big galleons at anchor there, and sacked the town. But, although England had asserted its naval supremacy hundreds of miles from home and Spain had been humbled, Essex did not complete his task. He failed to negotiate a ransom for the Spanish merchantmen bottled up in the inner harbour, which were eventually scuttled, and neglected to intercept some ships returning from the West Indies. Finally, he boosted his personal popularity tenfold by distributing the proceeds of the raid among his men instead of reserving them for the Crown. Elizabeth, who sought no glory for herself and regarded a costly campaign as a failure, was not impressed.

In 1597 she nonetheless permitted him to sail for Ferrol, a Galician port near La Coruña, charged with taking the place and destroying the fleet at anchor there. A rebellion had broken out in Ireland, and it was feared that the King of Spain would send some troops to reinforce it. Jointly commanded by Essex and Raleigh, the expedition proved a disaster, partly because of the terrible storms that raged throughout that summer. The weather off the French coast was so bad that Raleigh considered his men too exhausted to attack the Spaniards on their own ground, so he decided to sail for the Azores to intercept the Spanish colonial fleet. Thanks to lack of coordination between the English commanders, the Spaniards managed to slip through their cordon unscathed. Essex learned on his return that, had the Spanish fleet not been dispersed by the same storms that had rendered navigation impossible in the Bay of Biscay, it would have appeared off the English coast. The queen expressed her displeasure, whereupon Essex retired to the country to sulk. He missed a parliamentary session, refused to attend the Council, and even avoided taking part in the celebrations held to mark the queen's accession on 17 November, pleading illness. Although distressed by his absence, Elizabeth would not give way. It was not until December 1597, after a rift lasting four long months, that William Cecil effected a reconciliation between them.

The lull lasted only until mid-July 1598, when another storm broke out over who should take command in Ireland. The queen wanted to give the job to an uncle of Essex's, Sir William Knollys; Essex, not wanting to deprive himself of his kinsman's support at court, put forward another name and clashed violently with Elizabeth. Overcome with fury when she rejected his suggestion, he contemptuously turned his back on her. She, in turn, was so staggered by his insolence that she caught hold of him and slapped his face.

At that, the unthinkable happened: in a towering rage, Essex clapped his hand to his sword and shouted that he refused to tolerate such an affront and indignity from any woman. The two of them were hastily separated, and Essex, still vituperating, was hustled outside. He left for the country the same night. Incorrigible as ever, however, he wrote to Elizabeth accusing her of having 'broken all the rules of affection and gone against the honour of her sex'. Fearful of the queen's reaction – although she was, in fact, temporarily relieved at being rid of her hot-headed favourite and made no attempt to punish or even reason with him – his friends all counselled moderation and the absolute necessity of self-control and submission to the sovereign's will. 'Remember, I beseech you,' wrote his uncle, Knollys, 'there is no contesting between sovereignty and obedience. [...] Without her love you will be susceptible to the tongues of your enemies.'[11] Lord Keeper Egerton also tried to calm the young man down: 'Policy, duty and religion enforce you to sue, yield and submit to your sovereign.' Essex not only refused to heed this advice but was presumptuous enough to question the divine right of kings. 'When the vilest of all indignities are done unto me, doth religion force me to sue? Or doth God require it? Is it impiety not to do it? What, cannot princes err? Is an earthly power or authority infinite?'[12] Even to ask such questions was dangerous.

Elizabeth's continued failure to react was attributable to a sad preoccupation – perhaps the most distressing of her reign: William Cecil was dying. Although he had managed to leave his chamber to attend two Council meetings early that summer, he was compelled to take to his bed at the end of July. Elizabeth wrote him affectionate little notes but begged him not to reply because it hurt him so much to hold a quill, inquired after his state of health several times a day, and haunted his bedside, where she fed him a little gruel with, as he put it, 'her own princely hand, as a careful nurse'[13] – one of the feminine touches that so endeared the queen to her servitors. Cecil breathed his last on 4 August 1598, a few weeks before his old enemy Philip II. His last thoughts were of his sovereign, the queen who had summoned him to her side fifty years before, whom he had never left, and whom he still remembered as a vivacious young woman with long auburn hair. 'I hope to be in heaven,' he told his children, 'a servitor for her and God's Church.'[14]

Elizabeth closeted herself in her chamber and wept bitterly at the news of his death, but she could not afford to grieve for long: her army in Ireland had suffered a crushing and humiliating defeat. Affairs of state took precedence over self-communion.

13

𝔗𝔥𝔢 𝔖𝔢𝔱𝔱𝔦𝔫𝔤 𝔖𝔲𝔫

1598–1603

n 1560, only two years after Elizabeth came to the throne, the Earl of Sussex had warned her of the danger Ireland represented to her kingdom. An independent and hostile Ireland could serve as a base for her enemies, notably the Spaniards, and facilitate an invasion of England. Forty years later, as the century drew to a close, that warning was no less topical or relevant. Ireland remained as virulent and intractable a problem as ever. It was divided between four provinces, which were ruled by feudal chieftains, and the Pale, the English-occupied territory around Dublin. The viceroy, who represented the queen, wielded no real power. Guerrilla warfare, motivated less by religious or nationalistic considerations than by cultural differences, had steeped the island in blood for generations. The civil administration the English strove to impose on the Irish was as incomprehensible to the latter as the Irish way of life seemed unfathomable to the former.*

---

*Ireland, which had been converted to Christianity by St Patrick, occupied a

The truth was that the English regarded the Irish as a race of savages whose sole contribution to the public good was their whisky. The armed raids launched by the Irish and the repressive measures taken by the English were characterized by unimaginable brutality. The English justified their scorched earth policy, which included the indiscriminate slaughter of women, children and old men, by pleading the impossibility of waging a conventional war. They were dealing with an enemy who never joined battle on terrain suited to the deployment of infantry and cavalry. The Irish took advantage of their forests and bogs to mount ambushes, slit terrified soldiers' throats and disappear without trace.

On returning home, the survivors told of incidents so frightful that they discouraged potential replacements. The English found it so difficult to recruit soldiers for service in Ireland, and so hard to prevent them from deserting during the inevitable confusion attendant on embarkation or disembarkation, that they were reduced to employing Irish mercenaries – who themselves were tempted to desert at the earliest opportunity and return home with their weapons and the

---

unique intellectual status in Europe between the sixth and eighth centuries. Flourishing monasteries, scholars of great erudition, superbly illuminated manuscripts, spirited epic poems – all these helped to create a brilliant civilization. Then came the Danish and Norwegian conquest, the founding of the earliest Viking settlements, and a fierce struggle between the Scandinavian invaders and the indigenous Gaels. Their bloodthirsty rivalry led to cultural extinction. In 1166 a clan chieftain appealed for help to King Henry II of England. This marked the start of the English plantation and the problems that have dogged Ireland for eight centuries.

fruits of their military training. 'Pacification' proved illusory, as in all colonial wars, and every spell of relative peace was succeeded by a new explosion.

Unfortunately for Elizabeth, the end of her reign coincided with the emergence of a great Irish chieftain capable of uniting the clans against England. Hugh O'Neill, Earl of Tyrone, had been brought up in England and remained loyal to the queen for several years before turning against her. He combined a soldier's classical military knowledge with the speed, elusiveness and audacity of a guerrilla fighter. On 14 August 1598 Tyrone ambushed an English general, Sir Henry Bagenal, who had been sent with a substantial force of 3,500 soldiers to relieve the garrison of the Blackwater fort that formed part of Dublin's defences, killing Bagenal himself and 2,000 of his men. Panic reigned in Dublin, now besieged by bands of rebels, and Tyrone remained in complete control of the battlefield. If the Spaniards disembarked and supplied the artillery the Irish lacked, the English would be driven into the sea, so prompt action was required. Essex seized his opportunity.

Essex had not reappeared at court since the scene at the end of July, although he had accompanied Cecil's coffin at his solemn interment in Westminster Abbey, and his face, 'the saddest of the sad',[1] had impressed itself on those present. At news of the Blackwater disaster he wrote to the queen to offer his services and presented himself at Whitehall. She declined to receive him, intimating that he had 'played long enough upon her'; now it was her turn to amuse herself and keep him dangling. He had still not deigned to render her a genuine apology. In September he fell ill, however, and Elizabeth was concerned enough to send him her personal physician, for which Essex wrote her a letter of thanks couched in his most fulsome style. She forgave him and permitted him to return to court, but she did not forget.

Henceforward, her indulgence gave way to emotional detachment. The queen had overcome her feelings once more. Essex had been dealing with the woman in Elizabeth – not a mistress but a mother figure who was quick to smile and forgive; he would now, not that he realized it, be crossing swords with the sovereign in her. He thought he had triumphed yet again – imagined that his popularity with the lower orders had convinced her that it was dangerous to shut him out. And it is true that he was cheered by enthusiastic crowds whenever he rode through the streets. He had captured their imagination with his handsome appearance, his munificence and his courtesy. Won over by his love of literature, Cambridge had offered him the chancellorship. Self-assured and intoxicated by his own success, he ceased to heed Francis Bacon, who advised him yet again not to badger the queen and push himself forward so imprudently. It was not long before Bacon gave up, discouraged by his recklessness and obstinacy, and Essex lost the clearest-headed of his advisers.

He resumed his place in Council and his old habits, notably that of claiming the most remunerative posts for himself. Cecil's death had vacated the Mastership of the Court of Wards.* Elizabeth withheld it from Essex, not wanting to help him to increase his personal following. Cut to the quick, he vented his anger by writing her a letter that verged on insolence. Although she realized the potential danger inherent in a favourite who set himself up as her adversary, it would be a mistake to suppose that she was afraid of him. As she later explained to the French ambassador, the Comte de Beaumont: 'I feared that his impetuous nature and his ambition would embroil him in regrettable plans conducive to his own destruction. I gave him good warning and strongly advised him to cease to displease me and spurn my person with such insolence, and to be careful not to touch my sceptre, for I should be obliged to punish him in accordance with the laws of the realm, since my reprimands had been too gentle to frighten him, and my advice, no matter how affectionate and salutary, had not prevented him from going to his doom.'[2]

---

*The holder of this office acted as guardian of the orphans entrusted to the queen. He had to bring them up and educate them, usually in his own home, but his duties were extremely lucrative. He not only managed their assets and pocketed the income from them but sold them back to his wards when they came of age.

In spite of these skirmishes and after much hesitation, the queen entrusted Essex with command of the English forces in Ireland. This casts doubt on the validity of the reasons for her decision. Why entrust so difficult a mission to a man whose judgement had so often proved controversial? Was it her way of getting rid of an intimate whose appeal had waned and whose moods were getting on her nerves? Is it legitimate to suspect her, as some did, of a more machiavellian motive? A setback in Ireland would put paid to Essex's ambitions once and for all. This is doubtful, to say the least. Elizabeth had too exalted a conception of her role and her responsibilities. She would never have deliberately jeopardized her kingdom to destroy a courtier, and besides, as we shall see, she placed immense resources at his disposal.

Essex owed the appointment to other factors. He had already demonstrated his courage and powers of leadership, even if his various campaigns had not always turned out as well as might have been hoped. More importantly, his popularity gave him an incalculable advantage over the other candidates, who were anyway few in number. Men responded to his name with enthusiasm, and this disposed of the difficulty of raising a large force – an indispensable prerequisite of success. Everyone was eager to serve under Essex. Although the queen had strongly resented his lavish distribution of knighthoods during previous campaigns, his generosity had won him many supporters, all of whom saw him as their guarantee of a great future. Last but not least, he was hell-bent on the appointment – an attitude all the more remarkable because no one had ever disguised the difficulties of the undertaking.

Having made her decision, the queen stuck to it. Essex was briefly beset by doubt once his initial feeling of satisfaction had subsided, as witness a curious letter he wrote to the Earl of Southampton: 'Unto Ireland I go. The Queen hath irrevocably decreed it; the Council do passionately urge it, and I am tied to my reputation to use no tergiversation. And as it were *indecorum* [unbecoming] to slip the collar now, so it were *minime tutum* [thoroughly unsafe], for Ireland would be lost, and although it perished by destiny, yet should I be accused of it, because I saw the fire burn, was called to quench it, and yet gave no help.'[3] At night Essex succumbed to dire imaginings; by day his confidence returned. A victorious campaign would earn him renown, and renown was his supreme ambition. He would not draw back.

Essex was given command of a large, battle-hardened army of 1,400 cavalry and 6,000 foot soldiers, and 2,000 men were earmarked as replacements for the unavoidable losses to come. A treasurer-at-war furnished with considerable sums of money was detailed to accompany Essex to ensure that his troops were promptly paid, nor did the government skimp on arms and ammunition: it had to borrow the necessary funds at ten per cent from the City of London – a higher rate of interest than the queen had ever consented to pay before. The army's departure from the capital was a triumphal occasion.

Its new commander left Essex House on horseback, surrounded by a glittering escort, and headed north-west to the port of Chester, where he embarked. 'All the people left the fields to see him, and he was accompanied by the tears and prayers of many, the queen and some courtiers being offended by the contrast between the favour he enjoyed and that bestowed by the Parisians on the late Duke of Guise.'[4]

When he landed in Ireland, however, Essex's macho self-confidence evaporated. In London he had strongly advocated an immediate attack on Tyrone, O'Neill's fiefdom, and argued against engaging in any diversionary manoeuvres. Once on the spot and surrounded by the survivors of O'Neill's attacks, who gave him alarming reports of the Irish chieftain's skill and the ferocity of his men, he quailed. Without taking the precaution of notifying the Council in advance, he opted for stalling tactics.

Instead of launching himself at the enemy, he undertook a pacification campaign south of Dublin. Defeating a few local chieftains struck him as an easy way of putting the wind up Tyrone and depriving him of support. He did not know Ireland. The English colonists hailed him with joy, made him welcome in their homes and harangued him in Latin, whereas the Irish rebels, unseen and formidably effective, picked off stragglers, lured them into ambushes and enticed the earl's splendid army into the depths of their rain-sodden, slippery, treacherous terrain. Half-naked beneath cloaks of animal hide, their faces enshrouded by shaggy manes of hair, the savage clansmen had no need to give battle. Hundreds of their enemies, exposed to fevers and miasmas, contracted malaria and died. Others went astray in the mist-enshrouded forests and succumbed to ambushes, and still others deserted. Almost imperceptibly, without sustaining any spectacular defeat, Essex lost three-quarters of his force.

The queen was appalled by this news. 'Yet you must needs think that we have the eyes of foreign princes upon our actions and have the hearts of people to comfort and cherish — who groan under the burden of continual levies and impositions which are occasioned by these late actions — can little please ourself hitherto with anything that hath been effected. [...] Your two months' journey hath brought in never a capital rebel. [...] A matter wherein we must note that you have made both us and our Council so great strangers as to this day we know but by reports who they be that spend our treasure.'[5] What worried the queen still more was that Essex preened himself on these military operations and that, although she had forbidden him to, he continued to dole out knighthoods. Her anger was perfectly justified. By ignoring her instructions, Essex was risking military defeat in Ireland and a financial crisis in England.

Stung by the queen's reproaches and feeling that his reputation had been impugned, Essex adopted a precipitate and inexplicable course of action. Although he could put only 4,000 men in the field against the 10–12,000 deployed by Tyrone, he advanced to meet him. The Irishman sent him a messenger proposing a parley. Essex agreed to confer with Tyrone in private, but within sight of his officers. Tyrone rode out into the middle of the small river that separated the opposing forces while Essex, also on horseback, remained on the bank. Two days later a truce came into effect. Elizabeth was apprised of this by a very vague letter from Essex, which she received on 16 September. Extremely concerned by a move that to her smelt of treason, she expressed her dissatisfaction in the strongest terms and ordered him to do nothing before giving her a detailed account of the agreements reached. Essex, completely out of his depth by now, lost his head: he decided to leave for England and explain things to her face to face. Deserting his post without permission was an extremely grave step, but he had nothing more to lose. His panic and desperation were such that they blinded him to reality. One question remains: Was he going to court to beg the queen to forgive him, or to intimidate her?

Essex left Ireland on 24 September, escorted by a large number of officers, and reached London on the 28th. There he learned that the queen was at Nonesuch, some ten miles from the capital. He rode to the palace in haste and arrived at about ten in the morning, his face bespattered with mud. Not pausing to wash and change, he made straight for the queen's apartments and strode into her bedchamber unannounced. Elizabeth had just got up. Wigless and only half-dressed, with grey hair straggling around her weary face, which was still bare of cosmetics, the discomfited old woman's first thought on being confronted by Essex was that he was launching a *coup d'état*, and that the palace was surrounded by a substantial force. Although this seemed the only logical explanation for his tactless intrusion, she reacted with surprising composure. In dangerous situations her instinct never failed her.

Without batting an eyelid or losing her temper, she addressed him kindly, expressed concern at his appearance and suggested that he go and change while she completed her toilette. She summoned him an hour later, still as graciously, and dismissed him only when her midday meal was served. Essex, reassured and delighted by the apparent success of his unheralded visit, went off to eat and regaled his table companions with stories of Ireland and its frightful savages. Meanwhile, messengers dispatched to London by the queen returned with news that the streets of the capital were calm: not the smallest portent of an insurrection could be observed. Reassured, she sent for Essex again, and, changing her tone, got down to brass tacks: Why had he deserted his post? Dissatisfied with his explanations, she sent him to be thoroughly interrogated by the Council. At ten that night he was ordered to be confined to his room.

The interrogation was resumed the next day. He was accused of committing a series of delinquencies: quitting his post without permission, bursting into the queen's chamber unannounced, conducting the Irish campaign ineptly, and knighting dozens of his junior officers without the least justification. Was he endeavouring to create a following composed of men entirely devoted to his service? This last was a serious charge. The queen ordered Essex into the custody of Lord Keeper Egerton. He was conducted to York House, the minister's London mansion, and forbidden to leave or receive visitors. Even his wife was denied access to him. As ever in times of great tension, he fell ill. It was then, to everyone's anger and amazement, that the terms of his accord with Tyrone became known. Among other things, Essex had agreed that all the lands appropriated by the Crown during the previous two centuries should be returned to their original owners. This betrayal could no longer be ignored.

Elizabeth, who had never underestimated the fragility of power, refrained from precipitate action even now. She knew that Essex had retained his popular appeal, and a conversation with Francis Bacon vindicated her prudence. Bacon had abandoned all hope where the earl's political future was concerned. Their erstwhile relationship did not justify his continuing to owe more loyalty to Essex than to the queen, so he was quite candid with her. His affection for the earl did not blind him to his faults, he told her in the course of their first conversation, so he had to concede that Essex was not competent to fill certain posts. Sending him back to Ireland would, therefore, be a mistake. 'Send him back to Ireland?' the queen broke in. 'I would as lief marry you!' No, what she wanted was a judicial hearing, but she was doubtful as to the form it should take. Could the Star Chamber* be considered? That was what she wished to know.

Bacon advised her against a public trial. It would be difficult to adduce indisputable evidence, given that everyone know how many able generals had failed miserably in Ireland. Punishing Essex without solid justification might have the direst consequences. His incompetence and his startlingly inept initiatives had left his popularity intact. He was known to be sick and in solitary confinement. Before long, he would be said to be at death's door. Pamphlets in his favour were being secretly distributed and heated discussions were raging in the streets and taverns. 'Turbulent spirits' claimed that the treatment he had received was 'to condemn a man unheard, and to wound him on his back, and to leave justice her sword and take away her balance, which consisted of an accusation and a defence.'[6] All this agitation persuaded Elizabeth to tread with care. She decided to go to York House and form her own opinion of Essex's state of health, but he was genuinely too ill to speak with her. Accordingly, she had him read a Star Chamber declaration listing his delinquencies and gave orders that the conditions of his detention remain unchanged. Six months later Essex had regained his health but was no more endowed with common sense than before.

---

*The Star Chamber was a court composed of members of the queen's Privy Council, who were at liberty to invite other judges to join them and held their hearings in public. They met regularly to rule on all matters that might disturb the peace of the realm. Thus the Star Chamber and the queen's Council were two different institutions with the same membership.

He imagined that the queen was on the point of pardoning him. A decision had become imperative.

It was prudence rather than magnanimity that spared him the humiliation of a public trial. In June 1600 he was arraigned before a panel of judges and councillors. Kneeling bare-headed, he was charged with desertion and incompetence, with having disobeyed his sovereign's commands and conferred in private with the enemy. After an hour the Archbishop of Canterbury permitted him to rise, then to lean on the table, and finally to sit down on a stool. In the course of this interminable hearing, which lasted for eleven hours without a break, his conduct was dissected by each member of the panel in turn. He was informed that his offences were punishable by life imprisonment, but his admissions and prayers and his obvious repentance earned him clemency. He avoided the Tower. Stripped of all his offices and suspended from the Council, he was placed under house arrest in his own London residence.

Essex, realizing that he owed his salvation to the queen's indulgence, began to hope for a return to favour. He wrote her a series of imploring letters in his old courtly style. To be banished from her presence was to be 'condemned to perpetual night' and consigned to 'a sepulchre'. He redoubled his efforts: 'Haste, paper, to that happy presence, whence only unhappy I am banished; kiss that fair correcting hand which lays new plasters to my lighter hurts, but to my greatest wound applieth nothing.'[7] Elizabeth appreciated his style but was undeceived by it. She read the letter to

Bacon, adding in a disillusioned tone: 'What I took for the abundance of the heart I find to be only a suit for the farm of sweet wines.'[8]

Essex had failed to grasp that, susceptible to flattery and receptive to adulation as she could be, the queen never in the long run allowed herself to be ruled by sentiment. She had held Dudley at bay and resisted the insane temptation to marry Alençon. Her forbearance and indulgence towards Essex had been excessive, perhaps because the feelings he aroused in her were purer, but the spell was finally broken. She did not renew his farm of sweet wines, which she had granted him ten years earlier. This enraged Essex, who promptly abandoned all pretence of chivalry. The queen's mind, he told his friends, was 'as crooked as her body'.[9] He was now disgraced, ruined, infuriated, and a potential threat to her. She had agreed to spare him exemplary punishment and leave him at liberty despite her justifiable anger, whether out of lingering affection or fear of public disapproval. Her suspicions had been aroused, however, and the course of events was to prove them warranted.

Essex, whose grip on reality had never been very secure, proceeded to entertain the wildest schemes. He got it into his head that Robert Cecil was encouraging the Spanish Infanta, Philip II's daughter, to succeed Elizabeth, so he established contact with James, King of Scotland, and warned him of this. He offered to persuade Lord Mountjoy, who had been appointed commander-in-chief in Ireland after his departure, to bring the army home, thereby reinforcing his own position in the Council and enabling him to secure James's accession. Mountjoy, who was naturally cautious and on the point of re-establishing order in Ireland in any case, refused to engage in such a venture purely 'to satisfy my Lord of Essex's private ambition'.[10] Essex then proceeded to recruit a cabal of noblemen by holding out the prospect of ousting Cecil and putting their clique in power, boasting that his mere presence would be enough to silence the queen. However, his fantasies were becoming so notorious and absurd that he was soon reduced to the company of 'sword men, bold, confident fellows, men of broken fortunes, discontented persons and such as saucily used their tongues in railing against all men'. This led to his being summoned before the Council. When he declined to appear, pleading an indisposition, the queen sent four councillors to compel him to do so.

They reached the courtyard of Essex House to find it thronged with wildly excited men. When they confronted the earl on his doorstep and demanded an explanation, he replied that his life had been threatened and that his 'friends' had gathered to defend him. He invited the councillors into his library, whereupon his servants locked the doors. Trapped, the queen's representatives could hear his supporters baying for their blood in the courtyard below. Then silence fell: Essex had sallied forth into the street accompanied by a vociferous escort some two hundred strong.

He hesitated to set off for the palace of Whitehall, where Elizabeth was residing, at the head of such a meagre band. Convinced that he would recruit more supporters in the City, he made his way there. But people in the streets merely evinced surprise when he urged them to join him in combating a plot hatched by Cecil and his friends against the queen, the Church and himself, and they were equally unmoved when he shouted to them that the English Crown had been 'sold to Spain'. Thoroughly perturbed, Essex attempted to retrace his steps but found his route barred by the militia. He managed to reach the Thames and returned home by boat.

Meantime, the four councillors had been released by a member of his household who had either taken fright or come to his senses. This left Essex without any bargaining counters. Early that afternoon his mansion was surrounded by government troops under the command of the Earl of Nottingham. Called upon to surrender, Essex replied that he would 'the sooner fly to Heaven'. Nottingham then threatened to blow up the house. Essex eventually yielded at ten o'clock that night, when he emerged with a few loyal followers and surrendered his sword. The queen, who had vowed that she would not retire to bed until she knew Essex had been taken prisoner, was informed without delay.

She had remained surprisingly calm throughout the day, reassured by the sight of hundreds of armed men converging on the palace to defend her and camping around it all evening. When the members of her entourage were briefly alarmed by erroneous reports of an uprising in the City, 'she never was more amazed than she would have been to have heard of a fray in Fleet Street,'[11] Cecil reported, filled with pride and admiration for his elderly sovereign. Boissise, the

French ambassador, who went to the palace to congratulate her on Henry IV's behalf, found her undismayed at the events provoked by that 'mad ingrate'. In recounting them, 'she fell to laughing and jeering at the earl's progress through the city. [...] If he had come towards her, as people said, she had resolved to go forth and confront him, in order to know which of the two of them ruled. [...] In such cases, she added, one must banish all idea of clemency and adopt the most extreme measures.'[12] She then proceeded to discourse on a variety of topics in a carefree manner that won the Frenchman's admiration.

Elizabeth had demonstrated yet again that authority knows no gender. She had often annoyed those close to her by being too soft with Essex, by hesitating and changing her mind. Her quirks and crotchets had convinced him that he was dealing with a woman, a weak woman who would bow to a stronger will, but he failed to realize that no one had ever dominated Elizabeth either intellectually or emotionally. She had enough self-confidence to enjoy intellectual duels and brave contradiction, and she was too aware of the importance of her role to yield to temptations of the heart like poor Mary Stuart. Essex did not understand that Elizabeth had no need to play at being a man. She liked to project a feminine image that varied according to circumstances, ranging from the mistress to the virgin, from the sprightly dancer to the hieratic idol displaying itself to adoring crowds. But when her authority was threatened – as it was during the northern earls' rebellion, the Armada's onset or Essex's attempted *coup d'état* – every trace of feminine frailty vanished and she sloughed off her complex, ridiculous veneer of cunning, affectation and coquetry. What remained was a courageous and determined woman who readily wielded as much authority as the father she had always admired. It could even be argued that she possessed more natural authority than the latter, because hers was not based on fear or gratuitous cruelty.

Elizabeth, who been so reluctant to put the Duke of Norfolk to death and had so often postponed Mary Stuart's execution, did not intervene once Essex and Southampton, his chief accomplice, had been tried and condemned by their peers. The earl pleaded that he had only meant to warn the queen against her councillors, but this defence was easily demolished by the prosecutors. He was unanimously convicted of treason and the queen signed his death warrant the next day. Essex reacted with misplaced insouciance, going so far as to say that he would not demean himself by 'making any cringing submission' in order to obtain the queen's clemency. Some hours later, however, after his chaplain had threatened him with the fires of hell if he died unrepentant, he gave way. Having sent for Cecil and three other ministers, he made a detailed confession. He did not ask the queen for a stay of execution. On the contrary, he conceded that she would never be safe while he lived. The only favour he asked was not to be executed in public for fear, so he said, that the populace would cheer him. Handsome as ever, with his fair hair blowing about his shoulders and attired in a doublet with long scarlet sleeves, he mounted the scaffold on 25 February

1600. He displayed extreme contrition. 'My sins are more in number than the hairs of my head,' he declared. 'I bestowed my youth in pride, lust, uncleanness, vainglory and divers other sins.' For these failings he craved forgiveness of the Almighty, and 'especially for this my last sin, this great, this bloody, this crying and infectious sin whereby so many for love of me have ventured.'[13] The priest suggested that he recite Psalm 51, but after the second verse he broke off and cried: 'Executioner, strike home!' He was still commending his soul to God when the axe came down. Picking up the bloody head, the executioner displayed it to those present with a cry of 'God save the Queen!' A messenger dispatched to Whitehall to confirm that the execution had taken place found the queen seated at her virginals. She received the news in silence. No one spoke. Moments later she resumed playing.

Elizabeth pardoned some other conspirators, telling James VI that she was 'not so unskilful of kingly rule that I would wink at no fault'. She also winked at Cecil's correspondence with the Scottish king. The question of the succession, which had exercised people so often throughout her reign, no longer arose. Everyone knew that James would succeed her and that the queen wished it so, but that she would not announce it during her lifetime. Her certainty that naming a successor was the surest way of uniting malcontents still held good. She often mentioned Essex and always wore a ring he had given her, but although she regretted the manner of his death she never questioned the justice of his execution.

'Those who touch the sceptres of princes deserve no pity,'[14] she remarked to the French ambassador when Henry IV was faced with a conspiracy on the part of his faithful companion Marshal Biron. It came hard, as she knew from experience, but monarchs had to be able to sacrifice all personal affection when the safety of their realm and their successors was at stake.[15]

The closing years of a reign are a melancholy time. Elizabeth was now regarded as a hardy survivor. Although in good health, she was not unaware of her declining powers. She still danced the galliard, still enjoyed the chase and never appeared in public other than decked out in all her finery. But, alert and energetic though she could still be, her vitality was waning. In private the façade crumbled, disclosing the elderly woman she had become. When she appointed Egerton Lord Keeper she remarked that he would be the last of her reign. 'God forbid, madam,' Cecil exclaimed. 'I hope you will bury four or five more.' Her only response was to burst into tears and take refuge in her bedchamber. Forever at pains to dramatize her public appearances, she transformed the Parliamentary session of 1601 into a premature but nonetheless impressive ceremonial farewell, knowing that it would be her last.

At the end of the session, in the course of which she had had to make some political concessions, she invited a delegation to the palace. At that, a cry went up from 'the lower end of the House', where the younger members were sitting: 'No! All, all, all!' The queen construed their enthusiasm as a token of appreciation for the compromise she had agreed to, so she invited them all, trusting that the Council Chamber would be big enough to accommodate them. Having received them, she delivered what became known as her 'Golden Speech', in which she welcomed the affection they had shown her: 'I do not so much rejoice that God hath made me to be a queen, as to be a queen over so thankful a people.'[16] The parliamentarians listened to her on bended knee. She bade them rise and continued her address, in which she emphasized how beneficial their community of views and united actions had been. Far from being the speech of an absolute and over-bearing monarch, hers was that of a sovereign grateful for her subjects' assistance and support. All present were visibly affected by the sight of this woman nearing the end of her life as she looked back on a reign of forty years and, far from claiming credit for the blessings of internal peace and national strength, rendered thanks to Providence and the wisdom of her realm's inhabitants. A true artist, she ended by asking her ministers to ensure that every parliamentarian who wished to kiss her hand came forward and did so.

A sort of calm descended on the kingdom. Neither Spain nor Ireland constituted an immediate threat. Fits of melancholy notwithstanding, the queen continued to follow affairs of state and hold court. There was no doubt, however, that her sun was setting and that, as she herself had said so often, the rising sun was the cynosure of every eye. Despite the manifest greatness of her reign, her subjects were looking forward to a male successor.

On 21 January 1603 the queen betook herself to Richmond, the palace where she had been born. On 6 February, smothered in jewels and sumptuously attired in white taffeta embroidered with silver thread, Elizabeth granted an audience to the very first Venetian ambassador to be appointed during her reign. She reproached him for the Venetian Republic's long delay in lively, very personal terms. She was not, she said, 'aware that my sex has brought me this demerit, for my sex cannot diminish my prestige, nor offend those who treat me as other princes are treated.'[17] The ambassador stammered his congratulations on her healthy appearance, to which she made no reply. At the beginning of March, shocked and saddened by the death of the Countess of Nottingham, one of her few remaining old friends, she retired to her apartments, never to leave them again. Her cousin Sir Robert Carey, who came to pay his respects, found her 'sitting low on her cushions' and looking glum. 'No, Robin,' she said in answer to his enquiry, using the affectionate diminutive, 'I am not well.' Still refusing to take any medicine – her rejection of her physicians' advice had long accounted for her good health – she remained silent and pensive. Robert Cecil, who was very concerned, told her that she *must* take to her bed. No one told princes what they 'must' do,[18] she retorted

swiftly. Comte de Beaumont, the French ambassador, came to see her several times. She received him without ceremony, still seated on her cushions, and confessed to feeling prostrated by sorrow and weary of life. All her closest friends were gone; only Essex could have offered her the solace of filial affection, but Essex had betrayed her and no member of the younger generation had taken his place. Her loneliness matched her greatness. She remained like this for ten days, refusing to lie down or eat but drinking to relieve the dryness of her mouth and throat and sucking her forefinger. On 21 March she finally consented to go to bed. Archbishop Whitgift, her 'little black husband', as she called him, never left her bedside. She clasped his hand and seemed to find his voice and prayers soothing, but although she remained conscious she never spoke. When Robert Cecil sought her formal consent to James's accession, she made no response, neither by word nor by gesture; faithful to her policy of silence to the last, she said nothing. She died peacefully at three o'clock on the morning of Thursday, 24 March 1603, 'like a ripe apple from the tree', as her physician put it.

A courier galloped off into the darkness, bound for Scotland, where James received the news three days later. Early that morning Robert Cecil convened the Council to draft a proclamation announcing the queen's death and the Scottish king's accession to the throne of England. He read it out first on the green at Whitehall, then in front of St Paul's Cathedral, and a third time at Cheapside Cross. The ministers then proceeded to the Tower and demanded admittance in the name of King James I. The doors were duly opened. There were no public disturbances. James promptly wrote Cecil a letter authorizing the members of the Council to retain their posts and continue to transact current business. This peaceful transfer of power was a final vindication of Elizabeth's prudent policy of inaction. She had scored yet another triumph from beyond the grave.

Epilogue

The Scottish king's first act on becoming James I of England was to request the Council for sufficient funds to enable him to make a befitting entrance into his new kingdom. He was immediately sent £5,000 in gold and £1,000 in silver, together with some jewels, various ceremonial robes encrusted with pearls, and the late queen's wardrobe for his wife, Anne of Denmark. To enhance his prestige, he was also sent six geldings and a coach plus four spare horses. On 5 April, leaving his pregnant queen and his five children to their preparations, James set off from Edinburgh alone. He took a month to reach London. In the meantime, at a spectacular funeral service in Westminster Abbey, Queen Elizabeth had been laid to rest beneath the altar of the chapel built by the founder of the Tudor dynasty, Henry VII.

James I was too shrewd not to bend the past in a direction that suited him. He paid homage to Elizabeth, his political mother, and emphasized the legitimacy of his accession by commissioning a magnificent funerary monument in honour of her memory, but he also took the opportunity to reorganize the layout of the tombs in the abbey. Elizabeth's coffin was removed from its place of honour and transferred to the tomb of Mary Tudor. The two sisters now shared the same vault, but the white marble effigy represented Elizabeth alone, wearing

the robes reserved for the opening of Parliament and holding
the sceptre in her right hand and the orb in her left. More
significant still, the king sent to Peterborough Cathedral for
the remains of his natural mother, Mary Stuart, and accorded
her an even more imposing monument than that of Elizabeth.
James I's conscience was not too clean where Mary was
concerned, and he knew that his acquiescence in her execution
did not redound to his credit. Glossing over Mary Stuart's
guilt and representing her as a victim certainly did not excuse
her, but it did at least regild his ancestry and erase some of the
blemishes of the past. James also banned publication of those
parts of William Camden's *Annals* that dealt with his mother's
trial and execution.* The rewriting of history had begun.

Posthumous honours leave their impress and bear fruit.
Mary's criminal passions and political intemperance were
gradually forgotten, until all that people remembered were
the captive queen's misfortunes and death. Her horrific
execution by the headsman's axe gained an overpowering
hold on the popular imagination, especially as the victim
was a woman. This had not escaped Elizabeth, who many
times told her ministers, when they urged her to be uncom-

---

*William Camden, a scholarly historian born in 1553, wrote a complete
history of Elizabeth's reign. The final text appeared in 1629, the chapters
dealing with Mary Stuart having been watered down to suit the king.

promising, that a woman who ordered the death of another woman would seem monstrous to posterity. She was right to regard her cousin as a formidable enemy to punish by reason of her sex. Jules Michelet, referring to Mary Stuart and Marie Antoinette, emphasized this proven truth: '[Women] are often guilty; they are morally responsible; and yet, curiously enough, *they are unpunishable.* Woe to the government that sends them to the scaffold; it will never be pardoned for so doing. He that strikes them strikes himself; he that punishes them punishes himself.'[1]

It is true that the effect of Mary Stuart's execution was to rehabilitate her in the years following her death. In direct opposition to the person of Elizabeth, she gradually emerged as an essentially feminine figure, a victim of her own sensitivity, of the brutality of the outside world and her inability to wield the harsh and implacable authority required of a sovereign. Strangely, it was in Protestant England and Scotland that her memory first re-established itself. In England, as we have seen, this was attributable to the influence of James I, who, in order to uphold his legitimacy and, in particular, to prohibit any mention of Riccio, banned any work inimical to his mother's private life. In Scotland Mary regained her reputation by becoming the symbol of a vulnerable kingdom subjugated by England. Her folly and acts of violence were forgotten, and so was her subjects' unanimous wish to rid themselves of an incompetent queen; all that lingered in the memory was the image of a beautiful young princess cruelly put to death by her rival. In France, once religious disputes and the Guises' political ambitions had been quelled, Mary's legend was promoted by the poems of Ronsard and du Bellay and a whole dramatic industry. A plethora of tragedies appeared with Mary as their captive protagonist. French plays of the seventeenth and eighteenth centuries blithely skirted the Darnley and Bothwell episodes and concentrated on Norfolk's fatal passion – in fact they sometimes spiced up the horror by making the lovers (who never met) die on the same scaffold.

This wholly fictional heroine continued to win hearts over the centuries thanks to a proliferation of sentimental, pseudo-historical novels. In 1801 a manual for use in the upbringing of girls – one opposed to any ambition that transcended the family circle, of course – cited Mary as a paragon of all the most attractive feminine attributes, those qualities of grace and elegance, charm and gentleness which, by their very nature, rendered a woman incapable of proving her mettle in public life.[2] The adulteress, the accomplice in the murder of her husband and the tenacious and cunning rival had disappeared behind a smokescreen of platitudes and finer feelings.

On a more exalted literary level, that of Sir Walter Scott, Robert Burns and Friedrich von Schiller, Mary underwent another transformation. Her great and abundant passion, her total surrender to the heart and contempt for custom and convention made her the very embodiment of romanticism, her sins being excused by the cruel price she had to pay for them. It was no longer a question of morality; what interested those Protestant writers (just as it did Stefan Zweig, the great Jewish author, in the ensuing century) was not Mary's self-sacrifice in the Roman Catholic cause but her courage and passion. Schiller portrayed her confronting Elizabeth absolved of Darnley's murder by her feminine vulnerability to Bothwell's ardour. With her immutable beauty, erotic fervour and utter aversion to prudence, she triumphed over her English rival, who was portrayed as a patient, cunning, malign spider of a woman. Legend had given way to myth. As immensely successful in England, France and Italy as it was in Germany, Schiller's drama is still regularly performed throughout the world. It not only defined and determined Mary's character throughout the Romantic nineteenth century but continues to do so for a vast number of our contemporaries. This portrait of a woman wholly governed by instinct and emotion was consolidated by Stefan Zweig's conception of her.

Zweig, an extremely talented and experienced biographer, could not bring himself to criticize Mary Stuart in political terms. According to him, her personality was explicable only by her sex. Like Schiller, he made no attempt to acquit her. On the contrary, he did not question the authenticity – disputed by many historians – of Mary's love letters to

Bothwell. 'Mary Stuart as woman was wholly woman, first and last and for always, so that the greatest decisions forced upon her during her brief span took their shape from this deepest well-head of her being…and when she saw herself confronted by a choice between passion and honour her queenship was set aside to give place to the woman who chanced to sit upon a throne. The regal mantle slipped easily from her shoulders, and she stood naked and unashamed, as do so many other women who yield to the ardours of love.'[3] Seduced by his heroine, Zweig excuses all her mistakes and bends an implacable gaze on her rival, who was guilty of being 'not like other women'.[4] Proof of this, he says, can be found in portraits of her, which never display the serenity, candour and pride of a true sovereign. 'We feel that whenever she was alone, having doffed her robe of state and wiped the rouge from her wasted cheeks, there could have been no royal dignity left – nothing but a poor, solitary, uneasy, prematurely aged woman; the tragic figure of one who, far from being competent to govern a world, was unable to master even her own urgent distresses.'[5] Novelists, dramatists and poets will always prefer ardour to prudence and emotion to ambition, even at the expense of historical accuracy. It should be added that Mary Stuart is very exceptional in having, at different periods, inspired some outstanding literary champions whose popularity has not diminished in the course of time. Ronsard and du Bellay, Schiller, Zweig and even Sir Walter Scott are still read today, so her myth has been unceasingly nurtured and reinforced.

Elizabeth did not enjoy the same good fortune. Zweig, following in the footsteps of many others, made himself the spokesman of a tradition that assailed her reputation and has submitted her to a centuries-long process of revision whose severity stemmed from her improbable celibacy. Although the virgin queen eventually won the hearts of her subjects, her heirs regarded her as an old maid at best and at worst as a virgin in name alone. For, just as her contemporaries were disconcerted by her frequent pronouncements on the subject of her reluctance to marry, an attitude at odds with custom, so subsequent generations found it hard to reconcile the public figure with the woman. Everyone conceded that her personal authority would have been impaired by marriage, but how could any woman – any true woman – have sacrificed love and the joys of intimacy and motherhood for the sake of political power? Her femininity must have concealed some hidden vice. From the eighteenth century onwards, the chastity so inseparable from her charisma was no longer considered a virtue but the consequence of some physical malformation that enabled her to lead a scandalous private life. It was even insinuated that a male child had been substituted for little Princess Elizabeth, who had died young, and that the queen was consequently a man.

Her reputation was damaged still further by the accession of Queen Victoria in 1837. Victoria, a loving young wife who produced nine children in quick succession, enjoyed no real political power and inspired no fear in her own or the opposite sex. Elizabeth, an absolute monarch and desexualized figure, was vulnerable to criticism on two counts. It was not enough to condemn her in the name of eternal womanhood; her absolute power, not only legitimate but wielded with invariable moderation, was adjudged to be that of a usurper. One explanation for this hardening of opinion is that the first half of the nineteenth century was the period that witnessed the earliest stirrings of modern feminism. Needless to say, any progress in this respect was opposed by the overwhelming majority of the British people, Queen Victoria included. At one with their monarch, who considered her own position anomalous and laid stress on the effort it cost her not to 'go against common sense and decency',[6] the English were doubly reluctant to entertain an impartial conception of an all-powerful woman's glorious reign.

In the succeeding generation, enthusiasm for the baroque figure of Elizabeth was restricted to a little clique of Bloomsbury intellectuals in quest of an antidote to the Victorian climate. Virginia Woolf, in particular, was captivated by her teasing sexual ambivalence, her aptitude for playing the woman but reigning like a man, her relations with Dudley, Alençon and Essex, and, last but not least, her court, where men with the most alluring codpieces sported long hair and sparkling earrings and strutted around in doublets of elaborately embroidered silk. However, public opinion did not always agree. It was another half century before Elizabeth regained a dignity more in keeping with historical reality.

Although the present Queen Elizabeth, flanked by her husband and children, still conformed to the Victorian model at the outset of her reign, she evinced absolutely no desire to be compared to her glorious ancestor. Her Christmas address to the Commonwealth in 1953, broadcast from New Zealand, contained the following comment on the tendency to refer to her reign as a new Elizabethan age: 'Frankly, I do not myself feel at all like my great Tudor forebear, who was blessed with neither husband nor children, who ruled as a despot and was never able to leave her native shores.'[7]

Setting aside the fact that Elizabeth was invariably respectful of the parliamentary game of her day, so it was unfair to describe her as a despot and foolish to accuse her of insularity, it must be stated that her royal namesake's remarks did not accord with public opinion at home in England. To judge by films, historical novels and biographies on the subject, attitudes there were beginning to change. Women had long since acquired a full range of rights including the right to lead a life of their own choosing. They were gaining access to a wide variety of professions, and marriage and motherhood had ceased to be the ideal to which all aspired. Elizabeth I, who had governed her kingdom masterfully without a husband's support, seemed a forerunner worthy of emulation. The wind had veered, influenced less by literature than the cinema.

Thus the 1955 film starring Bette Davis, *The Virgin Queen,* ends with Elizabeth self-sacrificingly renouncing her love for Dudley. The final sequence shows the queen fighting back her tears as she walks to her desk with consummate dignity. Fifteen years later, notably in the BBC's six-episode television series in which Glenda Jackson scored a great success in the leading role, the queen was no longer defined by her various lovers, but by the major political crises that marked her reign. We are no longer confronted by the libidinous, hysterical, unstable Elizabeth of the nineteenth century, but by a modern woman – a strong woman – who quite rationally puts her remarkable career before all else.

'If Mary Stuart has remained somewhat ossified in her role as a pathetic victim, it may be because few female readers of historical novels and few playgoers or filmgoers care to identify with the Mary of the nocturnal murder at Kirk o'Field or the instigator of the foolish conspiracies at the end of her reign. Moreover, Mary is a figure always painted in black and white, either guilty or innocent.* Generally unfavourable during her lifetime, opinions of her mellowed after her execution. Her impulsive and disastrous marriages

---

*It was not until 1987 that an excellent and extremely fair biography of Mary Stuart appeared in France (Michel Duchein, *Marie Stuart* (Fayard)). Some years later the author gave free rein to his imagination but observed the distinction between the two genres by publishing a novel about his heroine

destroyed her career but failed to erode her legend. This was principally because, to a sentimental public, nothing is more admirable than amorous passion.

Elizabeth's complexity and originality have precluded such clear-cut verdicts. Interpretations of her character, both contemporary and posthumous, have been infinitely diverse, mainly because she never truly revealed herself. She was secretive about her feelings for her mother, her bizarre plan to marry Dudley to Mary Stuart, her flirtation with Alençon and her forbearance towards Essex. No one in her entourage ever ventured an explanation of those mysteries. She was described but not analysed. Finally, her subjects accepted, without necessarily understanding it, her refusal to bow to a woman's lot and marry. The surprising thing is that this decision benefited her not only during her reign but, after a very, very long wait, in the eyes of posterity.

ℜotes

1 The Bastard Princess

1. Report by Soranzano, 1554, in A Baschet, *La Diplomatie vénitienne au XVIe siècle* (Plon, Paris: 1862) p 121. The description of Elizabeth appears on p 128.

2 Mary Tudor: An Object Lesson

1. See G R Elton, *England under the Tudors* (Methuen & Co., London: 1969) pp 214 f.
2. Calendar State Papers, XII, p 162 (hereafter CSP), quoted in P Johnson, *Elizabeth I* (Holt, Rinehart & Wilson, New York: 1974) p 45, hereafter 'Johnson'.
3. Archives of Venice, quoted in A Somerset, *Elizabeth I* (Anchor Press, New York: 1991) p 53, hereafter 'Somerset'.
4. CSP, Spanish (1558–67), p 25, quoted in S Doran, *Monarchy and Matrimony. The Courtships of Elizabeth I* (Routledge, London: 1996) p 24, hereafter 'Doran'.
5. CSP, Spanish, p 372, quoted in Johnson, p 59.
6. Elizabeth, *Collected Works,* ed. L S Marcus, J Mueller and M B Rose (University Press of Chicago, Chicago: 2000) p 51, hereafter Elizabeth, *Collected Works*.
7. Elizabeth, *Collected Works*, p 52; speech of 20 November 1558.
8. Count de Feria's report, 14 December 1558, quoted in Somerset, p 57.
9. Speech by Sir Nicholas Bacon at the opening of Parliament on 25 January 1559.

3 The 'Reinette'

1. Letter from Throckmorton to Queen Elizabeth dated January 1561, quoted in A Fraser, *Mary Queen of Scots* (Delacorte, New York: 1970) p 110, hereafter Fraser.
2. Brantôme, *Sur la reine d'Écosse,* in *Œuvres complètes* (Bibliothèque de la Pléiade, Paris: 1991) p 80.
3. Fraser, p 162.
4. Fraser, p 162.
5. Johnson, p 105.

4 Handsome Dudley

1. Johnson, p 65.
2. T Thomson, *Sir James Melville, the Memoirs of His Own Life* (J S Stevenson, London: 1929), quoted in Johnson, p 111.
3. N Williams, *All the Queen's Men* (Macmillan, New York: 1972) p 70.
4. A Plowden, *Lady Jane Grey, Nine Days Queen* (Sutton, Stroud: 2003) p 158.
5. Elizabeth, *Collected Works*, p 73.
6. Elizabeth, *Collected Works*, p 81.
7. Catherine de Médicis, *Lettres,* ed. H de La Ferrière-Percy and G Baguenault de Puchesse, in *Documents inédits sur l'Histoire de France* (Imprimerie nationale, Paris: 1880–1943) II, p 256, hereafter Catherine de Médicis, *Lettres.*
8. D Wilson, *Sweet Robin, Robert Dudley, Earl of Leicester, 1553–1588* (Allison & Busby, London: 1997) p 83.
9. CSP, Spanish, pp 262–3, quoted in C Read, *Mr Secretary Cecil and Queen Elizabeth* (Knopf, New York: 1955) p 198, hereafter Read, *Mr Secretary Cecil.*
10. CSP, Spanish, pp 262–3, quoted in Read, *Mr Secretary Cecil*, p 198.
11. A Weir, *The Life of Queen Elizabeth* (Ballantine, New York: 1998) p 121, hereafter Weir, *Life of Queen Elizabeth.*
12. J E Neale, *Queen Elizabeth* (Harcourt Brace, New York: 1936) p 80, hereafter Neale, *Queen Elizabeth.*
13. Neale, *Queen Elizabeth*, p 82.
14. J E Neale, *Elizabeth and Her Parliaments* (Jonathan Cape, London: 1953–7) p 109, hereafter Neale, *Elizabeth and Her Parliaments.*

5 Mary Marries

1. CSP, Scotland, quoted in Fraser, p 261.
2. Fraser, p 263.
3. Fraser, p 227.
4. J Melville, *Memoirs of His Own Life* (London: 1929).
5. J M Herries, *Historical Memoirs of the Reign of Mary, Queen of Scotland, and a Portion of James Ist* (R. Pitcairn, Edinburgh: 1836).
6. Fraser, p 286.
7. Fraser, pp 309–10.
8. Fraser, p 310.

6 Political Assassination or Crime of Passion?

1. V von Klarwill, *Queen Elizabeth and Some Foreigners* (John Lane, London: 1928) pp 208–9, quoted in Doran, p 79.
2. CSP, Scotland, II, p 254, quoted in Fraser, p 284.
3. P F Tytler, *History of Scotland* (Edinburgh: 1870) II, p 400.
4. Fraser, p 278.
5. A Labanoff, ed., *Lettres, instructions et mémoires de Marie Stuart, reine d'Écosse* (C. Dolman, London: 1844) I, pp 374 f, hereafter Labanoff.
6. R K Marshall, *Queen of Scots* (Mercat, Edinburgh: 1986) p 131.
7. A Plowden, *Two Queens in One Isle. The Deadly Relationship between Elizabeth I and Mary Queen of Scots* (Sutton, Stroud: 1999) p 114, hereafter Plowden, *Two Queens*.
8. Neale, *Queen Elizabeth*, p 154.
9. L Marcus and J Mueller, ed., Elizabeth I, *Autograph Compositions and Foreign Language Originals* (University of Chicago Press, Chicago: 2002) pp 126–7, hereafter Elizabeth I, *Autograph Compositions*.
10. *Letters and Poems by Mary Stuart, Queen of Scots* (Philosophical Library, New York: 1947) Sonnet IX, p 68.
11. Labanoff, II, p 3.
12. Fraser, p 312.
13. Fraser, p 315.
14. Plowden, *Two Queens,* p 125.
15. H Fleming, *Mary, Queen of Scots* (Edinburgh) p 454.
16. Fraser, p 374.

17. A Teulet, *Relations politiques de la France et de l'Espagne avec l'Écosse au XVIe siècle* 3 vols (Plon, Paris: 1862) II, p 127, hereafter Teulet.
18. Teulet, p 130.

7 Lochleven

1. Elizabeth, *Collected Works,* p 119; letter dated 27 June 1567.
2. Neale, *Queen Elizabeth,* p 139.
3. Neale, *Queen Elizabeth,* p 139.
4. Labanoff, II, p 117.

8 An Unwelcome Visitor

1. A Plowden, *Danger to Elizabeth* (Sutton, Stroud: 1999) p 13, hereafter Plowden, *Danger*.
2. Plowden, *Danger*, p 15.
3. Neale, *Queen Elizabeth,* p 163.
4. Letter from Knollys to Cecil dated 14 July 1568, quoted in Read, *Mr Secretary Cecil,* p 404.
5. Labanoff, II, pp 129–30.
6. The Duke of Norfolk and Lady Dacre each had four children when they married. When the duchess died the duke became guardian to her sons and daughters. Since the two broods intermarried, this concentrated immense wealth in his hands.
7. Stefan Zweig, *The Queen of Scots* (trans. Eden and Cedar Paul) (Cassell (Hallam ed.), London: 1950) p 339, hereafter Zweig.
8. N Williams, *Thomas Howard, Fourth Duke of Norfolk* (Dutton, New York: 1965) p 141.
9. Plowden, *Danger,* p 86.
10. Elizabeth, *Collected Works,* p 125; letter dated 26 February 1570.
11. CSP, Scotland, p 684; quoted in Johnson, p 174.
12. P Chevallier, *Henri III* (Fayard, Paris: 1985) p 141.
13. Chevallier, *Henri III*, p 43.
14. Chevallier, *Henri III*, p 43.
15. J Spedding, *Life and Letters of Francis Bacon*, 7 vols (Longman, London: 1861) I, pp 97–8, hereafter Spedding.

16. Catherine de Médicis, *Lettres,* V, p 103; letter dated 10 November 1574.
17. Labanoff, III, p 6; letter dated December 1569.
18. Labanoff, III, p 19.
19. Labanoff, III, p 31; letter dated 19 March 1570.
20. Elizabeth, *Collected Works,* p 131.
21. Neale, *Elizabeth and Her Parliaments,* pp 263–4.
22. Neale, *Elizabeth and Her Parliaments,* pp 263–4.
23. Neale, *Elizabeth and Her Parliaments,* pp 263–4.

9 A Final Effort

1. *Elizabeth I and the Three Goddesses,* 1569, painting attributed to Hans Eworth in the Royal Collection and reproduced in *Elizabeth, the Exhibition at the National Maritime Museum* (Chatto & Windus, London: 2003) p 190, hereafter *The Exhibition at the National Maritime Museum.*
2. *'Pelican' Portrait of Queen Elizabeth I,* c. 1574, attributed to Nicholas Hilliard, Walker Art Gallery, Liverpool.
3. Neale, *Queen Elizabeth*, p 234.
4. Neale, *Queen Elizabeth*, p 233.
5. Neale, *Queen Elizabeth*, p 233.
6. Catherine de Médicis, *Lettres,* IV, p 103; letter dated 10 November 1574.
7. Johnson, p 110.
8. Catherine de Médicis, *Lettres,* VI, p 112; letter dated 9 November 1578.
9. Letter reproduced in Catherine de Médicis, *Lettres,* VI, p 203.
10. Weir, *Life of Queen Elizabeth,* p 320.
11. Catherine de Médicis, *Lettres,* VI, p 112.
12. Letter from Mauvissière dated 7 September 1579, quoted in C Read, *Mr Secretary Walsingham and the Policy of Queen Elizabeth,* 2 vols (Cambridge: 1925) II, p 19, hereafter Read, *Mr Secretary Walsingham.*
13. Weir, *Life of Queen Elizabeth*, p 322.
14. Weir, *Life of Queen Elizabeth*, p 323.
15. Historical Manuscript Commission, II, p 265, quoted in Somerset, p 310.

16. *Sur le départ de Monsieur,* in Elizabeth, *Collected Works*, p 302.
17. Elizabeth I, *Autograph Compositions*, p 152.
18. Read, *Mr Secretary Walsingham*, II, p 6.
19. Catherine de Médicis, *Lettres,* VI, p 374.
20. Catherine de Médicis, *Lettres*, VI, p 348.
21. Read, *Mr Secretary Walsingham*, II, p 45.
22. Read, *Mr Secretary Walsingham*, II, p 61.
23. Walsingham's correspondence in D Digges, *The Compleat Ambassador* (London: 1655), quoted in Read, *Mr Secretary Walsingham,* II, p 60.
24. Johnson, p 258.
25. Johnson, p 260.
26. Johnson, p 261.
27. Elizabeth, *Collected Works*, p 261.
28. Neale, *Queen Elizabeth*, p 252.

10 The Execution

1. F de Zulueta, *Embroideries by Mary Stuart and Elizabeth Talbot at Oxburgh Hall,* (1923), and M Swain, *Needlework of Mary* (London: 1973). The little monkey is preserved at the Victoria and Albert Museum, London, and reproduced in *The Exhibition at the National Maritime Museum,* p 226.
2. Labanoff, VI, p 51; letter dated November 1584.
3. Elizabeth, *Collected Works,* p 325; speech delivered on 30 July 1588.
4. Elizabeth, *Collected Works, passim.*
5. Labanoff, VI, p 181; letter dated 10 July 1585 addressed to M. de Mauvissière, the French amabassador.
6. Labanoff, VI, p 217; letter dated 6 September 1585.
7. Châteauneuf, *Mémoires,* in Labanoff, VI, p 151.
8. Manuscript preserved at the Public Record Office, Kew, and reproduced in *The Exhibition at the National Maritime Museum,* p 220.
9. Labanoff, VI, p 291.
10. Labanoff, VI, p 288.
11. Read, *Mr Secretary Walsingham*, II, p 23.
12. Read, *Mr Secretary Walsingham*, II, p 23.

13. Read, *Mr Secretary Walsingham*, II, p 38.
14. Fraser, p 570.
15. This description of the scene is taken from Bourgoing's journal, in R Chantelauze, *Marie Stuart, son procès et son execution* (Plon, Paris: 1876).
16. Elizabeth, *Collected Works,* p 284; letter dated August 1586.
17. Read, *Mr Secretary Walsingham,* II, p 52; letter from Walsingham to Cecil dated 6 October 1586.
18. Read, *Mr Secretary Walsingham,* II, p 53.
19. Elizabeth, *Collected Works,* pp 201–2; the queen's address to Parliament on 24 November 1586.
20. Elizabeth, *Collected Works,* pp 201–2; the queen's address to Parliament on 24 November 1586.
21. Elizabeth, *Collected Works,* p 292; letter from James VI to Elizabeth dated 26 January 1587.
22. J Morris, *Letter-books of Sir Amias Paulet* (London: 1874) p 361.
23. H Nicolas, *Life of Davison* (London: 1823) p 103.
24. Labanoff, VI, p 492; letter to Henry III dated 8 February 1587.
25. C Read, *Lord Burghley and Queen Elizabeth* (Knopf, New York: 1960) p 378.
26. Neale, *Queen Elizabeth*, p 276.
27. Elizabeth, *Collected Works*, p 296.

11 Elizabeth Triumphant

1. Johnson, p 226.
2. Johnson, p 236.
3. Johnson, p 248.
4. Cf. H Harrington, *Nugae Antique* (1779), in Johnson, p 233.
5. Neale, *Queen Elizabeth,* p 282.
6. C Martin and G Parker, *The Spanish Armada* (Norton, New York: 1988) p 165.
7. Elizabeth, *Collected Works,* p 326; speech on 9 August 1588.
8. C Hibbert, *The Virgin Queen, Elizabeth, Genius of the Golden Age* (Addison-Wesley, Reading: 1991) p 125.

12 Essex, or the Irresistible Appeal of Youth

1. Letter from Anthony Standen to Anthony Bacon, in T Birch, *Memoirs of the Reign of Queen Elizabeth* (London: 1754), quoted in Johnson, p 367.
2. Letter from Rowland Whyte to Sir Robert Sydney, quoted in Johnson, p 367.
3. Somerset, p 472.
4. Johnson, p 367.
5. De Maisse's diary quoted by L A Prévost-Paradol, *Élisabeth et Henri IV, 1595–1598,* (Michel Lévy, Paris: 1863) p 234.
6. Prévost-Paradol, *Élisabeth et Henri IV*, pp 166, 210 and 230. See also J Arnold, *Queen Elizabeth's Wardrobe Unlock'd* (Maney, Leeds: 1988) p 8.
7. C D Bowen, *Francis Bacon, the Temper of a Man* (Little, Brown, New York: 1963) p 68.
8. Spedding, I, p 289.
9. Somerset, p 477.
10. Somerset, p 502.
11. Neale, *Queen Elizabeth,* p 348.
12. Somerset, p 519.
13. Letter from William Cecil to Robert Cecil, in Johnson, pp 375–6.
14. Letter from William Cecil to Robert Cecil, in Johnson, pp 375–6.

13 The Setting Sun

1. Spedding, III, p 146.
2. Birch, *Memoirs of the Reign of Elizabeth*, II, p 506.
3. Johnson, p 392.
4. Laffleur de Kermaingant, *Mission de Jean de Thumery, sieur de Boissise* (Paris: 1886) p 483, hereafter Laffleur de Kermaingant, *Boissise.*
5. Elizabeth, *Collected Works,* p 392; letter dated 19 July 1599.
6. Somerset, p 536.
7. L Strachey, *Elizabeth and Essex* (Chatto & Windus, London: 1928) p 231.
8. Spedding, III, pp 135–6.
9. Johnson, p 405.
10. Somerset, p 539.
11. Somerset, p 543.

12. Laffleur de Kermaingant, *Boissise,* p 477.
13. Somerset, p 545.
14. Neale, *Queen Elizabeth,* p 388.
15. Neale, *Queen Elizabeth,* p 388.
16. Elizabeth, *Collected Works,* p 337; address on 30 November 1601.
17. Neale, *Queen Elizabeth,* p 391.
18. This account of the queen's last days appears in W Scott, ed., *Memoirs of the Life of Robert Carey, Written by Himself* (Edinburgh: 1808).

Epilogue

1. J Michelet, *Histoire de France* (Marpon & Flammarion, Paris) XII, p 158.
2. J West, *Letters to a Young Lady* (New York: 1806), quoted by M Dobson and N J Watson in *England's Elizabeth* (Oxford: 2002) p 100.
3. Zweig, pp 97–8.
4. Zweig, p 98.
5. Zweig, p 96.
6. Victoria to Gladstone, 6 May 1870.
7. Radio broadcast by Queen Elizabeth II, Christmas 1953.

Brief Bibliography

I Works and letters by the two queens

Elizabeth, *Autograph Compositions and Foreign Language Originals,* ed L S Marcus and J Mueller (University of Chicago Press, Chicago: 2002).

Elizabeth, *Collected Works,* ed. L S Marcus, J Mueller and M B Rose (University of Chicago Press, Chicago: 2000).

Lettres et Mémoires de Marie Stuart, ed. A S Labanoff, 7 vols (C Dolman, London: 1844); supplement by A Teulet, 1859.

Mary Stuart, *Letters of Mary Queen of Scots and Documents Connected with Her Personal History,* 3 vols, ed. A Strickland (London: 1842–3).

Letters and Poems by Mary Stuart, Queen of Scots (Philosophical Library, New York: 1947).

II Contemporary works

Birch, T, *Memoirs of the Reign of Queen Elizabeth,* 2 vols (London: 1754).

Brantôme, P de Bourdelles, abbé de, *Recueil des dames, poésies et tombeaux* (Gallimard, Bibliothèque de la Pléiade, Paris: 1991).

Catherine de Médicis, *Lettres,* ed. H de La Ferrière-Percy and G Baguenault de Puchesse, in *Documents inédits sur l'Histoire de France* (Imprimerie nationale, Paris: 1880–1943).

Chéruel, A., *Marie Stuart et Catherine de Médicis: étude historique sur les relations de la France et de l'Écosse dans la seconde moitié du XVIe siècle* (Hachette, Paris: 1858).

Herries, J. M., *Historical Memoirs of the Reign of Mary Queen of Scots and a Portion of James Ist* (Pitcairn, Edinburgh: 1836).

La Mothe-Fénelon, B de, *Correspondance diplomatique,* ed. C Cooper and A Teulet, 7 vols (Paris/London/Leipzig: 1838–41).

Melville, J, *Memoirs of His Own Life,* ed. J S Stevenson (London: 1929).

III Twentieth-century works

Black, J B, 'The Reign of Elizabeth' in *Oxford History of England* (Clarendon Press, Oxford: 1959).

Davis, G, 'The Early Stuarts' in *Oxford History of England* (Clarendon Press, Oxford: 1959).

Dobson, M, and Watson, N, *England's Elizabeth: An Afterlife in Fame and Fantasy* Oxford University Press, Oxford: 2002).

Doran, S, *Monarchy and Matrimony. The Courtships of Elizabeth I* (Routledge, London and New York: 1966).

Duchein, M, *Marie Stuart* (Fayard, Paris: 1987).

Elton, G R, *England under the Tudors* (Methuen & Co., London: 1969).

Fraser, A, *Mary Queen of Scots* (George Weidenfeld & Nicolson Ltd, London: 1969).

Johnson, P, *Elizabeth I* (Holt, Rinehart & Wilson, New York: 1974).

Neale, J E, *Queen Elizabeth* (Harcourt, New York: 1934).

Read, C, *Lord Burghley and Queen Elizabeth* (Knopf, New York: 1960).

——, *Mr Secretary Cecil and Queen Elizabeth* (Knopf, New York: 1955).

——, *Mr Secretary Walsingham and the Policy of Queen Elizabeth* (Cambridge: 1925).

Somerset, A, *Elizabeth I* (George Weidenfeld & Nicolson Ltd, London: 1991).

Starkey, D, *A Struggle for the Throne* (Harper Collins, New York: 2001).

——, *Elizabeth I: Apprenticeship* (Chatto & Windus, London: 2000).

Weir, A, *Mary, Queen of Scots and the Murder of Lord Darnley* (Ballantine, New York: 2003).

Williams, N, *All the Queen's Men. Elizabeth and Her Courtiers* (Macmillan, New York: 1972).

——, *A Tudor Tragedy: Thomas Howard, Fourth Duke of Norfolk* (Dutton, New York: 1965).

Wilson, D, *Sweet Robin, Robert Dudley, Earl of Leicester, 1553–1588* (Allison & Busby, London: 1997).

Wormald, J, *Mary Queen of Scots. A Study in Failure* (George Philip, London: 1991).

Zweig, S, *The Queen of Scots* (trans. by Eden and Cedar Paul) (Cassell, Hallam Edition, London: 1950).

Who Was Who

Anne Boleyn, Queen of England [1501–36]. Second wife of Henry VIII and mother of Elizabeth. Executed in 1536.

Bothwell, James Hepburn, Earl of [1535–78]. Scottish nobleman who headed the conspiracy that cost the life of Lord Darnley, Mary Stuart's husband. He married Mary in 1567 but was forced to flee from Scotland by the rebel lords and died in captivity in Denmark.

Catherine of Aragon, Queen of England [1485–1536]. Daughter of Ferdinand of Aragon and Isabella of Castile. Was married in 1501 to Arthur, Prince of Wales, and after his death to Henry VIII. In 1516 she gave birth to 'Bloody Mary' Tudor. Henry divorced her in 1533 to marry Anne Boleyn.

Catherine de Médicis, Queen of France [1519–89]. Wife of Henry II and mother of the last three Valois kings. All-powerful regent during the reigns of Charles IX and Henry III.

Catherine Parr, Queen of England [1512–48]. Last wife of Henry VIII. Her excellent relations with her stepdaughter Elizabeth deteriorated after her remarriage to Thomas Seymour.

Cecil, William [1520–98]. Secretary of State and principal adviser to Elizabeth. Ennobled in 1571, he became Baron Burghley.

Charles IX, King of France [1550–74]. Second son of Catherine de Médicis and Henry II. Succeeded his brother Francis II but was dominated by Catherine throughout his reign. Married Elizabeth of Austria but died without issue. The crown then passed to his brother, Henry III.

Darnley, Lord Henry Stewart, Earl of Ross, Duke of Albany and King of Scotland [1545–67]. Son of the Earl of Lennox and Margaret Douglas, he was a grandson through his mother of Margaret Tudor, the widow of King James IV of Scotland whose second husband was the Earl of Angus. He married Mary Stuart in 1565 and was murdered at Edinburgh in 1567. His son James ruled both Scotland and England.

Dudley, John, Duke of Northumberland [1502–53]. Son of Edmund Dudley, a member of Henry VII's Council who was executed by his successor Henry VIII. A privy councillor under Edward VI, John Dudley prevailed over Edward Seymour, the Lord Protector, and endeavoured to get the young king's sisters, Mary Tudor and Elizabeth, removed from the line of succession in favour of Jane Grey, who was married to his son Guildford. He failed utterly and was beheaded for treason.

Dudley, Robert, Earl of Leicester [1533–88]. Son of John Dudley, he did not suffer as a result of his father's machinations and became Elizabeth's longtime favourite. His wife's mysterious death proved an insurmountable obstacle to his marrying the queen.

Edward VI, King of England [1537–53]. Son of Henry VIII and Jane Seymour. During his minority, power was wielded by his uncle Edward Seymour, Duke of Somerset, and then by the Duke of Northumberland, who persuaded him to remove his sisters, Mary and Elizabeth from the succession in favour of his cousin Jane Grey.

Essex, Robert Devereux, Earl of [1566–1601]. Son of Lettice Knollys, whose second husband was Robert Dudley. Elizabeth's last favourite, he attempted a *coup d'état* against her and was executed.

Francis, Duke of Alençon, then of Anjou [1554–84]. Fourth son of Henry II and Catherine de Médicis. Elizabeth's last suitor.

Henry III, Duke of Anjou, King of Poland, King of France [1551–89]. Third son of Henry II and Catherine de Médicis. Succeeded his brother Charles IX in 1574, having been elected King of Poland less than a year earlier. Briefly a candidate for Elizabeth's hand. Murdered in 1589.

Henry IV, Duke of Bourbon, King of Navarre, King of France [1553–1610]. Premier prince of the blood and cousin of the last Valois kings, he married Margaret of Valois in 1572 and inherited the throne of France on the death of Henry III in 1589. Divorced and remarried Marie de Médicis. Father of Louis XIII. Murdered in 1610.

Henry VIII, King of England [1491–1547]. The second son of Henry VII and Elizabeth of York, he came to the throne in 1509. His second marriage to Anne Boleyn resulted in a break with Rome and the establishment of the Anglican Church. He had four more wives after Anne's execution: Jane Seymour, who died in childbirth; Anne of Cleves, divorced; Catherine Howard, executed; and Catherine Parr, who survived him. He had three children: Mary I, Elizabeth I and Edward VI.

James IV, King of Scotland [1472–1513]. His marriage to Margaret Tudor was at the root of the Stuarts' claim to the English succession.

James V, King of Scotland [1512–42]. He forged links with France by marrying first Madeleine, the daughter of Francis I, and then Mary of Guise, on whom he fathered Mary Stuart.

James VI, King of Scotland and King of England as James I [1566–1625]. Son of Mary Stuart and Lord Darnley. He became King of Scotland in 1567 after his mother was accused of being complicit in his father's murder and fled to England, where she was imprisoned and ultimately executed. He inherited the English throne on Elizabeth's death in 1603.

Jane Grey [1537–54]. Eldest daughter of the Duke of Suffolk and Frances Brandon and granddaughter of Charles Brandon and Mary Tudor, younger sister of Henry VIII. Her father-in-law, the Duke of Northumberland, tried to bypass Henry VIII's own daughters, Mary and Elizabeth, and put her on the throne after Edward VI's death. Her 'reign' lasted only nine days and she was executed after a year in captivity.

Margaret Tudor, Queen of Scotland [1489–1541]. Elder sister of Henry VIII. Married first to King James IV of Scotland and then to the Earl of Angus. Grandmother of Mary Stuart by her first husband and of Lord Darnley by her second.

Mary of Guise [1515–1560]. Daughter of Claude of Lorraine. The widow of the Duke of Longueville, she married James V of Scotland, by whom she had a daughter, Mary Stuart. She acted as regent of Scotland after her husband's death.

Mary Tudor, Queen of England [1516–58], popularly known as 'Bloody Mary'. The daughter of Catherine of Aragon and Henry VIII, she succeeded her half-brother Edward VI in 1553. Her marriage to Philip II of Spain in 1554 proved sterile and she died in 1558. Elizabeth succeeded her.

Mary Tudor, Queen of France [1495–1533]. The younger sister of Henry VIII, she married King Louis XII of France. On the latter's death she returned to England and married Charles Brandon, Duke of Suffolk. Grandmother of Jane Grey, the ill-starred nine days' queen, and of Catherine Grey.

Philip II, King of Spain [1527–98]. Son of Charles V and Isabella of Portugal. He married Mary Tudor in 1554, then Elizabeth of Valois, daughter of Henry II, and finally Anne, daughter of Maximilian II of Austria. His long struggle with Elizabeth culminated in the defeat of the Armada in 1588.

Seymour, Edward, Duke of Somerset [1500–52]. He owed his fortune to his sister Jane's marriage to Henry VIII. Appointed Lord Protector on the accession of his under-age nephew, Edward VI, he fell prey to a coup mounted by the Duke of Northumberland and was beheaded like his brother.

Seymour, Thomas, Baron Seymour of Sudeley [1510–49]. Younger brother of Jane Seymour, Henry VIII's third wife, and thus an uncle of King Edward VI. He married Catherine Parr, the queen dowager. On the latter's death he tried to marry Elizabeth while plotting against her brother. He was executed.

Stewart, James, Earl of Moray [1530–70]. Illegitimate son of James V and half-brother of Mary Stuart. He favoured her return to Scotland from France and was the most trusted of her advisers until she married Lord Darnley. He then withdrew from public life but returned to power as regent during her captivity in England. He was murdered in 1570.

Chronology

1533 Birth of Elizabeth Tudor, second daughter of Henry VIII.

1534 Breach between England and Rome.

1536 Death of Catherine of Aragon, first wife of Henry VIII and mother of Mary Tudor. Execution of Anne Boleyn, second wife of Henry VIII and mother of Elizabeth.

1537 Birth of Edward, son of Henry VIII and his third wife, Jane Seymour, who dies in childbirth.

1542 Birth of Mary Stuart. Six days later she accedes to the throne of Scotland on the death of James V.

1547 Death of Henry VIII and accession of his son Edward VI.
Death of Francis I of France and accession of Henry II.

1548 Mary Stuart betrothed to Francis, Dauphin of France.

1549 Mary Stuart arrives in France.

1553 Death of Edward VI. Mary Tudor accedes to the English throne.

1554 Mary Tudor marries Philip of Spain, son of Charles V.

1556 Charles V abdicates in favour of Philip II.

1558 Ferdinand I elected to head the Holy Roman (German-Roman) Empire.

Mary Stuart marries the Dauphin in Paris.

Mary Tudor dies. Elizabeth I accedes to the English throne.

1559 Accidental death of Henry II.

Francis II and Mary Stuart accede to the French throne.

1560 Death of Francis II. Charles IX succeeds him with Catherine de Médicis acting as regent.

Death of Amy Robsart, Robert Dudley's wife.

1561 Mary Stuart returns to Scotland.

1564 William Shakespeare born.

1565 Mary Stuart marries Henry, Lord Darnley.

1566 Birth of James, future King of Scotland and England.

1567 Lord Darnley murdered. Mary Stuart marries the Earl of Bothwell.

1568 Mary Stuart takes refuge in England.

1571 The Holy League defeats the Turks at Lepanto.

1572 Marriage of Margaret of Valois to Henry of Navarre, later Henry IV.

St Bartholomew's Day massacre.

1573 Henry, Duke of Anjou, brother of Charles IX, elected King of Poland.

1574 Death of Charles IX. Henry III abandons Poland and succeeds him.

1576 Death of Titian.

1577 Francis Drake sets out to circumnavigate the globe.

1580 Francis Drake returns to England.

1584 Death of Ivan the Terrible.
Death of Francis of Alençon, son of Henry II,
Elizabeth's suitor.
William of Orange assassinated.

1585 Death of Ronsard.

1586 Babington conspiracy.
Mary Stuart tried and convicted.

1587 Mary Stuart executed.

1588 Defeat of the Spanish Armada.
Death of Robert Dudley.
The Duke of Guise murdered.

1589 Death of Catherine de Médicis.
Henry III murdered.
Galileo appointed professor of mathematics at Pisa
University.
Henry of Bourbon, King of Navarre, becomes King
of France as Henry IV.

1592 Shakespeare stages *Richard III.*

1594 Henry IV finally crowned King of France.
Shakespeare's *Romeo and Juliet.*
Tintoretto dies.

1598 Treaty of Vervins between France and Spain.
Death of Philip II.

1599 The Earl of Essex placed under house arrest after
disgrace in Ireland.
Henry IV and Queen Margaret divorced.

1600 Henry IV marries Marie de Médicis.
Shakespeare's *Hamlet.*

1601 The Earl of Essex executed.
      Birth of Louis XIII.
1603 Death of Elizabeth.
      James VI of Scotland accedes to the English throne
      as James I.

Index

political education, 25; relationship with Thomas Seymour, 26–30, 40, 320; appearance, 26, 33, 94, 231, 288, 316–17; unmarried state, 30, 40, 52, 78, 82, 84–8, 93–4, 129–30, 158–60, 193–4, 283; and Mary Tudor's succession and coronation, 32–3, 44; pleases crowds, 33, 85, 250–1; and religion, 40–1, 52–3, 55–6, 58, 159, 199, 201–2; retires to country, 41–2; reluctance to name successor, 42, 58, 77–8, 88–9, 93–5, 130, 352; summoned to London, 42–3; popularity, 43, 46–7, 54, 214–15, 232–3, 283, 291; imprisonment, 43–8, 98; writes to Mary Tudor, 44–5; political marriage negotiations, 52–3, 86–8, 94, 129–30, 158–60, 193–203, 212, 239; shuns court, 55; accedes to throne, 55–7, 67–8, 234; political compromises, 58; permits Knox's return, 66; introspection, 78; collapses with smallpox, 82, 93; personal authority and political acumen, 83, 214–15, 232–3, 315, 317, 350–1; fertility, 86, 199, 221–2; treatment of Catherine Grey, 89–93; proposes Dudley's marriage to Mary Stuart, 95–6, 104–7; friendship and possible marriage with Dudley, 96, 98–105, 110, 114, 200, 212, 313, 320, 347, 366, 368; and Mary Stuart's marriage with Darnley, 107, 111, 113; fails to intervene in Scotland, 116, 121; and taint of illegitimacy, 126; reaction to Scottish revolt, 127; godmother to James VI, 133; reaction to Darnley murder, 138; letters to Mary Stuart, 157–8, 169; and succession of James VI, 158, 161, 207, 212, 242–3, 253–5, 268, 279, 352, 356–7; discovers potency of virginity, 160, 213; and Mary Stuart's flight

to England, 172–8; and Darnley murder inquiry and Mary Stuart's proposed marriage with Norfolk, 182–6, 189–90; backs Moray, 184–6; defeats rising of northern earls, 190–3, 198, 350; Pope excommunicates, 197, 200, 202; and Norfolk's execution, 206–8, 351; royal progresses, 213–14, 250–1, 284–7; policy over Netherlands, 215–19, 237, 239, 318; negotiates marriage with Alençon, 218–43, 245, 347, 366, 369; and Dudley's remarriage, 223–4; love of late nights, 224, 312; cruelty to Puritans, 232; stages festivities for Alençon, 240–1; letter from Mary Stuart, 249; refuses security measures, 250; understanding of James VI, 254; and Babington plot, 262–6; reluctance to execute Mary Stuart, 266–71, 351; and execution of Mary Stuart, 274, 276–80, 283, 313; attendance at plays and concerts, 287; attendance at divine worship, 288–9; delegation of authority, 290; mastery of public finance, 290–1; counters invasion threat, 295–6, 300–2, 350; and her courtiers, 302–6, 309; relationship with Essex, 312–15, 320–1, 324–30, 335–7, 346–7, 350, 366, 369; rebukes Polish ambassador, 315–16; and Cecil's death, 331; Irish campaign, 338–9, 341–2; confronted by Essex, 342–3; and Essex's rebellion and execution, 349–53; ceremonial farewell, 353–4; death, 356; transfer of power, 356–7; tomb, 359–60; posthumous reputation, 363, 365–9

Elizabeth II, Queen, 367
Elizabeth of Austria, 195n
Elizabeth of Valois (Queen of Spain), 63, 68